Be Heard & Be Trusted

*I help people experience enthusiasm, love,
and wisdom to fulfill big dreams.*

TOM MARCOUX
Personal Mission
Statement

Be Heard and Be Trusted

"Tom shows you how to be charismatic and persuasive."

Dr. JoAnn Dahlkoetter, author of *Your Performing Edge* & coach to Olympians

"Tom gives you powerful methods so you easily gain rapport, trust, and active responsiveness from important people."

David Barron, coauthor of *Power Persuasion* (www.Power-Persuasion.com)

Praise for Tom Marcoux's other work

"In *Communicate to Win*, Tom teaches potent tools for finding your voice and powerfully expressing yourself, essential for getting what you want in life."

Marcia Wieder, author of *Making Your Dreams Come True* and PBS celebrity

"Tom's *How to Heal When Life's Too Much*, helps if you are having a rough time. I'd recommend it to clients, colleagues, and friends."

Shannon Seek, Principal, Seek Solutions, author of *Organic Organizing Matrix*

"In *Online Secrets to Build Your Brand*, Tom [gets you] more cash per click."

David Barron, persuasion expert, coauthor of *Power Persuasion*

"Tom's *How Top Salespeople Double Sales in Half the Time*, provides me with new techniques that I use."

Steven Seitz, Sales Manager, Silicon Valley Conference Center

"Hiring Tom Marcoux as my media and marketing coach was the most valuable thing I've done in several years."

Dr. JoAnn Dahlkoetter, author of *Your Performing Edge* & coach to Olympians

Be Heard & Be Trusted

How You Can Use
Secrets of the Greatest Communicators
to Get What You Want

THIRD EDITION

formerly titled
Communicate to Win

Tom Marcoux

America's Communication Coach
AND
The Time-Leverage Detective

A QUICKBREAKTHROUGH EDITION

ISBN: 0-9800511-4-2 / 978-0-9800511-4-8

QuickBreakthrough Publishing is an imprint of Marcoux Media

More copies are available from the publisher:

Marcoux Media
(415) 572-6609
TomSuperCoach@gmail.com
www.TomSuperCoach.com

This book was developed and written with care. Names and details were modified to respect privacy where necessary.

Interviews and substantial excerpts by other authors are copyrighted by those authors and included herein with their permission.

❧ **This book was published using green technology.** The inks used contain no substances listed as hazardous air pollutants per §112 of the Federal Clean Air Act and emit virtually no volatile organic compounds (VOCs), unlike traditional books.

Disclaimer: No fiduciary relationship is created hereby between the reader and author or publisher. The author and publisher note that each person's situation is unique and that readers have the responsibility to seek consultations with health, financial, spiritual, and legal professionals when implementing any advice contained herein. The author and publisher make no warranties of any kind, and shall not be liable for any special, consequential, or exemplary damages resulting, in whole or in part, from the reader's use of, or reliance upon, this material.

Book design + photography by **Kunst+Aventur**
see *Collophon* at rear

Source: Be Heard + Be Trusted - II - 79 May 14, 2009 8:56 PM

Publisher's Cataloguing in Publication data

Tom Marcoux [1963– .]
    Be heard and be trusted : how you can use secrets of the greatest communicators
      to get what you want. – 3rd ed.
    xxiii, 370p. ; 20 cm.
    San Francisco, Cal : Marcoux Media, 2009
    Includes illustrations, bibliographical references, and indices.
    ISBN: 978-0-9800511-4-8 (pbk)
    1. Success in Business. 2. Self-actualization (Psychology). I. Author.
      II. Title.
    BF637.S8
    158/.1

Abstract: A system of persuasive communication techniques for use in business/life.

Indexer: G. Bambo

DEDICATION

*This
book is
dedicated to
the terrific book
and film consultant*

Johanna Mac Leod

ACKNOWLEDGEMENTS

My heartfelt gratitude to all my other team members. Thanks to the guest authors for their voices of great experience. Thanks to Linda L. Chappo, and to Sun Editing & Book Design (www.SunEditWrite.com) for editing. Thanks for comments from my father, Al Marcoux. Thanks to my mother, Sumiyo Marcoux, a kind, generous soul. Thanks to Kunst+Aventur for the book's cover, design, typesetting, and production logistics. Thanks to Higher Power, our readers, our clients, and our enthusiastic audiences.

SUMMARY OF CONTENTS

DETAILED CONTENTS

PART I, SECTION 1

PART II, SECTION 3

PART II, SECTION 4

PART III

PART IV, SECTION 1

PART IV, SECTION 2

PART V

Be a Credible Communicator, Make Honesty Your Policy! 159
Craig Harrison

Enhance Your Confidence and Self-Image 173
Dr. JoAnn Dahlkoetter

PART VI

Part VII

Part VIII

Part IX

PART X

Part XI

Part XII

The Beginning

How MUCH would your life improve if you could easily get people to say yes to you? What if you could easily get them to *want* to say yes?

- "Yes! You're hired. The job is yours."

- "Yes! Here's your raise and promotion."

- "Yes! I'll marry you."

- "Yes! Here's $200,000 to develop your entrepreneurial idea."

- "Yes! I'll buy your product."

What if you could get what you really want – faster than you ever imagined?

That was both the opportunity and the problem for my client Sarah. She confessed, "I need to improve my communication skills."

"How would that give you what you really want?" I asked.

For a moment, she frowned in thought.

"And what *do* you really want?"

"A raise and a promotion!" she said with sudden clarity.

"What would that take?"

"My boss would have to trust me with higher profile assignments."

In essence, Sarah didn't just want to improve her communication skills; she wanted to *be heard and be trusted.*

With my guidance, Sarah learned to use the skills found in this book. She learned methods to increase her confidence, speak well to authority, and feel higher self-esteem.

For 24 years, I have helped thousands of clients and audience members become great communicators. In fact, an earlier version of this book was accepted as a textbook by Cogswell Polytechnical College and included in that college's time capsule. The capsule is set to be opened in 2100. Even in 2100, the timeless principles of warm and trustworthy communication will be valuable.

In this book, we will cover story after story that highlight how many, including twelve billionaires and millionaires, communicate successfully to make things happen. You will also learn directly from the articles and comments of a number of other great communicators.

This book is filled with principles that can help you relate to people on a higher level of connection and cooperation.

> *As to methods there may be a million and then some, but principles are few. The man who grasps principles can successfully select his own methods. The man who tries methods, ignoring principles, is sure to have trouble.*
>
> RALPH WALDO EMERSON

Let's create your best year so far …

Part I, Section 1

How You Can Radiate Charisma and Get What You Want

WHAT TERRIFIC THINGS could be in your life if you were charismatic?

Imagine if you could easily gain people's agreement and cooperation. Top professionals come across as charismatic. *The American Heritage Dictionary* defines "charisma" as "personal magnetism or charm."

A charismatic person makes each of us feel like the *most important person in the room.* How is this done? The charismatic person listens to others and connects with their pain. A charismatic person often uses an effective story to engage people's emotions and open listeners to benevolent influence.

A charismatic person expresses compelling messages. Dictionary.com defines "compelling" as "to force or drive, especially to a course of action … to overpower … to have a powerful and irresistible effect, influence." We want to overpower inertia, low moods, and procrastination. We want to take action consistently to create the best possible situations in our own lives.

An interviewer said to me, "I'm not comfortable with the idea of 'force.'"

"All right, let's focus on having a good intention first," I replied. "Instead of force, let's aim to 'move' a person's emotions.

"For example, when I was ten years old, my piano teacher knew how to persuade me to practice. She helped me see how much I improved when I practiced. She moved my emotions so that I could feel and enjoy the benefits I was getting. She also cleverly had me practice a song that I really *wanted* to play."

In essence, my piano teacher was a compelling communicator. She was *heard and trusted* by me. And that's what you'll learn how to do in this book.

For compelling communication, you need to do two things, to:

1. Seize the attention

2. Create a connection

We want our communication to be not merely pleasant, but *compelling*. We want people to cooperate with us, to take action in the direction we're proposing. To help you make this year the best year of your life so far, we will explore the C.O.M.P.E.L. process.

C – Connect with the listener's pain

O – Open with genuineness

M – Maximize leverage

P – Pull with a story

E – Ease

L – Lift

"Be so good—they can't ignore you," said writer-actor-comedian Steve Martin in response to the question, "How do you gain big success?" With this book, *you* will become *so good* at influencing people. And, I will add, *be so trustworthy* that they want to do for you.

Let's move on. Let's learn how to be charismatic and influential.

CONNECT WITH THE LISTENER'S PAIN

Where does it hurt?

Did your attention go to your body? Did you feel tension in your neck area?

To make your message compelling, you need to uncover your listener's pain.

Ask someone what he or she wants. The easiest way for the person to reply is to say, "What I *don't* want is to stay in this job. Here's what I do *not* like in my current situation." The person talks about what causes pain.

> *What I have in my heart must come out;*
> *that is the reason I compose.*
>
> LUDWIG VAN BEETHOVEN

Beethoven reminds us that what is in our hearts must come out. Similarly, as great communicators we need to help our listener *express* his or her heartfelt pains and desires. By helping your listener identify "where it hurts," you can help her achieve a transformation.

The power of transformation reminds me of the journey of Gay Hendricks, the bestselling author of *Five Wishes* and cofounder of The Hendricks Institute. Years ago, when he was a 300-pound tobacco addict in a horrible marriage, he felt the need to reinvent himself. He says that what sustained him was a deep inner knowledge of where he was going – toward a life of soul awareness and creative fulfillment. Today he has a fit, 180-pound frame, over six feet tall.

Gay was blocked. His blockage was made of conflicted feelings: he couldn't decide whether to continue studying in the University of New Hampshire counseling program or follow his desire to be a writer. Dwight Webb, an insightful professor of his, suggested, "Why not write about counseling?"

Was there any reason Gay could not put his feelings and inner experiences into poems and articles connected with his profession? The answer was that he could do both things he loved. He could pursue psychological counseling *and* writing.

Gay's poems were published in counseling journals and caught the eye of a professor at Stanford University, who helped Gay gain a fellowship to that institution for his doctorate. Gay went on to a 25-year academic career and wrote over 20 books.

When I contacted Gay a while ago, I discovered that he had found fulfillment as a screenwriter-filmmaker and as a seminar leader through The Hendricks Institute. Gay's journey shows that it is an "and" universe, not a "this or that" universe.

The point is that Gay's professor Dwight Webb provided great coaching. He *listened* to Gay's pain and shared a new way to view the situation.

> *The only service a friend can really render is*
> *to keep up your courage by holding up to you a*
> *mirror in which you can see a noble image of yourself.*
>
> GEORGE BERNARD SHAW

When you really want to be heard and be trusted, focus on something that will benefit the other person. Be the person's friend. Take the appropriate actions to help him or her.

With a number of my clients, we focus on the transition from novice salesperson to *coach-to-action*. As George Bernard Shaw points out, you as the coach can hold a *friendly mirror* up to your listener, who will then be able to see a noble image of the self. This noble image can inspire the listener to agree to whatever you're offering. And as the coach, you can help the person enjoy more in life and work.

> *It is above all by the imagination that we achieve perception and compassion and hope.*
>
> URSULA LEGUIN

First, connect with the listener's pain. Then, with the knowledge you have gained, you can focus on helping. You can help people *imagine* a better personal future.

> *People in general are starved for the experience of being heard.*
>
> GORDON LIVINGSTON, M.D.

Get what you want by giving people what they crave: to be heard.

Principle:

Connect with the listener's pain and show that you have the remedy.

Power Question:

How can you gently ask questions that allow you to identify the listener's pain?*

OPEN WITH GENUINENESS

When you are content to be simply yourself
and don't compare or compete,
everybody will respect you.

LAO-TZU

"We don't need you to be perfect; we need you to be genuine," I say to my graduate students who seek to be better public speakers and pitch-givers.

Do what you said you were going to do,
when you said you were going to do it,
in exactly the way you said you were going to do it.
You won't ever get any better business advice than that.
Be there when you said you would be there.
Deliver when you said you would deliver.
Call when you said you would call.
Be a person who can be counted on
by keeping his word every time.

LARRY WINGET

Have you ever been afraid that when you are giving a speech, your mind might go blank or you might lose your place? *The solution is, be genuine.*

* To get the maximum benefit from this book, devote at least 20 seconds to writing down the answer to each Power Question in your personal journal.

When I coach CEOs and company presidents in how to give speeches, I help them express genuineness. This helps the CEO connect with the audience and motivate team members.

Here are comments from Rich Fettke on how you can recover during difficult times. *If you are prepared to recover, your genuineness can carry the day.*

Learn to Recover

RICH FETTKE

Years ago, I was just beginning skydiving lessons. My instructor Bill said, "If you go into a tumble, you must stop, be aware, and resume control – by arching your body and holding it."

When we were high above the clouds, Bill and I stood at the door. I yelled the protocol, "ready, set, go!" We jumped. As we fell away from the plane, I arched my body. Bill held my arms and we leveled out, nice and stable.

We practiced letting go of each other and then connecting. At six thousand feet, it was time to separate and fly far enough away from each other so we could open our parachutes.

The farther I got from Bill the more nervous I became. I thought: "What if my chute doesn't open? What if I do something wrong? What am I doing alone out here?" I quickly reached for my ripcord, and found myself spinning and flipping out of control! In desperation, I kept reaching for my ripcord, yelling, "Where is it?!" I was in such a tumble I couldn't see how far I was from the ground. It felt like minutes since I last saw Bill and all I could think was "I'm going to hit the ground!"

Then I remembered Bill's advice, "Stop, be aware, and resume control." I stopped my panic, arched my body and instantly I was under control and my front side was facing the ground. I pulled my ripcord and let out a yell of joy as my parachute unfolded above me.

I notice how many of us go into a *tumble* in our daily lives. We don't know where we are and what we really want. We keep trying harder and harder and focus on how busy we are and how overwhelmed we feel. Now, I use Bill's advice, I stop for a moment to be aware of my confusion or stress, then I can resume control and turn my attention to solutions instead of problems.

Rich Fettke, author of *Extreme Success*

www.Fettke.com

The lesson of recovery applies whether you are talking with one person or speaking to a group.

Four ways to recover:

1. If you mispronounce a word, say, "Oh, I don't use that word every day." Then slowly say the word again.

2. If you lose your place, respond with something like, "My train of thought just derailed. I'm waiting for a crane." *The idea is to pick a gentle phrase that might include a bit of humor.*

3. If you make an error, remark, "That's not what I meant to say. What I meant was … "

4. If English is your second language and you see that people haven't understood what you've just said, use a synonym. One of my students mispronounced "result." I invited the student to say "outcome."

During one class, when I was teaching the method of saying, "My train of thought just derailed," I suggested that the students come up with their own comments. My graduate student Joseph Hsieh suggested, "Oh, I need a moment; my brain doesn't have enough RAM."

Ah, the first step in humility: Listening.

DR. MICHAEL BERNARD BECKWITH

rendered by Chris Sehenuk

Now will you ask for directions?

A crucial part of genuineness is true caring & listening

Listening is one of the best ways to show how important we feel another person is. To listen well, we need to avoid listening blockers. (Authors Paul J. Donoghue and Mary E. Siegel write about the habits that block listening.)

Listening blockers

1. Judging

A friend talks about her ex-husband again and again. You are thinking: "Enough already! Can't you move on?"

2. Defending

Your roommate suggests that you do more to help keep the place clean. You yell back, "I do chores around here! Two weeks ago, I … "

3. "Me, too!" – one up

You say, "Yes, finals are tough for me, too. In fact, I have eight classes." When the person you are talking to has only five classes, this comment is "one up" (or "one better").

The solution to our own listening blockers is to observe our behavior. If you find yourself responding with judging, defending or "Me, too! – one up," pause. Be quiet. Then say something like,

1. So, how do you feel about the situation?

2. That must have been frustrating for you.

It often helps to ask a gentle question that returns the conversational spotlight to the other person.

What do we live for,
if it is not to make life less difficult for each other?

GEORGE ELIOT
(pen name of Mary Ann Evans)

Principle:

Show your genuineness and put the person at ease.

Power Questions:

How can you reveal that you are genuine? What brief stories demonstrate how much you care about people and perform supportive actions?

MAXIMIZE LEVERAGE

What do most of us want? We want the greatest benefit for the least effort. In fact, for many individuals, getting something for nothing would be just fine. Others realize that giving and receiving is a natural law.

This is where leverage comes in. The person you're talking with wants to avoid effort and pain – and still gain benefits.

Show how your ideas and solutions maximize the person's leverage. At one conference I attended, a tax accountant said that he would show us how to gain $5,000 a year with only a bit of extra effort. He had our attention.

How can we find out what will truly gain the attention of our listener?

> *Inspiration usually comes during work,*
> *rather than before it.*
>
> MADELEINE L'ENGLE

Let's do the work. In your personal journal, write down two quick responses to each of these questions:

- What is most important to my customer (my friend? my spouse?)

- What does the person want?

- What does the person want to avoid?

- How can my solution give the person the greatest benefit for the least effort?

As stated in Madeleine's quote, it is during the process of writing the answers to these questions (doing the work) that we will often find the inspiration.

Questions help you discover what matters most to your listener. Here in this comment from Aaron Parnell are some vital questions:

Living with Vitality

AARON PARNELL

The key thing about most of our fitness goals is that we have a trifecta of bliss associated with our ultimate aspirations.

In order to provide the best guidance, I need to know how my clients want to look, feel, and what they want to be able to do. For example, one of my clients wanted to look like a supermodel and play a good game of racquetball. It was important for me to establish her fitness regimen on two tracks, because fitness for the sport of your soul doesn't always lead to the star-quality super-body of your dreams.

With all health goals, you have to ask yourself these three questions: "What do I want to be able to do?" Second, "What do I want to look like when I'm doing that or what do I want to look like at all?" This will naturally lead to: "How do I want to feel?" With these essential elements as your nucleus, it naturally leads to a constellation of power-sources to surround yourself with.

Close your eyes, search your soul, and imagine yourself at your extraordinary best.

1. What food and nutrition choices will *feed* that person?

2. What recreational and fitness activities will *prepare* that person?

3. What lifestyle and social networks will *support* that person?

4. What rest and restorative solutions will *invigorate* that person?

5. What spiritual, emotional, professional and personal guidance will *inspire* that person?

Though not always easy, your vision makes your priorities clear – and the process of achieving true vitality becomes simple.

Aaron Lloyd U. Parnell, author of *Living with Vitality – The Dynamic Power of Extraordinary Health*

(650) 347-4565
www.AaronParnell.com

Principle:

Show how your solution provides the person with the greatest benefit for the least effort (leverage).

Power Questions:

What is it about your solution that provides the greatest benefit? How can you ask questions to discover what the person most desires?

PULL WITH A STORY

"Tell me a story!" Millions of children throughout the world say this every day. A story gives us an experience. The story reaches us on our subconscious and emotional levels. The story goes around people's natural resistance.

We have been conditioned to respond favorably to stories. With a dash of suspense, tension, and release, your story can influence your listener.

> *If you can dream it, you can do it.*
>
> WALT DISNEY

> *It all comes down to the story you tell yourself.*
>
> TOM MARCOUX

> *Facts go in our brains. Stories go in our hearts.*
>
> SANDRA BLOCH

A good story …

    1. Begins with a *grabber*

    2. Has *suspense*

    3. Has *vivid details*

    4. Includes *word pictures*

5. Ends with *"What I learned was … "*

6. Has a *call to action*

A word picture creates an image. To a friend who likes puppies, I said, "When I'm waiting for you, I feel like a puppy on a raft in the middle of the Atlantic Ocean, never knowing whether a rescue ship is going to appear." My comment touched her heart.

A story with a goal *gives us the chance to earn the ending.* We go through the trials and suffering along with the main character.

> *Character cannot be developed in ease and quiet.*
> *Only through experience of trial and suffering*
> *can the soul be strengthened, vision cleared,*
> *ambition inspired, and success achieved.*
>
> HELEN KELLER

We want to earn the happy ending. We want to see how the hero with good intentions struggles and then earns the positive outcome.

A story helps you make your point powerfully. The following anecdote is one of the signature stories I tell my audiences.

> We need to be careful about the stories we tell ourselves – and the stories we tell others. At one point, my wife and I went on the Disney Cruise. We went to refresh ourselves, and I also went on the cruise to find more stories. "I need a story," I felt. "I need an adventure."
>
> When I was younger, I did stunts. I'd hang on the hood of a speeding truck, a cherry-red classic Chevy truck going 60 miles an hour. Not any more! So now I need an adventure.

"Let's go on a cruise and go snorkeling for the first time!" It looked good on paper. So I go snorkeling with my sweetheart. It's the Bahamas, and it's 83 degrees at eight o'clock in the morning. It's hot, so she tells me that the water will be warm. But the water is relatively *cold*. And I discover what happens in cold water. First thing I learn: What is worse than a cramp in your right leg?

"A cramp in both legs," says an audience member.

Yes! You're right here with me. A cramp in both legs. So now I have terrible, horrible pain that I cannot solve with a "to-do" list or a "guilt" list. I cannot solve this by doing it harder – "Let's move the legs harder!"

It looks like a mile back to the beach. I've got to let go. I've got to relax. I've got legs that don't work, and they hurt like fire. So I start to use my arms. Thank goodness for Red Cross swimming lessons! I do the sidestroke. And my sweetheart – yes, she's better at snorkeling her first time than I am. *(Women in the audience laugh.)* She's towing me a little bit, too. That's comforting.

Eventually, we get back to the ship and our cabin. And I discover the second thing that happens in cold water: things shrink! *(Audience chuckles.)* My hand has shrunk. My wedding-ring finger has shrunk. *(Audible gasps.)*

My wedding ring is now lost in hundreds of yards of water and sand. My wedding band is gone! And I'm thinking, "All right, I teach this stuff. Mental discipline. My ring has gone back to the universe.

Someone will find it who needs it more than I. I have had this ring for seven years. It has served me well. It is time for a change. *(Audience members are chuckling.)* I will flow. I teach about Taoism in my Comparative Religion class. I will flow. Be like water! The ring is in the water. It is in the sand; it is not on my hand.

I discovered: All men make mistakes; married men just find out about it sooner. *(Audience laughs).*

My wife tells me, "You do not go into water with jewelry on!" I am not into jewelry – and now jewelry is not on me!

So I call up the ship's Guest Services and say, "My wedding ring is somewhere in hundreds of yards of sand and water." The person says that I can come by and fill out the form. There's always a form. There's a form for losing your wedding ring.

The next day, I go to the Guest Services desk. I'm thinking, "It's okay. It's all right. I've had it for seven years *(whimper of sadness)*." So I talk with a new person at the Guest Services desk. "I'm here to fill out the form. I lost my wedding ring."

"Where did you lose it?" he asks me.

"I was on the island tram. And I was at the snorkeling lagoon … "

"Is this your ring?" *(Audience gasps.)*

And here is the ring. *(I hold up my hand with the wedding ring.)*

To me, it is a miracle. And it reminds me of what Albert Einstein said:

> *"There are two ways to live: you can live*
> *as if nothing is a miracle; you can live as if*
> *everything is a miracle."*

We have a choice. And so, what are the stories you are telling yourself? What are the stories you tell others?

Are you telling yourself stories so that you can have a year where *nothing can stop you this year?**

You can see how this snorkeling-adventure story illustrates my point about the stories we tell ourselves and others. Be careful about the stories you tell yourself and the stories you tell others. *Tell good stories – miraculous stories.*

I often tell audiences, "Just about everyone in this room has a good story about something that went well – a lucky break, a miracle, even like when you're thinking about someone and the person calls you on the phone." Then I invite the audience to place their hands over their hearts and feel their hearts beating. Finally, the audience joins me in saying the four powerful words Dr. Martin Luther King, Jr., shared with us all: *"I have a dream."*

Remember to pull the listener in with a good story.

Principle:

Use a story to eliminate resistance.

Power Question:

What stories can seize the attention of your listener?

* *

*This is an excerpt from my speech related to my book *Nothing Can Stop You This Year!* Visit TomSuperCoach.com.

EASE

What do you wish was easier in your life?

Imagine how it would be if the person you were talking with thought you could bring ease into his or her life. This person would likely be receptive to your comments.

As a verb, "ease" implies going forward gently: to ease into something. Dictionary.com defines *ease* (as a noun) as "freedom from labor, pain, physical annoyance, concern, anxiety, difficulty, great effort, stiffness, constraint, formality or financial need." Ease relates to "tranquil rest; comfort; a quiet state of mind; and plenty."

Wow! Let's have some of that! To set a person at ease is a powerful way to be heard and trusted.

rendered by Chris Sehenuk

I *love* complimentary peanuts!

The twin killers of success are impatience and greed.

JIM ROHN

Don't rush the person you're talking with. *Show patience.* The point is to make it easy for the person to buy your product or idea.

We make things easy by asking a gentle question and *listening* to the potential customer. For example, one salesman approached me by saying, "I know a lot about your work." And without showing any patience, he launched right into his pitch. I did *not* buy the advertising he was offering.

It would have helped if he had replaced his supposed "efficiency" by saying something gentle and easy. He could have said, "Our advertising process reaches four major cities in your target area. What message would you like to bring to those people?" Then he could have listened to my response. This would have made the process easy. I would have replied with something like, "That's a good question. I would like them to know about my new book, and that I'll be appearing at X and Y, and I am offering a special value and discount with … " A gentle question would have made it easy for me to "sell myself" on the idea of using his type of advertising.

Great communicators know to avoid rushing the person they're talking with. Again, show patience and make your listener feel at ease.

A charismatic person sets a listener or an audience at ease. Now, Dr. Tony Alessandra discusses charisma.

Charisma: What is It? What Will it Do for You?

DR. TONY ALESSANDRA

You're squirming in your seat, wondering if the next speaker can possibly be less inspiring than the preceding one, when, suddenly, the room falls silent. Looking poised and confident, the next presenter smiles, and then begins. Instantly, it's clear that he's *good*: His strong, measured voice, his relaxed tone, his precisely articulated and well-chosen words, and even his classy but understated appearance seem to fixate the crowd.

You think, "Wow! Who *is* this guy?" And then you realize it's just not what he is saying, or how he looks.

It's his *whole* being.

As his voice and gestures signal that he's nearing the high point of his remarks, you feel yourself soaring, rationally as well as emotionally, along with the ideas he presents so passionately...so much so that you know you'd probably follow him to a convention of cannibals if that's where he wanted to lead you. This guy *has* it!

Appeal to Mind and Emotions

But *what* does he have? What do real leaders have that can inspire you and draw you to them, that can cause you perform beyond expectations to accomplish *their* goals? Is it speaking well...or being socially adroit...or projecting an attractive, exciting image?

Actually, it's all that – and *more*. And for lack of a better term, we often group such qualities under the term *charisma*. I've been studying, teaching, and writing about human behavior, especially in business, for more than 20 years now. As a result, probably like you, I know charisma when I *see* it...even if it's sometimes hard to pinpoint. But here's my definition: *Charisma is the ability to positively influence others by connecting with them physically, emotionally, and intellectually.*

In brief, it's what makes people like you and enjoy being around you...even when they don't know much about you. This personal magnetism can exist at the level of mass movements – such as politicians and evangelists – or in the small-scale encounters of everyday life, such as the shop owner who makes you feel so comfortable and valuable that you cheerfully drive a few extra miles to her store.

I'm convinced that, contrary to popular wisdom, charisma is not something you're born with, like having blue eyes or brown eyes. Instead, I think our personalities consist, let's say, of a series of containers, like cups or glasses. Some are nearly empty; some brimming; yet others are partially filled to varying degrees. Together, they constitute our potential charisma.

If all the glasses were filled to the top, you'd be so charismatic people would think you were a god … and you'd probably think so, too. But nobody has a complete set of totally full glasses, although some really gifted people – JFK or, say, Churchill – may have come close to this ideal. But, for most of us, the glasses are filled a bit erratically, though we *can* add to them.

Here, as I see them, are the seven main components of charisma – or, the "glasses," if you will:

- *Your silent messages* … You unconsciously send out signals to others. Maybe you look them right in the eye, or maybe you stare at your shoes when you talk. Perhaps you slump your shoulders, or maybe you square them confidently. You may fail to smile naturally or shake hands firmly, or you might dress in a way that's not *you*. All these shape your image and affect the people you want to lead.

- *Your persuasive talent* … No idea, however great, ever gets anywhere until it's adopted. Charismatic executives can distill complex ideas into simple messages so that even the guy who sweeps the floor understands what the company stands for and why that's important.

- *Your ability to speak well* … You may have a zillion terrific ideas, but who will know if you can't articulate them?

- *Your listening skills* … Rarely taught and infrequently practiced, listening is nonetheless a key to communicating and making others feel special in your presence.

- *Your use of space and time* … Again, though it's often overlooked, use of spatial and temporal territories can make or break relationships.

- *Your ability to adapt to others* … Building rapport means understanding other people's personalities, then adapting your own behavior to increase compatibility.

- *Your vision and ideas* … Regardless of how strong and persuasive a speaker you are, how adept you are at connecting with others, how well you listen, use your space or time, or send out silent signals, you've *still* got to have something to say … or you'll just be an empty suit.

So, it's not a single ingredient that makes a person charismatic, and, more important, charisma isn't based on IQ, genetics, social position, wealth, or luck. Instead, it can be learned.

Why Charisma Matters

Learning to improve your charisma is more important than ever. Why?

Change calls for strong, mesmerizing leaders. In our age of start-ups, acquisitions, turnarounds, mergers, de-mergers, new regulatory climates, and all other sorts of rapid, unpredictable change, especially in business, that's truer than ever.

Television and our general emphasis on the visual make char-ismatic people more effective. (Remember: The physical is a big component of "the silent message" glass.)

Our expectations have risen. We've come to demand more from people than mere competence. When even the local car dealer or supermarket manager can be seen as articulate, personable, and persuasive in a slick TV ad, we no longer readily accept those who squirm, stumble over their words, and don't quite look us in the eye.

The old-fashioned kind of hierarchy, the command-and-control environment, is passé. Even the highest-ranking officials need more than their title to get people to accept their ideas. Instead, in this era of "empowerment," when empathy and support are revered, charis-matic people stand out because they're communicators who are able to see things from another's perspective and, thus, continually seek to find the common ground.

Those with personal magnetism, or charisma, are usually self-con-fident optimists. Viewing almost all problems as solvable – focusing on *desired results* rather than *possible failures* – helps encourage people to step forward and convert fear into challenge.

All of these are reasons for you to try to greatly improve your cha-risma. In subsequent articles, I'll give tips on how to raise the levels in each of your seven charisma "glasses."

But, for now, remember that even if you never get a chance to head a corporation, spearhead a movement or even hold office in the local PTA, you can use your charisma, present or future, to do good for yourself and others, to make for positive change in ways large and small.

Connecting with People

A person who develops his or her charisma is likely to do well in all aspects of life. That's because, on several different levels, they better connect with people. By definition, the charismatic person is more other-directed, more empathic. That gives them more personal power – and that's a big plus for anybody.

Take basketball star Michael Jordan, certainly one of the most charismatic athletes of recent times. Despite being the most heralded professional player of his era, he quit the hardwoods to play minor-league baseball for a time. He didn't make it to the big leagues, but he didn't strike out with his millions of fans, who may have thought his ill-starred tenure with the Birmingham Barons made him, if anything, more human.

As you seek to improve you charisma and personal power, remember that when people feel someone is *making* them do something, they're often frustrated and resentful – and as a result, they dig in their heels. The truly charismatic person strives to create feelings of collaboration and equality. They approach others interactively and try to give them a choice.

Testing this doesn't require a big, important issue. Everyday tasks will suffice. For example, saying, "Copy this report" is a mild form of coercion from a position of power. But asking "Would you mind copying this report?" or "Do you have time to copy this report right now?" is more interactive.

Similarly, you can't successfully order employees to "Be more productive!" or "Improve your efficiency!" But you *can* organize them into teams, for instance, or create suggestion systems that really work, and give people more information about the company's profits and losses.

In addition, recognize another person's achievements, contributions, and particular skills. Catch someone doing something right!

And celebrate those successes. Everyone wants to feel that they're on a winning team.

Be aggressively optimistic and willing to be the first to do something and to take the heat if it doesn't work out. Charismatic people have heard all the bromides about why you can't rock the corporate boat (*"We've never done it that way before." "It's too radical a change."*), but they just pay less attention to them.

Instead, they relish a challenge, not just for themselves but for their followers, too, who wish to take risks and be allowed to make some mistakes. So if you give your people some control over resources and influence over how to do a task, you'll help them build self-confidence.

In fact, the charismatic person often good-naturedly challenges, prods, and pokes as he or she encourages others to stretch themselves. Again, take Michael Jordan. He's said to, even in practice, be the loudest, most demanding player on the court, goading the other Bulls to give their all. It's his way of being inspirational; he never stops competing, even when no one is keeping score.

The potential to be charismatic leader is within you, too. And ... the payoff for doing so has never been higher.

Dr. Tony Alessandra, has authored 17 books translated into over 50 foreign language editions, recorded over 50 audio and video programs, and delivered over 2,000 keynote speeches since 1976. This article has been adapted from Dr. Alessandra's book, CHARISMA: *Seven Keys to Developing the Magnetism that Leads to Success.* If you would like more information about Dr. Alessandra's programs, or about Dr. Alessandra as a keynote speaker, contact him at:

(800) 222-4383
www.Alessandra.com/products

Above, Dr. Tony Alessandra emphasized the importance of our silent messages and listening. These two elements are crucial to helping your listener feel at ease.

Principle:

Set the person at ease and you will gain cooperation.

Power Questions:

How can you set the person at ease? How can you ask a gentle question and then listen? (Remember, listening demonstrates that you are trustworthy and that the speaker's well-being is important to you.)

LIFT

What four words have lifted the hearts of millions of people for decades? Martin Luther King, Jr., said them: "I have a dream." I'm mentioning this again because *great communicators tell inspiring stories to themselves and other people.*

Dr. Wayne Dyer, the bestselling author of *Inspiration*, tells how he left the security of the bimonthly paychecks he received as a college professor to go out on his own. In 1976, he decided that he would buy a large number of copies of his first book, entitled *Your Erroneous Zones*, appear on local media shows and leave his books at stores across America on consignment. He used his own savings to purchase the books and pay travel expenses for his wife, his daughter, and himself. As the months went by, the number of interviews he was asked to give rose to 15 a day, and bookstores began to reorder the books from his publisher.

A publicity expert had told Wayne that he would not sell enough books without a network television appearance, but Wayne proved him wrong. In one year, Wayne accomplished what seemed impossible: without his making one major television network appearance, his book debuted on the *New York Times* Best Seller List at position number eight. Wayne concludes, "I received more money in the first year I was out on my own without the security of a regular paycheck than I had in the entire 36 years of my life before then."

Many people have succeeded and later said, "I didn't know that it couldn't be done." In the same way, you can use the secrets and methods in this book to give you the edge you need to *make impossible dreams come true*. It all starts with having a dream. A dream can *lift* our souls and fill us with the energy to take action.

Principle:

Lift people's hearts. Mention a dream and express your enthusiasm.

Power Question:

How can you demonstrate that what you're doing or offering is exciting and full of powerful benefits?

CONCLUSION TO PART I, SECTION 1

In Part I, Section 1, we explored the C.O.M.P.E.L. process:

C – Connect with the listener's pain

O – Open with genuineness

M – Maximize leverage

P – Pull with a story

E – Ease

L – Lift

The greatest communicators truly connect with their listeners because they express genuineness. As I quoted earlier:

> *When you are content to be simply yourself*
> *and don't compare or compete,*
> *everybody will respect you.*

LAO-TZU

The idea is to focus on expressing your genuine concern for the person's well-being.

> *I don't know what your destiny will be, but one thing I do know: the only ones among you who will be really happy are those who have sought and found how to serve.*

ALBERT SCHWEITZER

Find out the listener's pain and discover how you can be helpful. This is a prime way to be heard and be trusted.

In Part I, Section 2, we will see how twelve billionaires and millionaires have used the C.O.M.P.E.L. principles.

Part I, Section 2

How Billionaires & Millionaires Use C.O.M.P.E.L. Principles

HERE ARE the C.O.M.P.E.L. principles once again:

C – Connect with the Listener's Pain

O – Open with Genuineness

M – Maximize Leverage

P – Pull with a Story

E – Ease

L – Lift

BILL GATES

One of the founders of Microsoft, he is among the most influ-ential technologist of the digital era.

Bill Gates uses the principle *Maximize Leverage.* He said,

"The first rule of any technology used in a business is that automation applied to an efficient operation will magnify the efficiency. The second is that automation applied to an ineffi-cient operation will magnify the inefficiency." And, "As we look ahead into the next century, leaders will be those who empower others." And, "Often you have to rely on intuition."

Bill Gates uses the principle *Connect with the Listener's Pain.* "If you show people the problems and you show people the solutions they will be moved to act." And, "The digitization of the economy, whether it's work, meetings being recorded digi-tally, moving away from paper documents more and more so all forms are digital, that's happening at full speed. In the home, it's moving even TV onto the Internet … And we're finally getting all of our experiences with information into that digital realm."

Bill Gates aims at the principle of *Ease.* In his May 2007 address to 100 CEOs, he said, "Group meetings: We've got a thing called Roundtable that gives you a 360-degree view of a meeting room … And there are a lot of people taking advanced camera technology and allowing a meeting either to be par-ticipated in remotely or easily recorded [so] somebody can go back and then take, say the transcript and find the part that they're interested in. Things where you improve meetings, the efficiency, reduce the number of people who need to go, things like that have a surprisingly big impact on digital work style productivity."

Finally, *Maximize Leverage* again: "[About the Internet and advertising] The ability to target the ads, to have somebody indicate an interest, and even for the advertiser to have a better understanding of who's there viewing the ads, and easily see what impact they're having, do people click on it, what immediate action do people take, this is a real change … And because advertising is so key to the whole mechanism of capitalism where you're matching buyers and sellers, the revolution in these markets really is quite an impactful thing."

He continues, "After all, advertising funds a lot of the great content creation that gets done. And so now we see this in the world of software where some things will have these ads brought in as well. We've got a lot of companies investing very heavily in this: Yahoo!, Google, Microsoft, many others on a global basis. And your ability as an advertiser to understand who you're getting to, and to pick a particular audience will be dramatically different in this new world.

Even as reading goes online, what would have been print-type advertising gets targeted, and as TV goes to the Internet, like that AT&T platform, you're getting this same capability. And so a lot of change [is] in the ads themselves and how you think about getting those out there."

OPRAH WINFREY

She is one of the most powerful women in America by virtue of her immensely popular daytime talk show and magazine.

Oprah Winfrey uses the principles of *Open with Genuineness* and *Connect with the Listener's Pain*. After the author James Frey said on the "Larry King Live" show that he had made up some of his book, *A Million Little Pieces*, Oprah apologized for a phone call she had made to the show in which she supported the book. Soon after that, on her own television show Oprah apologized to her national audience for defending James Frey. "I made a mistake and I left the impression that the truth does not matter, and I am deeply sorry about that because that is not what I believe," she said.

When Frey later appeared on her show, Oprah said to him, "It is difficult for me to talk to you because I really feel duped … More importantly, I feel you betrayed millions of readers … As I sit here today, I don't know what is true, and I don't know what isn't."

It was reported that during her interview with James Frey, Oprah was near tears. Her audience gasped, moved by her obvious sincerity and regret.

Being genuine and apologizing sincerely is compelling. It inspires trust. Oprah knows the power her book club wields. When she selected Frey's book for the club, over three million copies were sold. Since then, Oprah has been careful to avoid memoirs because she feels that publishers do not properly vet the books.

Oprah's sincere good will captivates her audiences. Oprah said, "What I'm interested in doing now is creating a lasting impact … My efforts [are] going into schools because education is freedom." In 2007, Oprah dedicated $40 million to open The Oprah Winfrey Leadership Academy for Girls in South Africa. She said, "When you educate a girl, you begin to change the face of a nation. The school is going to change the trajectory of their lives."

JACK CANFIELD

Cocreator of the Chicken Soup for the Soul *series of books and products, among the most successful lines in the self help arena.*

Jack Canfield uses the principle of *Maximize Leverage*. He said, "There are two things that build self-esteem. One is quality of relationships, where you feel lovable and you're making a difference in the lives of others. And the other is achieving things … People who ask confidently get more than those who are hesitant and uncertain. When you've figured out what you want to ask for, do it with certainty, boldness and confidence." Jack and his partner, Mark Victor Hansen, used the principle of *Ease*. They envisioned their book, *Chicken Soup for the Soul*, topping the *New York Times* Best Seller List. They cut out a copy of the list from the newspaper and modified it, adding the name of their book to the top of that list. As a team, they did double the number of media interviews either of them could have done alone. They encouraged each other consistently.

MARK VICTOR HANSEN

Cocreator of the Chicken Soup for the Soul *series of books and products, among the most successful lines in the self help arena.*

Mark Victor Hansen's famous phrase is, "Don't think it, ink it!" This is in line with the principle *Maximize Leverage*. He listens to educational audio programs while he exercises. He said, "Most people's goals are too low and too slow." Also, "Your problems are good. They are power in disguise." And, *"If you're overstressed it's because you're underasked.*" He means that we need to ask for what we want.

Mark Victor Hansen and his coauthor, Robert Allen, wrote, "Each person is DNA-coded to solve something for themselves and others ... Marketing is storytelling. Whoever tells the best story gets the sale."

As a side note: Mark's mentor was Buckminster Fuller, who said, "Real wealth = Ideas x Energy."

BRIAN TRACY

Brian Tracy is a bestselling author and public speaker who has helped over 4 million people achieve their goals.

Brian Tracy used the principle of *Lift* as he raised himself from poverty. He said, "Your decision to be, have and do something out of the ordinary entails facing difficulties that are out of the ordinary as well. Sometimes your greatest asset is simply your ability to stay with it longer than anyone else." And, "Those people who develop the ability to continuously acquire new and better forms of knowledge that they can apply to their work and to their lives will be the movers and shakers in our society for the indefinite future." For example, Brian Tracy learned how to do real estate deals by reading every book on real estate that was available at the public library. Today, he still reads hundreds of books and magazine articles to keep his knowledge current and increase his effectiveness. This inspired me; in one year, I read 109 books.

ANTHONY ROBBINS

For the past three decades, Anthony Robbins has served as an advisor to leaders around the world as a recognized authority on the psychology of leadership, organizational turnaround, and peak performance.

Anthony Robbins uses the principle of *Connect with Your Listener's Pain.* He said, "In life you need either inspiration or desperation." And, "When you are grateful, fear disappears and abundance appears." And, "It's not the events of our lives that shape us, but our beliefs as to what those events mean." Also, "One reason so few of us achieve what we truly want is that we never direct our focus; we never concentrate our power. Most people dabble their way through life, never deciding to master anything in particular … Take control of your consistent emotions and begin to consciously and deliberately reshape your daily experience of life." Finally, "The way we communicate with others and with ourselves ultimately determines the quality of our lives."

WARREN BUFFET

Legendary investor often ranked among the wealthiest people in the world. His partnership with Bill Gates has resulted in the creation of the world's largest philanthropic foundation.

Warren Buffet uses the principle of *Lift.* He said, "Someone's sitting in the shade today because someone planted a tree a long time ago." Also, "It's better to hang out with people better than you. Pick out associates whose behavior is better than yours, and you'll drift in that direction." And, "A public-opinion poll is no substitute for thought." Also, "It takes 20 years to build a reputation and five minutes to ruin it. If you think about that, you'll do things differently … If you can tell me who your heroes are, I can tell you how you're going to turn out in life." Also, "I call investing the greatest business in the world because you never have to swing. You stand at the plate. The pitcher throws you General Motors at 47! U.S. Steel at 39! and nobody calls a strike on you. There's no penalty except opportunity lost. All day you wait for the pitch you like. Then when the fielders are asleep, you step up and hit it."

Journalist Larry Kanter described Warren Buffet's strategy: "Ignoring both macroeconomic trends and Wall Street fashions, [Warren Buffet] looks for undervalued companies with low overhead costs, high growth potential, strong market share and low price-to-earnings ratios, and then waits for the rest of the world to catch up."

DONALD TRUMP

Eminent real estate developer, casino mogul, reality TV host, and business celebrity.

Donald Trump wrote, "One of the prime determinants of success in life and business is the ability to make quick, definite decisions. And I'll be blunt: If you cannot or will not respond to this offer [at his Trump University Web site] before the deadline, this package is not for you. Knowledge, even insider knowledge and success secrets like what I've described here cannot make a success out of anyone who lacks the courage to make decisions … and make them quickly. Quick, decisive action truly is one of the most important qualities you must have before you can lead the good life."

In this compelling communication, Donald Trump is using the principle of *Pull with a Story*. How? Trump paints a picture [or story] of what a leader is like: "courage to make [quick] decisions." Trump also wrote, "I don't do it for the money. I've got enough, much more than I'll ever need. I do it to do it. Deals are my art form."

SUZE ORMAN

New York Times number one bestselling author, known as "America's most trusted personal finance expert"

Suze Orman uses *Connect with the Listener's Pain*. She said, "A big part of financial freedom is having your heart and mind free from worry about the what-ifs of life."

And, "People first, then money, then things." Also, "In all realms of life it takes courage to stretch your limits, express your power, and fulfill your potential … it's no different in the financial realm." She adds, "Courage is the ability to face danger, difficulty, uncertainty or pain without being overcome by fear or being deflected from a chosen course of action." She wrote, "Truth creates money, lies destroy it."

STEVE JOBS

A visionary cofounder of Apple, his successes include the Macintosh, Pixar Animation Studios, and the iPod.

Steve Jobs uses the principle *Maximize Leverage*. "The only way to do great work is to love what you do. If you haven't found it yet, keep looking. Don't settle. As with all matters of the heart, you'll know when you find it." Also, "When Apple came up with the Mac, IBM was spending at least 100 times more on R&D. It's not about money. It's about the people you have, how you're led, and how much you get it … It's really hard to design products by focus groups.

"A lot of times, people don't know what they want until you show it to them."

Jobs also said, "We think basically you watch television to turn your brain off, and you work on your computer when you want to turn your brain on." Also, "We used to dream about this stuff. Now, we get to build it. It's pretty neat." And, "Remembering that I'll be dead soon is the most important tool I've ever encountered to help me make the big choices in life. Because almost everything – all external expectations, all pride, all fear of embarrassment or failure – these things just fall away in the face of death, leaving only what is truly important. Remembering that you are going to die is the best way I know to avoid the trap of thinking you have something to lose. You are already naked. There is no reason not to follow your heart."

Steve Jobs also uses the principle of *Lift*: "Be a yardstick of quality. Some people aren't used to an environment where excellence is expected … Sometimes when you innovate, you make mistakes. It is best to admit them quickly, and get on with improving your other innovations." Also, "I have looked in the mirror every morning and asked myself: 'If today were the last day of my life, would I want to do what I am about to do today?' And whenever the answer has been 'No' for too many days in a row, I know I need to change something."

WALT DISNEY

Legendary entertainment innovator in animation and motion pictures and the creator of the theme park.

Walt Disney focused on the principle of *Lift*. He said, "I don't want the public to see the world they live in while they're in the [Disneyland] Park. I want them to feel they're in another world … I would rather entertain and hope that people learned something than educate people and hope they were entertained." And, "I believe in being an innovator … We keep moving forward, opening new doors, and doing new things, because we're curious and curiosity keeps leading us down new paths." Walt also said, "Laughter is America's most important export."

RICHARD BRANSON

Billionaire, founder of Virgin and 300 Virgin companies, including the Virgin brands of cell phones and air travel. He is currently in the final phases of deploying a service for commercial space travel.

Richard Branson uses the principle of *Maximize Leverage*: "A business has to be involving, it has to be fun, and it has to exercise your creative instincts … If you can run one business well, you can run any business well." Also, "I want Virgin to be as well-known around the world as Coca-Cola … I have enjoyed life a lot more by saying yes than by saying no."

Branson also noted, "Business opportunities are like buses, there's always another one coming … I never get the accountants in before I start up a business. It's done on gut feeling … "

Branson explains, "I have always lived my life by thriving on opportunity and adventure. Some of the best ideas come out of the blue, and you have to keep an open mind to see their virtue … Fantasizing about the future is one of my favorite pastimes … My biggest motivation? Just to keep challenging myself. I see life almost like one long University education that I never had – every day I'm learning something new."

CONCLUSION TO PART I, SECTION 2

From these examples, we see that top people in all kinds of industries approach life by using empowering principles.

When you use the C.O.M.P.E.L. principles, *nothing can stop you.*

In Part II: *Greatest Communicators Handle Fear & Mistakes with Skill – Bouncing Back Stronger than Ever*, we cover essential skills that will make you twice as effective.

Let's move forward …

Part II, Section 1

Great Communicators
Handle Fear & Mistakes with Skill
Bouncing Back Stronger than Ever

WHAT IF you could handle fear and get it out of your way? How amazing and fulfilling would your life be?

As you learn how to handle fear, you will become someone who is heard and trusted. Top professionals are heard and trusted because people believe that they can handle fear with grace and strength.

The greatest communicators have a special advantage: *they are skilled in communicating with themselves.* They talk to themselves in ways that *get them into action.*

How do you talk to yourself about your fears? Many people have become paralyzed by fear. If they have read some idea about how to deal with their fear, trying to apply that idea merely frustrates them.

*Fear defeats more people than any other one thing
in the world.*

RALPH WALDO EMERSON

The good news is that this section will help you *work* with the fear and *transform* it into something you can use to lift your life to a higher level of success and fulfillment.

*Courage is not the absence of fear, but rather the judgment
that something else is more important than fear.*

AMBROSE REDMOON

What could be more important than fear? Living your life with joy and fulfillment.

*I don't believe people are looking for the meaning of
life as much as they are looking for the experience of
being alive.*

JOSEPH CAMPBELL

In this section, I will share three powerful processes for handling fear:

1. Reduce Risk

2. Power Thought/Physiology Method (the Three-Fs)

3. Solution-for-Error Plan

Fear affects much of what we do and what we avoid doing. Some of us are truly diminished by the fear of being hurt. But if we have ways to deal with pain, we become stronger. We experience more freedom.

This discussion about fear is vital if you want to be a great communicator, someone who is heard and trusted. Great communicators deal with their own fears and they help their audiences handle fear, too. Great communicators guide audiences to move beyond fear to real freedom.

Here are Dr. Fred Luskin's comments on how to *free ourselves* from pain by engaging in the process of forgiveness.

Nine Steps of Forgiveness

DR. FRED LUSKIN

My book *Forgive for Good: A Proven Prescription for Health and Happiness* is a primer on how to make peace when things you choose or things chosen for you do not work out well. When painful things happen you have a choice. I teach people to make more forgiving choices. I do this because I understand that as a function of life everyone will have painful experiences as well as pleasant ones. It is a singular power to be able to handle what comes your way without getting lost in blame and suffering. We do not know what the game of life has in store but we do know that forgiveness is one way that provides strength to get back into the game.

As Director of the Stanford Forgiveness Projects my forgiveness methodology has been tested and shown to be successful through a number of research projects. We have demonstrated that forgiveness can reduce stress, blood pressure, anger, depression, hurt, and increase optimism, hope, compassion, physical vitality, and forgiveness. We have worked with people who have been lied to, cheated, abandoned, physically injured, beaten, abused or had their children murdered. Forgiveness training made a significant difference in many of their lives. What follows is our nine step method of teaching and becoming forgiving.

Nine Steps to Forgiveness

1. Know exactly how you feel about what happened and be able to articulate what about the situation is not OK. Then, tell a couple of trusted people about your experience.

2. Make a commitment to yourself to do what you have to do to feel better. Forgiveness is for you and not for anyone else.

3. Forgiveness does not necessarily mean reconciliation with the person that upset you, or condoning of their action. What you are after is to find peace. Forgiveness can be defined as the "peace and understanding that come from blaming that which has hurt you less, taking the life experience less personally, and amending your grievance story."

4. Get the right perspective on what is happening. Recognize that your primary distress is coming from the hurt feelings, thoughts, and physical upset you are suffering now, not what offended you or hurt you two minutes – or ten years – ago.

5. At the moment you feel upset practice stress management to soothe your body's flight or fight response.

6. Give up expecting things from other people, or your life, that they do not choose to give you. Recognize the "unenforceable rules" you have for your health or how you or other people must behave. Remind yourself that you can hope for health, love, friendship and prosperity, and work hard to get them. However, you will suffer when you demand these things occur when you do not have the power to make them happen.

7. Put your energy into looking for another way to get your positive goals met than through the experience that has hurt you. I call this step finding your positive intention. Instead of

mentally replaying your hurt seek out new ways to get what you want.

8. Remember that a life well lived is your best revenge. Instead of focusing on your wounded feelings, and thereby giving the person who caused you pain power over you, learn to look for the love, beauty, and kindness around you. Appreciate what you have more than attending to what you do not have.

9. Amend your grievance story to remind you of the heroic choice to forgive.

Dr. Fred Luskin, author of *Forgive for Good and Forgive for Love*
www.LearningToForgive.com

When we know how to deal with great pain, we can free our personal energy. With more energy, we can take our lives and our businesses to higher levels.

The most successful people, those who enjoy personal fulfillment, are skillful in the ways they handle fear. They realize this truth:

We fear the thing we want the most.

DR. ROBERT ANTHONY

CONCLUSION TO PART II, SECTION 1

Sometimes, people say they want something and then discover that they have failed to take even the smallest actions toward fulfilling their stated goal. Subconsciously, they may be engaged in a tug-of-war of conflicting desires and fears.

Here's the secret: When you bring your feelings about your fears into the open by using the three processes I share in this section, you will have the power to leap forward and create your life on a higher level.

In the next section, you will learn how to reduce risk. This will enable you to take effective action.

Part II, Section 2

Reduce Risk

WHAT LIES BELOW the paralysis many people face when confronted with tough decisions? It is fear. They think, "I'll be hurt."

> *You block your dream when you allow your fear*
> *to grow bigger than your faith.*
>
> MARY MANIN MORRISSEY

What is the faith you need? Faith that you will adapt. How can you have this faith? You prepare.

> *Courage is easier when you're prepared.*
>
> TOM MARCOUX

Now I'll share with you powerful ways to prepare, with the *Reduce Risk System.**

....

* I note that this process manages the risk of failure by managing fear, not risk *per se*. This process reduces perceived risk, thereby enabling one to take effective action.

The most powerful way to handle fear is to *communicate effectively with yourself.*

Researchers note that we communicate with ourselves constantly throughout the day. Random thoughts keep arising: "That worked," or "I can't do that because … " Unfortunately, much of what we think is fear-based.

Author Gene Bedell identified five *buying anxieties:*

1. Reluctance to give up options

2. Fear of making a mistake

3. Social pressures

4. Fear of losing

5. Perceived cost

What does this have to do with handling fear? A lot! When you handle each of these five *buying anxieties,* you empower yourself to take action. So I created a system to reduce risk. We use the R.E.D.U.C.E. process:

R – Revise options

E – Envision solutions to mistakes

D – Disengage from the fear of loss

U – Unleash yourself from social pressures

C – Cover the cost

E – Engage rehearsal

To show how the process works, I will tell you how my client Stephanie went from paralysis and fear about hiring an editor for her new book to taking effective action.

REVISE OPTIONS

Handle the reluctance to give up options

"What if I pick the wrong editor?" Stephanie asked, her voice choked by fear. She thought she had only two options: to pick the best editor or to fail by picking the wrong editor.

Stephanie's black-and-white thinking was keeping her paralyzed. I helped her realize that she could *revise her thinking* about her options and see that she had more than two choices.

Stephanie converted the idea of "best editor" into "good or excellent editor." She reduced the negative emotional charge carried by her fear of failure. With this viewpoint, she *could* take action.

Stephanie set up a four-step plan:

1. Identify her criteria.

2. Contact the local editors' association.

3. Interact with 10 editors.

4. Request to see 500-word samples of the work of three prospective editors.

> *Luck affects everything.*
> *Let your hook be always cast;*
> *in the pool where you least expect it,*
> *there will be a fish.*
>
> OVID

An old phrase says, "Success goes to the activist." By taking action, Stephanie moved through her fear toward a better life. The life she envisions includes ultimately becoming an author of bestselling books. She needs to learn her craft first, so she must find an excellent editor for her current book.

Once, an interviewer mentioned to me, "You have been talking about revising options. Some of my friends face too many options. In fact, they complain, 'I don't have one focus. I wish I had wanted to become a doctor or something like that. At least I would have focused on one thing. But I don't like any one thing that much. What can I do?'"

I replied, "I help a number of clients and audience members who are confronted with this dilemma of too many options and 'I'm not passionate about anything in particular.' We focus on two useful strategies."

Strategies to handle the "I don't have one focus" problem

1. If you're an idea-person, team up with "implementers."

2. Keep a few projects progressing simultaneously.

The idea-person teams up with "implementers"

Some people are idea-people. They can come up with good ideas, but they're *not* interested in becoming experts at the tasks that are involved in implementing those ideas. It helps when idea-people team up with implementers.

Some people are "starters." Implementers are "finishers." They get a lot of joy out of finishing a task well. For example, one of the typesetters of my books loves to complete projects to his standard of excellence. He is an implementer (among other talents). I have no interest in learning how to use typesetting software, so it's best for me to hire someone who will do a terrific job with the typesetting. I'm an idea-person who loves to write.

Keep a few parallel projects progressing simultaneously

For those people who say that they get bored easily with just one project, the solution is to have a few parallel projects progressing simultaneously. This keeps the person feeling constantly renewed because she can rotate the projects.

For example, at this moment I am involved with these projects:

1. I am typing the words of this book (project one).

2. My graphic novel writer is adapting a screenplay that I wrote (project two).

3. My illustrator in Japan is revising the cover of my children's book (project three).

4. My illustrator in San Francisco is revising the character illustrations for my science fiction feature film trilogy (project four).

5. My printer in Maine is printing one of my books (project five).

One interviewer asked me, "Aren't you spreading yourself too thin?"

I replied, "Because I have a number of dreams, I have devoted time and energy to learning the skill of *delegating*. So my projects can progress while I'm not there."

The important idea is to *keep vigilant, watching for one project to become "red-hot."* The way work flows is that at certain times, some projects become popular or gain an almost miraculous momentum. At that point, it is wise to pull back to some degree from the other projects and put the appropriate attention, money, time, and resources into the *red-hot project.*

ENVISION SOLUTIONS TO MISTAKES

Handle the fear of making a mistake

My client Stephanie tells herself that at the worst, she could hire a second editor to correct the first editor's errors. That is a *solution.* This is a strategic plan because Stephanie realizes that *she can recover from a mistake.* She has a plan.

> *To live a creative life, we must lose*
> *our fear of being wrong.*
>
> JOSEPH CHILTON PEARCE

Let's bring this down to financial considerations. Based on her last book's performance, Stephanie thinks she can make a profit of at least $3,000. (And she has a plan to market this new book in more profitable ways.) So if the first editor makes a mistake and Stephanie must hire a second editor at $700, she still clears $1,600.

The solution here is to prepare for what could go wrong. Make sure that you can do fine if you go through a bumpy time.

> *Aim for success, not perfection. Never give up your*
> *right to be wrong, because then you will lose the ability*
> *to learn new things and move forward with your life.*
>
> DR. DAVID M. BURNS

DISENGAGE FROM THE FEAR OF LOSS

Handle the fear of losing

> *Let the fear of danger be a spur to prevent it;*
> *he that fears not, gives advantage to the danger.*
>
> FRANCIS QUARLES

The solution is to think the situation through. How could you lose? How could you *prevent* that loss from happening? And if you do lose, how could you still be okay?

You can reduce the risk of a debilitating loss by using the full R.E.D.U.C.E. process. We have already seen how Stephanie avoided the big fear of losing too much money. Even if she has to hire a second editor, she can still clear $1,600. Stephanie's fear is reduced.

Next, I guided her to a vendor who can do print-on-demand, so Stephanie's first order can be for only 30 books for a fee of approximately $150. In this way, she reduces her fear still further by selecting a small action.

> *Make [your] first action step so tiny and non-threatening that you stop being afraid … If you want to lower your fear level, lower the danger level.*
>
> BARBARA SHER

Now Stephanie can have a friend send an e-mail to a local editors' guild's list of members. This is a small step toward hiring her first editor.

When we lower the danger level, reduce fear, and take action, we create opportunities for success and feelings of fulfillment.

In talking with successful people, I have discovered that they have developed skills for dealing with rejection. In fact, many say that it is their ability to face and persist through rejection that has made the difference in creating their massive success.

Researchers note that the fear of rejection relates to feelings of the loss of self-esteem. In seeking to avoid these feelings of loss, many people avoid situations in which rejection may happen. Now Dr. Elayne Savage guides us to avoid miscommunication and misperceptions, so that we can become stronger and avoid the pitfalls of rejection.

Riding the Runaway-Rejection-Train and Missing the Relationship Boat

ELAYNE SAVAGE, PHD

Isn't it amazing how business and personal relationships can so quickly hit a snag and get off course? The culprits? Miscommunication, Misunderstandings, Mistakes, Missteps, Misreadings, and Miscues. Someone's meaning isn't clear. You try to guess and misread their intent. You bring in your own perceptions and interpretations. You find yourself playing the frustrating game of 'fill-in-the-blanks' and there's at least a 50% chance you're wrong. Unless you clarify, personal and work relationships suffer.

The Prism of Our Misconceptions

We see things through the prism of our misperceptions. Our interpretations pass through a filter containing our private storehouse of experiences accumulated since childhood. These early experiences color our beliefs about the safety of our world and the people in it.

These experiences, when positive, teach us to trust the intentions of others. If they happen to be rejecting experiences, however, we become wary, protecting ourselves from further hurts.

Here's how it happens. You are walking down the hallway at work. You pass a senior colleague who doesn't say hello. What do you tell yourself? Do you go through your emotional checklist?

- "Do I have a stain on my shirt or food in my teeth?"

- "Did I do a bad job on that last report?"

- "They don't like me."

- "Oh no, I'm going to be fired."

Fired! How quickly you go there. Isn't it fascinating how we 'fill-in-the-blanks' with self-doubt and self-rejection when we don't know the real explanation. And to make matters worse, we tend to ruminate on these misconceptions, dwelling on them for hours or days.

Most likely the explanation is that your colleague was wrapped up in his or her own thoughts and didn't see you. It would help if you could put yourself in the other person's shoes. If you find yourself still dwelling, what would it take to clarify the situation and clear the air?

Feeling Like the Bull's-Eye in a Target

The times when we find ourselves in the center of our universe we tend to make the situation all about us. We take someone's comment or action as a personal affront. No wonder we feel like the bull's-eye in a target – just waiting for the dart's sting. And perhaps even expecting it.

Getting hurt leads to protecting ourselves from more hurt. When we feel like a target, vulnerable and unprotected, it's hard not to take it personally. And it takes some work to get out of the center, put ourselves in the other person's shoes, imagine what might be going on for them.

The Dance Between Taking Things Personally and Rejection

Taking things personally involves feeling disrespected and rejected, feeling blamed, slighted or personally attacked. We get our feelings hurt by misinterpreting the meanings of others. We see the actions of others as a personal affront, believing someone wants to hurt us. We let our emotions be controlled by what somebody says or does (or what they neglect to say or do.)

The tendency is to protect ourselves, pulling back, even to the point of 'disappearing.' One woman describes how she "goes invisible, contracting into a pinpoint, withdrawing from everybody and everything."

Sometimes the tendency is to snap at the 'offender,' attack back, or explode in a blaze of rage. And you know this isn't helpful for productive relationships.

When you're feeling snubbed, hurt, and rejected, how will you react the next time you see that person? Will your hurt show on your face or body language? Might they interpret this as judgment or disdain? Or will it look like 'attitude' to them. Now it's the other person's turn to 'fill in the blanks' with messages from their own prism of misperceptions.

Talk About Vicious Cycles!

Each person affects and is affected by the other person's behavior. Reciprocity is the effect of behavior on subsequent behaviors. One response begets another in a circular process of relating.

For example, Jane says something to John. John thinks Jane means something negative or critical. He doesn't check it out. John's response is to protect himself and he withdraws. Jane feels rejected by his withdrawal and reacts by getting hurt or angry. In other words, the behavior of each person affects the behavior of the relationship. Jane doesn't do it to John. John doesn't do it to Jane. They do it with each other.

Getting Off that Runaway-Rejection-Train

All too often confusing behaviors don't get addressed, checked out, and clarified. Soon you don't know what to say or how to say it. So you don't say anything. The relationship becomes strained, you begin to feel awkward and uncomfortable.

Next, you're avoiding or limiting contact with them. They may tell themselves you are ignoring them. Ignoring feels like disrespect. Disrespect feels like a rejection. And once both of you get on that runaway-rejection-train, it's hard to get off.

Misunderstandings and hurt feelings lead to bitterness and resentment. There is no space left for connection.

It's best to deal directly with the issue and the person. The idea of 'confronting' is surely scary. However, confronting the situation is not the same as confronting the person. You could start by identifying and addressing the awkwardness. At least that's an entree back into a respectful relationship. You might say: "I've noticed that it's been awkward between us lately. I wonder if it has felt the same for you? I'd like our relationship to get back on track. Can we talk about how we can make this happen?"

Here are some tips for not boarding the rejection-train in the first place:

Elayne Savage's 10 Sure-Fire Ways To Avoid Rejection

- Remind yourself, it's more about the other person than it is about you.

- Separate the "personal" from the "professional."

- Don't presume – clarify and check things out.

- Don't try to read someone's mind – or expect them to read yours.

- Put yourself in the other person's shoes. How might they be feeling?

- Remember: you really do have choices.

- Be direct. Ask for what you need.

- Practice "time outs" to collect your thoughts. Even counting to 10 helps.

- Try rejecting rejection for a change.

- And *don't take it personally*

Elayne Savage, PhD, is The Queen of Rejection. Professional Speaker, Communication Coach and Author of *Don't Take It Personally! The Art of Dealing with Rejection* and *Breathing Room – Creating Space to Be a Couple*

(510) 540-6230
www.QueenOfRejection.com

Successful people become skillful in dealing rejection. They make sure that any fear of possible rejection does not stop them from making the next phone call and meeting the next person.

Just imagine: *What would you do if you had no fear?*

Grab a sheet of paper or your journal and write down your answer.

My client Marina wrote, "I would call the local college's illustration department and find a good student to illustrate the children's book I've written."

Your life will change when you experience this process: *Every year I live a new year.* I do new things. *I move beyond fear.* Remember …

> *Do the thing we fear, and death of fear is certain.*
>
> RALPH WALDO EMERSON

Create an environment in which you can rehearse. If you fear public speaking, join Toastmasters. Do something proactive. For example, the popular comedian Don Rickles discovered his comedy act by dealing with hecklers.

> *A man of courage is also full of faith.*
>
> MARCUS TULLIUS CICERO

Take a step forward. You will lift your spirits and the spirits of those around you.

> *There is no duty we so underrate as the duty of being happy. By being happy we sow anonymous benefits upon the world.*
>
> ROBERT LOUIS STEVENSON

We discover that we can enjoy happy times when we learn to move beyond fear. We do *not* let the fear of loss control us. We remember to think the situation through.

- Identify how to prevent a loss.

- Plan how we can recover *if* a loss occurs.

Let's move on to the next step …

Unleash Yourself from Social Pressures

Handle social pressures

Stephanie wants the approval of other authors in her industry. She also wants to position herself for greater success. A solution is for Stephanie to hire *two* editors on purpose. She then has double the possibility of getting her work to rise to the level of excellence.

The greatest communicators realize that fear subsides when you devote yourself to the process and *focus* in the moment.

> *The way you overcome shyness is to become so wrapped up in something that you forget to be afraid.*
>
> LADY BIRD JOHNSON

The point here is that Stephanie can immerse herself in the process of refining her book's text. She can view the corrections noted by the first editor, make revisions, and improve the quality of her book. Then she can give her revised draft to a second editor, the "last-eyes editor."

The most productive people in any field realize that in order to improve, you need to practice your craft. It is likely that Stephanie's next book will be better than her current book. We learn by doing.

We can also learn to deal with criticism of our earliest work. Some people feel social pressure because they fear that they cannot recover from the criticism of their early work.

I worked with a client, a filmmaker, who found that someone had taken excerpts from her first film and placed them on YouTube.com. She developed her own answers to criticism:

- "Did you laugh?"

- "Works for some; doesn't work for others."

- "That was at the beginning of my career."

- "That's a part of my body of work."

Just knowing how she would be able to respond to any criticism lowered my client's fear level. With less fear, she was free to devote her energy to her current work. Do you see how being prepared for criticism can *free up your personal energy?*

COVER THE COST

Handle perceived cost

"How much does it cost?" Some salespeople dread this question. If the perceived cost of any project is too high, a person is unlikely to take action. However, when you want to be at your best, you must uncover the *real cost of inaction.*

The real cost of inaction can be the loss of an opportunity. Or it can be the pain of remaining stuck in a rut. Not taking action can create stagnation. That is the real cost of inaction.

The real cost hurts. Imagine being stuck in a dead-end job, or being stuck in your own small business and barely hanging on.

Now that we know the real cost of inaction, we can carefully and strategically plan our next move.

> *If a problem can be solved with money, it is no longer a problem. It is an expense.*
>
> HARVEY MACKAY

This is how Stephanie steps up, reduces her risk and takes action: when she thinks through her options and runs the numbers, she discovers that she can handle an additional cost if it proves necessary. As we saw earlier, if she must hire a second editor to make up for the first editor's mistakes, she will have invested $1,400 – and she can still clear $1,600. This realization makes it easier for Stephanie to take action.

Engage in Rehearsal

> *Fear helps us when we use it as a springboard for preparation and as energy for heightened senses.*
>
> TOM MARCOUX

What is a prime cure for nervousness? Rehearsal. After years of speaking to audiences, I still get occasional pre-speech jitters. My solution? Whenever I have a driver to take me to a speaking engagement, I rehearse in the car.

> *It is no use saying, 'We are doing our best.' You have got to succeed in doing what is necessary.*
>
> WINSTON CHURCHILL

The necessary thing is to move forward. Taking action is necessary. *Rehearsing is necessary.* Taking action does not make us immune to mistakes, but using the R.E.D.U.C.E. process makes it possible to avoid much damage.

Strive not to be a success, but rather to be of value.

ALBERT EINSTEIN

When you focus on giving value, you can let go of the fear that you're not perfect.

CONCLUSION TO PART II, SECTION 2

In this section, we have explored the way to lessen the risk of any action through the R.E.D.U.C.E. process:

R – Revise options

E – Envision solutions to mistakes

D – Disengage from the fear of loss

U – Unleash yourself from social pressures

C – Cover the cost

E – Engage in rehearsal

When you reduce risk, you significantly reduce your resistance to action.

Part II, Section 3

Power Thought / Physiology Process
(The Three-Fs)

A man who is afraid will do anything.

JAWAHARLAL NEHRU

We can use this insight. We can take our fear and convert it into empowering energy by using the *Three-Fs* process:

Find your fear ⇨ *Flip it* ⇨ *Forward It.*

See the process below and fill in your own answers per the table on the next page.

The idea of "relaxing into" tells us that there are some things that we *cannot* solve with action. For example, to recover from the stress and strain of a hectic day, we actually need to disengage from our schedule of rushing around and just relax. So sometimes "what I can do" becomes simply to take six minutes for quiet time.

When I'm on a train, I set my timer for six minutes. I do some deep breathing and repeat a relaxing phrase in my mind. This brightens my day.

The Three-Fs Process

	Find It	Flip It	Forward It
Question	What are you afraid of?	What do you really want?	What can you do? What can you relax into?
Example	"I'm afraid of inadequate funds to support my spouse and me in retirement."	"I want an abundance of funds for retirement."	"Make a list of my talents. Look into how I can use these talents on a part-time basis and … "

Judge each day not by the harvest you reap,
but by the seeds you plant.

ROBERT LOUIS STEVENSON

By having a daily six-minute quiet time, you plant seeds of success. Similarly, you plant seeds by using the Three-Fs process to transform your experience of fear into a sense of power.

Now I'll share a personal example to show you the Three-Fs process in action. My sweetheart likes roller-coasters. Over the years, I found myself wanting to avoid being knocked about by this kind of thrill ride. Let's see how this looks.

THE THREE-FS PROCESS

Find It ⇨ *Flip It* ⇨ *Forward It*

What are you afraid of?

Adding discomfort to my day by being knocked about by a thrill ride.

What do you really want?

To enjoy time with my sweetheart, doing what she likes to do.

What can you do? What can you relax into?

This brought me to the point of discovering what I could do to *forward it* – to move forward from fear into fulfillment.

Fortunately, I saw a documentary about roller-coasters. I learned that many roller-coaster fans actually enjoy the queasy experience of zero gravity as the roller-coaster goes over the peaks on the ride. They call that moment "airtime."

I resolved to take the empowering word "airtime" with me on the next roller-coaster ride with my sweetheart. When we went through the zero-gravity times, I told myself, "This is airtime. People like this." And something amazing happened: I got a whole new interpretation of the thrill ride experience.

Now I have my favorite roller-coasters at Walt Disney World: Rock 'n' Roller Coaster and Expedition Everest. I also appreciate Top Gun at Great America in California. By having an empowering thought, I changed my experience of the event.

Let's notice that the Power Thought/Physiology Process (Three-Fs) begins with a question. In response to this question, you have a thought. Effective thoughts actually change your physiology in a way that benefits your life.

You are today where your thoughts have brought you;
you will be tomorrow where your thoughts take you.

JAMES ALLEN

CONCLUSION TO PART II, SECTION 3

Use the Three-Fs process to change your thoughts and experiences. In this way, you can use fear as a springboard to a higher level of personal success and fulfillment.

Part II, Section 4

Solution-for-Error Plan

WHAT IF you had no fear of making mistakes? Would you try more things? Would your career take a leap forward?

Great communicators are effective because they take action, learn, and improve through feedback. If you do nothing, you cannot improve.

My clients use the Solution-for-Error Plan to gain these terrific benefits:

- Live an extraordinary life

- Remove self-defeating patterns

- Eliminate guilt feelings

You can live an extraordinary life

Top achievers who experience deep satisfaction and fulfillment have effectively learned how to stretch themselves, make mistakes, and learn so they can improve their performance.

The secret is that when we make a mistake, we quickly learn from it and do better. This is the reason I have developed the *Solution-for-Error* process.

> *An error doesn't become a mistake*
> *until you refuse to correct it.*
>
> ORLANDO A. BATTISTA

> *I have missed more than 9,000 shots in my career. I have lost almost 300 games. On 26 occasions I have been entrusted to take the game winning shot, and I missed. And I have failed over and over and over again in my life. And that is precisely why I succeed.*
>
> MICHAEL JORDAN

> *Anyone who doesn't make mistakes*
> *isn't trying hard enough.*
>
> WESS ROBERTS

The people who take leaps forward in their lives engage in calculated risks. An old phrase says, "The person who never makes a mistake always takes orders from one who does." I have seen the value of this idea from talking with highly effective people. Entrepreneurs, and company presidents take calculated risks. They have employees who keep their heads down and seek only security. These employees prefer to accomplish routine tasks.

> *Creativity is allowing yourself to make mistakes.*
> *Art is knowing which ones to keep.*
>
> SCOTT ADAMS

Researchers note that society provides big rewards to people who express their creativity and natural brilliance. Producers, actors, presidents, CEOs, and entrepreneurs are rewarded with astronomical salaries, bonuses, and residual income.

The idea is to harvest wisdom from your experiences. Think of the old phrase, "Good judgment comes from experience. Experience often comes from bad judgment." Let's harvest wisdom from our own experiences.

The Solution-for-Error Plan helps us to impact our subconscious minds quickly and powerfully with the lessons we need to learn so that we experience deep understanding. In this way, we empower ourselves.

> *When I did [the feature film] 1941, I felt I was made of Teflon. I felt that anything I put on film was going to succeed. I felt invincible. And in a sense, at that point in my life, the best thing that could have happened was the drubbing that 1941 got both from the critics and the public … I sobered up so quickly. [On 1941] I had gotten so precious … I should have had a second unit film the Ferris wheel [miniature special effects … I was taking 20 takes on simple insert shots]. I couldn't let go. I couldn't share the workload with anyone. And I learned the greatest lessons of my career just from the experience of 1941 … I went from the disaster of 1941 to my first day of shooting on Raiders [of the Lost Ark]. In a sense, Raiders rescued me from getting self-involved with 'Oh dear, the movie is going to be a failure and all the critics will hate it' … By the time I did Raiders, I was humbled. Every shot was storyboarded. I was 14 days under schedule … Raiders of the Lost Ark was probably the most prepared I have ever been in my career to direct a movie, and it paid off.*

STEVEN SPIELBERG

I noticed that my clients felt limitations because of certain ideas they had read in books. Those books included good ideas, but the ideas were not integrated and hands-on. Many books do not give us a way to play with the material and feel it. Again and again, I've noticed people communicating lovely ideas that were merely rationally-oriented. To make massive progress, you need to feel it. As James Brown sang many years ago, "I feel good!"

With this insight, I developed the Solution-for-Error Plan to overcome the limitations that can arise in people from their mere reading of ideas in books.

Remove self-defeating patterns

Would your life leap forward to more enjoyment and greater success if you could break your self-defeating patterns? The Solution-for-Error Plan helps us pay attention to what went wrong and how to fix it.

For novice salespeople, self-defeating behaviors include devoting too little time to study and rehearsal, and then winging it. Winging it often leads to missed sales. Top producers study, rehearse their presentations and close more sales. With the Solution-for-Error Plan, we identify beneficial behaviors that can lead to breakthroughs.

Eliminate guilt feelings

How much lighter would you feel if you could eliminate guilt feelings?

The Solution-for-Error Plan helps us quickly develop a game plan for doing better. It is a planning process that allows us to escape from the endless loop of vague guilt feelings. Through this process, we can identify ineffective behaviors and focus on correcting them. We can say, "Okay, I blew it that time, but now I know how I can do better next time."

Psychologists have pointed out that punishment can often be ineffective because it only stops a behavior without providing productive alternative behavior. The Solution-for-Error Plan helps us identify the solutions, or productive alternative behaviors, so that we feel relieved and empowered.

> *You always pass failure on the way to success.*
>
> MICKEY ROONEY

> *Nobody has a problem; it's only a decision waiting to be made. If my so-called "problem" is the result of a bad decision that I made yesterday, then all I have to do is make another decision – a better decision – today!*
>
> ROBERT H. SCHULLER

> *As a general rule the most successful man in life is the man who has the best information.*
>
> BENJAMIN DISRAELI

Some of the best information only becomes available when you take action and discover how you function in new and challenging situations. You learn where your natural brilliance is and which areas you need to improve. You may also learn that it is better to delegate certain tasks to people who have a natural talent in an area in which you do *not* excel.

> *A discovery is said to be an accident meeting a prepared mind.*
>
> ALBERT VON SZENT GYORGYI

Many of the most successful people have noted that we learn more from a mistake or failure than from a successful outcome. The Solution-for-Error Plan helps you squeeze any experience and get the learning from it. You learn from what went wrong so you *can* correct it.

> *Failure is success if we learn from it.*
>
> MALCOLM FORBES

Before we go any further, I will show you the form that my companies use. We dare to achieve; occasionally, therefore, a situation turns out in a disappointing manner. The point is to learn, plan a better approach for future action and move on.

> *You miss 100% of the shots you don't take.*
>
> WAYNE GRETZKY

> *It's better to explore life and make mistakes than to play it safe. Mistakes are part of the dues one pays for a full life.*
>
> SOPHIA LOREN

What if a 10-minute method could help you squeeze an experience or tough situation and learn what you need to learn from it? That method is the *Solution-for-Error Plan.*

Let's go into action and learn the Solution-for-Error Plan from this fictional example.

Solution-for-Error Plan (example)

Step 1

What's the error and what led to it?

Started a business with another person, with whom I did not develop a full written agreement. We were friends. We trusted each other as friends and thought that we were compatible as business partners.

What were the painful consequences, or the feelings you want to avoid?

It broke my heart when I found that I could not rely on my business partner to carry the ball when I was tired. I felt abandoned. Finally, the business was failing because it needed both of us to have full dedication in the startup phase.

Step 2

How can you avoid the error? What can you do better?

I can (a) study what I need in a business partner, (b) hold a number of meetings with any potential partner, (c) hire a well-respected consultant to help assess whether we are compatible as business partners, and (d) write a full agreement, including an exit strategy.

Step 3

How can you compensate for your own tendency?

My tendency is to jump right in and not take time to look at all potential problems. I can compensate for that tendency by hiring someone (who is highly recommended) to walk through the potential consequences with me.

Step 4

What did you do right?

I took action. I learned what does not work for me. Now that I know what my tendencies can create, I can be careful in similar situations.

Step 5

What does the solution look like? What does it feel like?

I gain the right business partner, whom I can trust. My ideal is the partnership of Walt Disney and his brother, Roy O. Disney.

Step 6

What are the benefits of the solution to you? To the team?

I will save myself from heartache and stress. With the right business partner, my quality of life will improve. I won't have to stay at the office all the time. I'll have time for my family. My team will feel better and be more productive when I am not stressed out.

Step 7

How can you reward yourself for taking action?

I will make relaxation appointments for myself: time for reading, taking hot baths, and walking in nature.

Now let us investigate the Solution-for-Error Plan in greater detail.

WHAT'S THE ERROR AND WHAT LED TO IT?

I chose the word *error* with care. As we noted earlier,

> *An error doesn't become a mistake*
> *until you refuse to correct it.*
>
> ORLANDO A. BATTISTA

The first step is to face up to the error. We must acknowledge that we had something to do with the situation. We need to pay close attention to the details of what happened and then write down the error. Write what caused you to feel bad or what action you failed to take. For example, a workshop participant wrote, "I allowed myself to get tired, so that I was irritable later."

Many people respect the one who admits an error and says, "With what I know now, here is my new plan … "

What led to the error?

Note the steps that led to the error. They may be something like staying up too late, or procrastinating on doing research to prepare for a first meeting with a potential client.

What were the painful consequences or feelings I want to avoid?

Identify the feelings related to the error that you want to avoid. For example, "I want to avoid feeling angry"; "I want to avoid feeling wronged"; or "I want to avoid feeling ignored." You can begin the process of dropping these feelings when you write them down in your Solution-for-Error Plan.

To create behavior change, we often need to stop and become aware of the price we have paid for the error. We need to recognize the error's consequences. The consequence of an error can be, "I feel that I failed the job interview because I didn't prepare beforehand by studying the company."

The good news is that as soon as you identify the error and what led to it, you have power that you didn't have moments before. You can take action from this moment onward to do better in life.

Now you're ready for the next question.

How Can You Avoid the Error? What Can You do Better?

Fear is the father of courage and the mother of safety.

HENRY H. TWEEDY

Errors frequently occur because we didn't do something or we didn't prepare for a situation. We need to take preventative, proactive steps, which are like preventative medicine. This is proactive: you need to go out there and do it first, to prevent negative consequences from happening.

Consider every mistake you do make as an asset.

PAUL J. MEYER

Many of us remember procrastinating on a school paper until the night before it was due. Then we berated ourselves, telling ourselves, "I'll never let it get this bad again." Does this sound familiar? Does it remind you of how you prepare the paperwork for your taxes?

With the Solution-for-Error Plan, you'll have a powerful incentive to avoid letting this happen again, because you're going to remember how much pain the error caused. Also, you'll remember all the good things you can create in your life by taking proactive steps. You will have leverage on yourself in both directions: pain and joy (or pleasure).

An important component of this step is to note due dates for your proactive steps.

What can we do better?

In order to do better, we often need a team. In a team of people, one person can compensate for another's shortcoming.

Sometimes it helps to have a *post-game review*. For example, one friend told me about an error he experienced during a memorial service. A group of people gathered on a 70-foot yacht for the spreading of ashes in the ocean. Later, my friend told me, "I wasn't thinking straight. The grief had distracted me. If I was thinking clearly, I would have asked my wife to wear a life-jacket. No one wore life-jackets. Fortunately, no one fell over the side, even though the ocean was rough."

My friend was concerned about his oversight. He told me, "I am repeating this story to you so *I* learn the lesson."

Learning the lesson is the purpose of answering the question, "How can you avoid the error? What can we do better?"

How Can You Compensate for Your Own Tendency?

> *Harvest wisdom from an error and you are twice blessed: you won't repeat the error and you know what to compensate for.*
>
> TOM MARCOUX

Know your tendencies and compensate for them.

People who accomplish more and feel inner peace have a different perspective on the mistakes they make. They understand that life is constantly offering us lessons. If we don't learn the lessons, the opportunities for learning (what we call our "problems") are repeated until we learn to take effective action. So we do well when we learn to compensate for a troublesome personal tendency.

To compensate is to make a correction. A salesperson may talk too much, leave out a detail, forget to ask for the sale, or miss the chance to engage a new person in conversation (and miss the resulting referrals). This salesperson can compensate by turning each mistake around. If he or she talks too much, the turn around is to listen more.

In your personal journal, write down some of your mistakes and find the turn around for each mistake. You'll make surprising progress when you follow through with this process.

WHAT DID YOU DO RIGHT?

A balanced view of our actions often reveals that we did something right. This section reminds us that there are certain behavior patterns we should keep.

Sometimes we take the right action and something still doesn't work. Perhaps the interviewer was feeling ill, so the meeting went poorly in spite of our preparation. We don't always know. In any case, we need to *keep up our morale* by acknowledging our correct efforts.

Buckminster Fuller, who was considered a genius, emphasized the value of learning from mistakes:

> *If I ran a school, I'd give the average grade to the ones who gave me all the right answers, for being good parrots. I'd give the top grades to those who made a lot of mistakes and told me about them, and then told me what they learned from them.*
>
> BUCKMINSTER FULLER

> *Constant effort and frequent mistakes are the stepping stones of genius.*
>
> ELBERT HUBBARD

> *[For my first album, Virgin Records] gave me no budget – practically no budget. I said 'Prince, I will choreograph for you for free; you write me a song' … I worked with Kool and the Gang – [and I said] I need rhythm tracks; for your next tour [I'll choreograph for you]. I would go on and on, and I would barter deals …*
>
> PAULA ABDUL

Paula Abdul's first album was a big success, due in large part to the quality she gained with her bartered deals. But during her successful career as a popular music icon, she was not immune to feelings of self-doubt.

> *[I had] the real scary feeling of 'Oh, no, I'm a fraud. I'm just waiting for them to find out. Fraud, fraud, fraud, fraud. Because I never knew that everyone else does the same thing. You end up becoming who you are by actually jumping into that circle of fear and doing it. And that's how you end up believing in yourself.*
>
> PAULA ABDUL

We learn from Paula that the process is about doing and learning as you go.

We do not wait for the absence of fear. We use fear to help us learn what we need to do better.

This reminds me of how persistent Randy Pausch was in pursuing his childhood goal of becoming an Imagineer. He pushed beyond the first rejection letters that came to him from Walt Disney Imagineering. He continued in his efforts and eventually worked with Walt Disney Imagineering on Disney's *Aladdin*. Randy said:

> *The brick walls are there for a reason: they are there to give us a chance to show how badly we want something. Because the brick walls are there to stop those people who don't want it badly enough.... If you lead your life the right way, the karma will take care of itself, the dreams will come to you.*
>
> DR. RANDY PAUSCH

When we focus on what *we did right*, we often discover that we can feel good about some of our efforts. With this encouragement, we have the energy to refine our approach for the next occasion.

WHAT DOES THE SOLUTION LOOK/FEEL LIKE?

If we think happy thoughts we will be happy. If we think miserable thoughts, we will be miserable.

DALE CARNEGIE

Identify what you can do that will prevent a similar error from occurring in the future. Perhaps you can rehearse or write out your sales pitch. You might find that exercising or changing your diet will provide you with more energy. These are actions you can use to replace self-defeating actions.

What are you going to get after you change your behavior? Are you going to serve more people, make more money, win an award or earn a vacation in Hawaii? You can use the Solution-for-Error Plan for every area of your life. You can use it to enhance your personal and business relationships.

Ask yourself, "What do I want to feel?" One client wrote, "I want to feel connected. I want to feel on course with my purpose." Often we want to feel powerful, strong, healthy, and joyful. It is crucial to target the feelings you want that the Solution can provide. You *can* feel prosperous, successful, and good about yourself.

WHAT ARE THE BENEFITS OF THE SOLUTION?

Possible benefits, to you, to the team:

- I feel closer to my loved one.

- I have great job interviews.

- I feel relaxed.

- I feel the tension drain from my shoulders.

- I feel at peace more often during the day.

Here's an example of a valuable benefit, noted in this e-mail message from a client:

> Tom, I had another social success after applying some of the techniques I learned in your workshop and book. I am on the social committee here at work. We had our company Thanksgiving lunch and Potluck last Thursday. I was on the decorating committee, and as it turned out, ended up being the hostess as well. As people brought in the food, they started asking me where to put things, and – Well, I ended up directing things. There was one moment of panic. I had left for a few minutes, to wash my hands and as I came back I heard the roar of voices. The room had been filling up in my absence, and the voices seemed to reach a deafening volume (anxiety attack), but I took a deep breath, told myself this was an improvisation of a party-scene where I was the confident hostess, and walked in. I used your method of 'Act as if.' Someone came up to me to ask if there was anything that still needed to be done,

and that helped me get started directing things once again. Thanks Tom, for helping me through another tricky situation.

My client acted as if she were a confident hostess. With more practice, she is likely to find that she eventually *feels* like a confident hostess.

> *You gain strength, courage, and confidence by every experience in which you really stop to look fear in the face. You must do the thing you think you cannot do.*
>
> ELEANOR ROOSEVELT

When you focus on the real benefit, you feel the energy to take an appropriate risk. We need to remember to take action in the manner of a person who believes in himself or herself. When start to trust yourself, other people follow along and trust you, too.

How Can you Reward Yourself for Taking Action?

What tangible reward will you immediately present to *yourself* for changing your own behavior? I call this a *self-reward*. For example, I sometimes associate the purchase of a book with the successful accomplishment of a specific action. During my seminars, audience members suggest self-rewards such as a warm bath, reading a book, and getting a neck massage.

A special form of reward

The power to transcend fear comes from our burning desire and intense interest in *doing the actual work*. The work itself needs to be intrinsically enjoyable and valuable to us.

> *If you think that the finished book is of greater value than what you learned from the writing process, you are mistaken.*
>
> TERRY BROOKS

> *If you don't think there is magic in writing, you probably won't write anything magical.*
>
> TERRY BROOKS

Many people would like to have written a book. But the effective writers I know *like* to write. Find what *you like doing*.

Principle:

Use the *Solution-for-Error Plan* to help you learn and move on.

Power Question:

If you knew that you could not fail, what would you attempt? (If you learn from each experience, there is no failure.)

On the next page, find a blank copy of the *Solution-for-Error Plan* form for your repeated use.

SOLUTION-FOR-ERROR PLAN

Step 1. What's the error and what led to it? What are the painful consequences, or the feelings you want to avoid?

Step 2. How can you avoid the error? What can you do better?

Step 3. How can you compensate for your own tendency?

Step 4. What did you do right?

Step 5. What does the solution look like? What does it feel like?

Step 6. What are the benefits of the solution to you? To the team?

Step 7. How can you reward yourself for taking action?

© *Tom Marcoux, TomSuperCoach.com*

CONCLUSION TO PART II, SECTION 4

In Part II, Section 4, we explored the *Solution-for-Error Plan.*

> *What is your peaceful preference? … What is the course of action that adds most to your present peace?*
>
> HUGH PRATHER

We can make choices that enhance our quiet strength.

In Part III: *How to Help People Feel at Ease and Want to Say "Yes!" to You*, we will cover gentle ways to remove resistance and help you become influential.

Let's take the next step …

Part III

How to Help People Feel at Ease and Want to Say "Yes!" to You*

WHEN I was in Walt Disney World, I wanted to get something done that was different and against the stated policy. To gain people's cooperation, I made sure to tune in to *their* language.

At a fantasy photo concession, I wanted a photo in which my friend and I looked like we were flying, but Disney World policy indicated that photos needed to show the customer performing a skydiving motion. I said to the person taking photos, "This photo is a fantasy anyway. Have us flying, just like Peter Pan."

My friend had whispered in my ear, "Just like Superman." But as part of my strategy, I *avoided* saying anything about Superman (a Warner Bros/DC Comics character). By using the language of Disney, thereby making it easy for them to honor my unusual request, I gained agreement to my suggestion.

<hr>

* Formerly titled *Communicate to Win.*

We will use the W.I.N.–T.H.E.–P.R.I.Z.E. process:

> W – Walk up the chain of command

> I – Impress the person that you're staying

> N – Nudge politely

> T – Tune in to language

> H – Hone your approach

> E – Establish your credibility

> P – Persist

> R – Record notes

> I – Itemize "this or that"

> Z – Zero in on de-escalating

> E – Encounter the reputable

Let's move forward …

WALK UP THE CHAIN OF COMMAND

At the bottom of the chain of command of any organization, you have clerks, whose role is only to respond to stated policies. To get action that is beyond the organization's policy, you need to go up the chain of command. Politely ask, "Please connect me with your supervisor." If the clerk says, "I'm sorry. That person is not in today," you can respond, "Please pass me to someone on the same level as your supervisor or above," or, "That's not going to get me satisfaction today."

To get what you want, you may need to stretch. This reminds me of the experience of Jack Canfield, bestselling coauthor of the *Chicken Soup for the Soul* series. He began giving seminars many years ago, and he was having some financial trouble. He went to another speaker and asked, "How do you get $800 a day?" This was a large sum in those days.

"I ask for it," the speaker replied.

Jack described his clenched feelings as he tried to get the words out the next time he was asked, "What is your fee?" He was in the clutch of fear. Finally, he managed to say, "Ughhhh – $800 a day."

"Okay," the person replied. In that moment, Jack became an $800-per-day speaker. Now he makes $35,000–70,000 per keynote address.

Jack was surprised that the person said "okay" so readily. That same outcome often happens when we gently press for what we want.

Principle:

Move up the chain of command to interact with one who has the authority to solve the problem.

Power Question:

What words feel better for you to use when you ask to talk with someone in authority?

IMPRESS THE PERSON THAT YOU'RE STAYING

> *Do what you feel in your heart to be right – for you'll*
> *be criticized anyway.*
>
> ELEANOR ROOSEVELT

Make sure that your words and tone impress the person that you are not going away. You can say, "So, what does your firm do to take care of good customers who have been inconvenienced?" You can follow up with, "Perhaps I need to talk with your supervisor or someone higher up to get satisfaction today."

In addition to making it clear that you will not give up, you must stay polite. If you lose your temper, the person can "write you off." Instead, by politely but firmly holding your ground, you will get help towards a solution.

Principle:

You can gain a solution by impressing the person that you will stay, and by politely requiring satisfaction.

Power Question:

Who will help you rehearse polite but firm statements?

Nudge Politely

A hotel refused to let people check into their rooms before three in the afternoon. I said, "You have two guests who have been awake for 48 hours. Either we're going to have to fall asleep in the first aid section, or you can provide the service that (name of the hotel firm) is so famous for and find us another room. Do you need to talk with your manager about this?" Within three minutes, the room was found.

My use of the phrase "the service that (name of the hotel firm) is so famous for" was a form of verbal aikido. Aikido is a martial art in which you use your opponent's force against him. Basically, you guide the opponent in the direction he is already going. The use of verbal aikido ties in with the principle, "nudge politely."

Non-resistance, non-judgment, and non-attachment
are the three aspects of true enlightenment.

ECKHART TOLLE

The effective person avoids creating resistance in the one she's dealing with. If you get angry or insult the person or company, you hurt yourself by creating resistance. As in aikido, it is better to gently but firmly guide the person towards the outcome you prefer.

Principle:

As in aikido, it often helps to nudge a person in the direction in which you want him or her to go.

Power Question:

How can you clearly and politely communicate what you want?

Tune in to Language

Have you noticed that organizations have buzzwords? When you use them, you create the feeling that, "Yes, we're in this together."

Some doctors use language to keep a distance from their patients. Their language shows, "We're in the know, and you're not," or "We're in the 'in group.'"

Using the appropriate language can help you gain what you want. Study the language of the profession of the person you want to influence. Use his or her language to develop a rapport.

In my book *Nothing Can Stop You This Year!* I introduce my concept, the Ease-Through™. Many people try to push their point and encounter resistance. The pusher tries harder, and the other person *resists* harder. The pusher wants a breakthrough, like a karate punch to a board.

With the Ease-Through, you just remove the board. This is the power of effective language. Avoid saying, "I want a refund!" Ask instead, "So, how does Acme Company keep loyal customers happy?"

> *Nothing is softer or more flexible than water,*
> *yet nothing can resist it.*
>
> LAO-TZU

Principle:

Use the other person's language to develop a rapport with him or her.

Power Question:

What sources of information can you go to, such as a Google Search, before your meeting so that you can be prepared to speak in the other person's language (use their buzzwords)?

HONE YOUR APPROACH

How can you be at your best when you need to influence someone?

Dictionary.com defines *hone* as "to make more acute or effective; improve; perfect: to hone one's skills."

A powerful way to hone any skill is to *have winning experiences*. A workshop or a private coaching session is an ideal place for this to occur. For the clients I coach, I invite them to send me 10 specific questions *before* the coaching session. Then we focus on their specific areas of concern.

In my workshops, I have coached participants in how to have a vocal tone that is firm *and* friendly. A friendly, firm approach is to have a pleasant tone and repeat gently, "Thanks for your efforts on this. And we still need to get me satisfaction today. Who has the power to help keep your loyal customer happy about this situation?"

At the center of your being you have the answer; you know who you are and you know what you want.

LAO-TZU

To get to the quiet center of our being, many of us take deep calming breaths, pray or meditate before calling or seeing an opponent.

To the mind that is still, the whole universe surrenders.

LAO-TZU

To have a friendly, firm approach, *you need to know your own natural rhythms and take care of yourself*. When you talk with someone, you need to have a reserve of patience and calm energy. For example, Sylvester "Sly" Stallone, actor and screenwriter of *Rocky*, started out and discovered his own creative rhythms. Sly said, "In New York, I wrote from midnight to the morning.

I wrote my most nihilistic material. I went through my [Edgar Allen] Poe period."

On the other hand, Sly took a different approach to the screenplay for *Rocky*. He said, "To write *Rocky*, I wrote early in the morning. I was writing from 6:00 in the morning until 12 noon … I use a big pencil because at the end of six hours you're writing like this [holding the pencil in his fist] … If I had a problem writing, I told my subconscious mind, I want you to solve it by morning."

We notice that Sly Stallone used all his resources, including his subconscious mind. As a sidenote, Sly said, "Redemption is one of my themes. I never met anyone who didn't want a second chance." He took a big chance when he added 41 pounds to play a washed-out sheriff in *Copland*, and he also took a big pay cut for the role, from the $20 million he received for *Daylight* to $60,000. He emphasized, "In the great quest of self-satisfaction … I would always go to the unsafe zone … I believe in taking risks – every time out." Sly's performance as the sheriff in *Copland* was considered excellent by many critics and audience members.

An important part of honing your approach is to take a good look at how you are *interpreting* what is going on around you. Here are Ellen Bass's comments on how to make a working relationship flow harmoniously:

A New Plan

ELLEN BASS

I am a writer and have worked collaboratively for many years. Recently, I was working on a project with a coauthor. As the project progressed, so did our squabbles. I pride myself on my excellent collaborative skills, so this breakdown in amicability really bothered me. I found myself complaining every evening at the dinner table – I was annoyed by her pickiness, her insistence on her own way, and her inability to appreciate my contributions. Finally I couldn't stand hearing myself complain any longer.

The next morning I took a deep breath and said, "Look I have a new plan. I'm going to tell you what I think and why I think it. Then, if you disagree, we'll just do it your way." Although I was fed up, I forced myself past my impatience to the deeper truth: This is going to be terrific anyway. In the big picture, these tiny decisions don't matter.

My coauthor looked at me blankly, but didn't argue. Throughout the day as questions arose. I stated my opinion, gave my reasons, and added, in a pleasant voice, "It's your call." Near the end of the day she looked up from her computer and said, "I just want you know I'm reordering this section the way you wanted it."

Ellen Bass, is the author of *The Human Line* and coauthor of *The Courage to Heal*. Ellen Bass teaches in the MFA program in poetry at Pacific University and at conferences and workshops nationally and internationally.

www.EllenBass.com

To get people to want to say "yes" to you, *learn to ask gentle questions.* Using gentle questions is one of the best parts of a positive, effective approach. Author Gene Bedell wrote about these powerful questions:

1. Yes, I understand those are your company's needs. But what are *you* looking for? What's most important to you personally?

2. Let's project into the future. What do you visualize as the ideal outcome? How would things work if you could write the script and everything went as you'd like it to go?

3. It would help me understand what the best outcome in the future would be if you'd describe what you don't like about the current (or past) situation. From a personal standpoint, what change would you like to see?

4. I'm sure you're looking at other options. What do you personally like about the best options you've seen so far?

Gene Bedell emphasizes that people buy something to fulfill their *personal* needs. You learn how to persuade a person when you *know* details about her. Gentle questions open the door.

Principle:

Hone your approach by taking a good look at how you interpret what happens. Then find and practice methods to empower yourself.

Power Questions:

How can you adapt to what is going on so that you recover from what bothers you? How can you re-interpret what is going on so that you can approach the situation calmly? How can you lower your own stress levels?

Establish Your Credibility

You can't follow someone who isn't credible,
who doesn't truly believe in what they're doing
– and how they're doing it.

GAYLE HAMILTON
(Pacific Gas & Electric)

How do you get better treatment from a clerk? People treat a caller better when he or she has some social standing. On only two occasions, I have found it necessary to say, "I'm a national speaker who talks with corporations on customer service. I write for a number of newsletters and I would prefer to continue my good impression of your firm. So how can we handle this detail?"

Sometimes, it helps if you demonstrate that you have influence. The ability to influence others (especially those who can have an impact on the company's bottom line) can be an important factor in credibility.

An interviewer asked me, "But if you say that you write for a number of newsletters, aren't you bullying the person you're talking to?"

"I'm glad you asked me this," I replied. "It reminds me of my work with a number of clients. It helps to know and to feel in your bones the difference between being assertive and being aggressive. I helped one particular woman become assertive. When her parents were having difficulty getting a fair amount from an insurance company to repair their car, she learned to say, 'That's not working for us. Can you do better than that?' This statement is assertive. You notice that it is polite but firm."

A friend told me, "In this time of the Internet, you can create instant credibility. In one day you could start your own e-newsletter and send it to your friends. Then you could say something like, 'I write for a publication called *The Customer Service Journal*."

Remember, if you have some influence with people who are important to the company you're dealing with, you may get the treatment and results you want.

Principle:

Establish your credibility.

Power Question:

How can you express your credentials in a way that gets the person concerned about what you might report?

PERSIST

> *Being deeply loved by someone gives you strength;*
> *loving someone deeply gives you courage.*
>
> LAO-TZU

This quote identifies a source that many of us can use to have the strength to persist.

There is one way to get what you want: persist. When you are willing to go up the chain of command to the CEO, you are strong. You will get some form of satisfaction. Why? Because as you go up the chain of command, you will encounter the vice president, for example, who feels that her time is valuable. She wants the situation resolved quickly so she can return to leading her department. Also, the higher up you go, the more power the person has to *override* any stated policy.

Principle:

Persist. There is no substitute.

Power Question:

How can you persist? Would it help if you use a phone call, e-mail, a letter, contact a television consumer advocate … ?

RECORD NOTES

How can you save $100,000 on a significant deal? Write notes for each important conversation. Author Roger Dawson knows someone who saved $100,000 when he asked the other person to check his notes. The person did not have thorough notes, and Roger Dawson's friend prevailed.

> *All problems become smaller if you don't dodge them,*
> *but confront them.*
>
> WILLIAM F. HALSEY

We need to confront any hesitation we may have to writing notes. The benefit of recording notes far outweighs any discomfort.

When you have good notes, you can often get your way because the other person may have failed to take any notes. You can say, "Would you check your notes? According to my notes of January 22nd, at 12:45 p.m. we discussed X and Y and resolved to do Z."

Often upon closing a transaction, I request that a memo be e-mailed or faxed to my office to confirm the solution.

Principle:

Record notes of each interaction with a company's personnel.

Power Question:

What will you use (a notebook, binder, computer file, or contact management program) to record your notes?

ITEMIZE "THIS OR THAT"

How can you influence a person to give an answer in your favor? Provide a "this or that" solution.

For example, you could say, "It would help me feel better if your company provided me with a refund or a coupon for this."

Make it easier for the person to say "yes." Give her a choice between two specific options, both of which would satisfy you.

It is only with the heart that one can see rightly, what is essential is invisible to the eye.

ANTOINE DE SAINT EXUPÉRY

Antoine's comment reminds us that we need to get to the heart of the matter. What do you *really* want? And how can you express that as an easy "this or that" solution?

Principle:

Make it easier to get a "yes" by providing two options.

Power Question:

How can you phrase two options that make it easier for the person to say "yes" than "no"?

ZERO IN ON DE-ESCALATING

What can save you time and tension? Use de-escalating language.

At the beginning of your transaction, speak gently. For example, some years ago I helped a family member deal with a company. I said to the clerk, "Oh, we just need a little adjustment here, only 20 dollars." The magic de-escalating word was *adjustment*. I did not say, "I want my family member's money back." I avoided the phrase, "Give me a refund!"

> *Contributing to other people's happiness provides us with meaning and pleasure … an unhappy person is less likely to be benevolent.*
>
> TAL BEN-SHAHAR

If you use intense or escalating language, you are likely to make a person unhappy. When you use de-escalating language, you contribute to his or her well-being. You find a way to create cooperation. You help the person to do a good job. In the spirit of cooperation, you gently suggest solutions – which benefit you.

Principle:

Begin by using de-escalating language.

Power Question:

How can you re-phrase comments in ways that make the other person feel at ease?

ENCOUNTER THE REPUTABLE

It's better to hang out with people better than you. Pick out associates whose behavior is better than yours, and you'll drift in that direction.

WARREN BUFFET

When you work with established, reputable firms that build their business on repeat customers and referrals, you will get satisfaction. However, let's face it together: there are some firms that truly do *not* care. Stay away from them.

Over the years, I have appreciated the excellent customer service of Franklin-Covey (makers of day planners) and Walt Disney Resorts. Both companies train their employees in excellent customer service.

The Disney organization's training program is entitled *Traditions*, to emphasize the core value of service. Disney employees are trained to call customers *guests*. For example, on the Disney Cruise that my sweetheart and I enjoyed, many details were orchestrated to delight us. Even the way the ship's cabin was decorated provided charming surprises. The artistry included towels that were formed into cute, attractive animals. When I returned and spoke to my next audience, my one-word comment about the Disney Cruise was, "Woooooow!"

Principle:

Encounter the reputable firms that build their business on repeat customers and referrals.

Power Questions:

How can you get information about a company before you purchase its product or service? Will you study blogs? Visit consumer-advocate Web sites?

CONCLUSION TO PART III

In Part III, we explored the W.I.N.–T.H.E.–P.R.I.Z.E. process:

W – Walk up the chain of command

I – Impress that you're staying

N – Nudge politely

T – Tune in to language

H – Hone your approach

E – Establish your credibility

P – Persist

R – Record notes

I – Itemize "this or that"

Z – Zero in on de-escalating

E – Encounter the reputable

Without discipline, there's no life at all.

KATHERINE HEPBURN

*You really have to love yourself
to get anything done in this world.*

LUCILLE BALL

The above quotes remind us to be disciplined and to advocate for ourselves. It takes discipline and effort to prepare before your next interaction with a person on the other side who may seem to be your opponent. With effective preparation, you may be able to defuse the situation so that you do *not* have an opponent. Instead, you have an associate, with whom you can achieve a mutually beneficial outcome.

Remember to persist. Be friendly and firm as you reach beyond policy.

In Part IV, Section 1, *How Great Communicators Overcome the #1 Obstacle to Happiness*, you will learn how to communicate with yourself in ways that create success and fulfillment.

Let's start to enjoy more happy moments …

Part IV, Section 1

How Great Communicators
Overcome the #1 Obstacle to Happiness

WHAT IS the number one obstacle to happiness? I will answer this question in a moment.

First, here's a *crucial detail*: Please know that a profound truth may often be disguised as something that sounds simple. You may have a reaction like, "Oh, I've heard that before." But the essential question is, have you *done anything* with that knowledge?

There's an old phrase: "To know and not to do is not to know."

So, what is the number one *obstacle to happiness*? It is *not* to be in this moment, now.

What does that mean? If you're worrying about the future or feeling guilty over the past, you are *not* in this moment.

How do you get into this moment? Gratitude.

For example, I am grateful for the computer into which I'm typing these words. I'm grateful that you are reading this book.

I am grateful that I have a purpose and dreams, and that I am committed to them.

What does this number one obstacle to happiness have to do with the secrets of the greatest communicators?

The answer is – *everything*.

If you're not focused in the moment, your listener can sense that you're distracted. She might assume that you do not care about her.

> *The way we communicate with others and with ourselves ultimately determines the quality of our lives.*
>
> ANTHONY ROBBINS

How do we communicate powerfully with ourselves? We carefully choose the questions we ask ourselves.

If you're worrying, "How am I doing?" the audience can sense that. Switch to, "How can I serve you? How are *you* doing?"

The solution is to bring yourself back to the *present moment*. This became clear to me one year when I injured my back. The pain was so bad that I grunted involuntarily in agony a number of times. A concerned friend asked me, "How are you doing?"

I replied, "Making the most of this moment." This was a truthful reply. The pain in my back varied from moment to moment. When I rose from a chair, I would feel a disabling, stabbing pain in my lumbar area. But when I walked, the pain was less.

One powerful way to focus on the moment is to silently repeat, "Be in the moment."

> *I don't believe people are looking for the meaning of life as much as they are looking for the experience of being alive.*
>
> JOSEPH CAMPBELL

Immerse yourself in this moment. Enjoy what is here *now*.

I never lose sight of the fact that just being is fun.

KATHERINE HEPBURN

Learn to get into this moment. Use a phrase like *Be here now* to help you let go of distracting thoughts.

rendered by Michael Capozzola, colored by Lindsay Morita

A man is rich in proportion to the number
of things he can afford to let alone.

HENRY DAVID THOREAU

Henry's quote reminds us that we may need to let go of a particular thought in order to immerse ourselves in the present moment.

Get into this moment. Say to yourself, "I am grateful for … " People who are grateful radiate charisma and good will. They are fun to be around.

My clients report that they tell themselves:

- I am grateful to be talking with Janet now.

- I am grateful for this job.

- I am grateful for this opportunity to speak to this audience.

> *The quickest, easiest way to connect with*
> *God is to express your gratitude.*
>
> M.J. RYAN

Expressing *gratitude can restore a relationship.* At one point, my father was upset with me. He would not come to the telephone when I called my parents' home. Prior to this, he had stopped using e-mail. So I found a different way to connect. I sent him a happy-looking card that depicted Kermit the Frog playing the banjo. I wrote:

> *Dad,*
>
> *Happy today. Thank you for holding me to high standards. This has made my life better.*
>
> *Love, Tom*

This heartfelt message helped my father feel better. Soon we were talking on the phone and meeting again in person.

Sometimes it takes extra effort to connect with gratitude. Some of us say, "How can I be grateful? My brother has just died." The process of grief can overwhelm our perception.

While I was writing this book, a close friend (like a brother) died. I found that I didn't know from moment to moment whether I would choke up with grief or smile while remembering my friend's loving kindness and sense of humor. There were moments when I felt grateful for the opportunities to share time with him before he died.

In class, I told my graduate students the truth about my sadness over my dear friend's death. I could see in their faces that many of them had gone through a similar grieving time. This strengthened our connection. I said, "I may lose my voice for 30 seconds. But that's okay … we'll keep flowing forward."

> *It is natural – you need to smile to your sorrow because*
> *you are more than your sorrow.*
>
> THICH NHAT HANH

So even while I was experiencing intense grief, I flowed with each moment.

> *We do not remember days, we remember moments.*
>
> CESARE PAVESE

During this time of grief for my friend, I learned to flow with my feelings. And after a time of tears, I felt drawn to uplifting thoughts and experiences, such as soothing music.

> *Follow your bliss, and doors will open for you*
> *that you never knew existed.*
>
> JOSEPH CAMPBELL

This is such a hopeful idea! I have seen it come true many times in my life. I wrote a screenplay that impressed the California Motion Picture Commissioner, and three years later he secured (at no cost) an American Eagle airplane and an airport runway for a feature film I was directing. I followed my bliss, and amazing and unexpected doors opened for me.

HAPPINESS AND GOALS

Tal Ben-Shahar, author of *Happier* (the source material for Harvard University's most popular course) wrote, "The proper role of goals is to liberate us, so we can enjoy the here and now … Happiness is the overall experience of pleasure and meaning."

Now let's look at happiness in the context of big success.

> Jaws *is something that I'll never forget. It is something that I don't want to repeat … The experience of making* Jaws *was horrendous for me … I am completely grateful to the audience embracing the movie and the movie being such a phenomenon – which basically gave me what I had always dreamed about – which was (a) being a movie director and (b) having final cut. And* Jaws *gave me freedom.*
>
> STEVEN SPIELBERG

Be happy in the here and now. Focus on the process. Each day has ups and downs. Celebrate each small victory.

> *I am an extraordinarily lucky person, doing what I love best in the world. I'm sure that I will always be a writer. It was wonderful enough just to be published. The greatest reward is the enthusiasm of the readers.*
>
> J.K. ROWLING

From this quote, we see that J.K. Rowling, the fabulously wealthy author of the *Harry Potter* books, knows that she simply loves writing!

> *Keep a gratitude journal. Every night, list five things that happened this day that you are grateful for. What it will begin to do is change your perspective of your day and your life … Be thankful for what you have … If you can learn to focus on what you have, you will always see that the universe is abundant; you will have more. If you concentrate on what you don't have, you will never have enough.*
>
> OPRAH WINFREY

One day, Bob Greene, Oprah's trainer, asked her, "When was the last time you experienced joy?" Oprah thought for a while and replied that it had been seven years. This question inspired her to modify her show and take it to a higher level, to "help people lead better, more meaningful lives."

Here's a secret: Find ways to experience some joy each day. My clients have noted their joyful moments:

- Listening to music that reminds me of a fun concert I attended

- Talking with my spouse

- Going for a walk

- Writing my novel for a half-hour as soon as I get home from work

With my audiences, I emphasize, "Make it a game you can win." It's up to you. You can schedule some moments every day to devote to something that brings you joy, comfort, meaning or peace. I travel a lot, and I find that even devoting three minutes to quiet time on a train brightens my whole day.

Brighten your day. Raise your morale so that you radiate good will. Please write "Quiet time," or "15 minutes painting my picture," or something that brings you *joyful moments* into your day planner.

Principle:

Focus on this moment – *now*.

Power Question:

How can you use a certain phrase to remind you to return to the present moment? (*Example:* "I am grateful to be talking with Janet now.")

CONCLUSION TO PART IV, SECTION 1

In this chapter, we identified the number one obstacle to happiness as *not* being in this moment, now. Great communicators pay close attention to ensure that they serve their listeners by being present. Listeners appreciate and respond to such conscientious attention.

In Part IV, Section 2, *Truth No One Will Tell You–Secrets to Empower Yourself Through an Economic Crisis*, you will learn to lead yourself so that your day-to-day experiences are filled with strength, courage, and compassion.

Let's take a powerful step forward.

Part IV, Section 2

Truth No One Will Tell You
Secrets to Empower Yourself Through an Economic Crisis

HOW CAN YOU empower yourself to be strong during any crisis? At the time this is being written, American and global markets have been hit with a historic recession. Numerous families and individuals have suffered due to job losses and losing homes to foreclosures. Now what?

Imagine uncovering a lost secret that President John F. Kennedy wanted to reveal but could not before he died. On the day he died, Kennedy was scheduled to give a speech. Here is what he intended to say:

> *Leadership and learning are*
> *indispensable to each other.*
>
> JOHN F. KENNEDY

Kennedy's quote gives us the clue that we need in any crisis. *We need to learn to lead!* You must lead yourself and others to a state of feeling calm.

Do you want to feel better and stronger? Do you want your life situation to improve? Read on.

You cannot allow the media to lead you. The media sells advertising, and, in a nutshell, bad news sells. News broadcasts don't emphasize millions of people arriving home from work and kissing their spouse and hugging their children. Instead, broadcasts feature comments about foreclosures and the 14,000 jobs lost at Acme Corporation. The old journalism phrase is: "If it bleeds, it leads."

Don't be led by the media. You must lead yourself so you feel stronger and take powerful action. And you have already begun. I applaud you for reading this book. You're choosing to impact your mind with positive and inspirational material.

> *Your true freedom flows in your choices*
> *of your own programming.*
>
> TOM MARCOUX

In fact, you are programming yourself to improve your life situation right now. No one else can do it for you.

This section, *Truth No One Will Tell You*, explores the four reasons people fail to express the truth. These include:

1. They don't know the truth.

2. They don't want you to know the truth so they can exploit your weakness.

3. They care about you and want you to avoid getting hurt.

4. They can only guess about what is best for you because *your inner truth* is only revealed by *your answers* to effective questions.

An interviewer asked: "Which people are not telling the truth?" Many of us discover that, intentionally or not, the people who do not tell us the truth that could empower us include co-workers, family members, friends and politicians. Your life is truly in your hands. So we will focus on the L.E.A.D.S. process because you need to be a person who *leads*.

L – Listen

E – Engage

A – Act

D – Decrease downers

S – Shift to inner sources of happiness

LISTEN

To keep your job in tough economic times or to gain a new job, you need to be an effective listener. People trust and like individuals who listen well. We *confront the myth*: to be successful, one needs to be a smooth talker. The truth is: one needs to be an *effective listener*. To get someone to calm down, you need to make sure the person feels that you truly heard him or her.

A manager will often try to retain the people he or she likes during a bad business cycle or crisis. The people who have no rapport with management are the ones who are laid off first. Being an effective listener (and thereby creating a good connection) is also applied when convincing an interviewer that you are an ideal candidate for a new job.

> *People do not care how much you know*
> *until they know how much you care.*
>
> JOHN MAXWELL

To listen well is more than just keeping one's mouth shut.

Effective listeners

1. Turn their body so that their heart faces the other person's heart.

2. Lean forward.

3. Make listening sounds like "mm-hmm."

4. Mirror feelings by saying things like "That sounds frustrating."

5. Confirm that they understand by saying "So you want ________. Do I have that about right?"

Also, you must listen well to yourself.

As I mentioned, people can only guess about what is best for you because your inner truth is only revealed by your answers to effective questions. To get to the *Truth That No One Will Tell You*, you need to provide your own answers to some tough questions, starting with these:

Truth-Revealing questions

1. What do you really want?

2. What do you want to feel?

3. Where are you grieving?

4. How can you take better care of yourself now?

5. Where are you "contracting"?

6. How can you have some "expansion" in your life?

Pull out your personal journal or a sheet of paper and answer these questions.

What do you really want?

This is where your inner truth begins. Unfortunately, many of us have given up on hoping for something better in life. But you must understand that the past does not determine your future. Dr. Wayne Dyer emphasizes that the past is merely the wake behind a metaphorical boat. The wake does not drive the boat. The wake (the past) is not the engine of the boat. So put your fears and your preconceptions into a metaphorical drawer for a moment. Just imagine: If the Genie from Aladdin were next to you, what would you wish for? Write it down.

What do you want to feel?

Cognitive scientists often note that people take certain actions because they think something will yield certain feelings. Why do many people want a relationship? Because they want to feel loved and have a warm connection. Why settle on an unfulfilling job? Many people have the strong desire to feel safe and secure. Entrepreneurs often have an intense desire to get something done. Such entrepreneurs will endure feelings of uncertainty in order to press on for the accomplishments they crave. Empower yourself by uncovering what you really want to feel. Write your answer to "What do you want to feel?" in your personal journal.

Where are you grieving?

As I mentioned, this section of the book is being written during an extreme recession. Many people are grieving lost jobs, lost retirement funds and so much more. I can relate to such grieving because I was laid off from two jobs some years ago. In fact, that gave me part of the fuel I needed to build three companies. My advice: Find out where you are grieving then look for the *turnaround*. The turnaround is a way to reframe the situation so that you have new possibilities. For example, I took the situation "I was laid off" and *turned it around* to "How can I build a company so that I can earn multiple streams of income?"

How can you take better care of yourself now?

This much is certain: The only way to ride out a recession is to take care of yourself day by day. Be sure to get the basics: rest, sleep, exercise, good nutrition, time with friends and loved ones, quiet time, and meditation or prayer. These will also contribute to calm feelings.

Where are you "contracting"?

To contract is to pull back. Have you ever seen a turtle ducking his head back into his shell? The turtle ducks out of fear of being hurt. People also contract when feeling fearful. The problem is that contracting often hurts. It can feel like we're missing out on fun or fulfillment. At present the news media is filled with stories about how consumers are spending less. This makes sense for many families. I hold a powerful phrase in my thoughts:

Low overhead equals freedom.

RAYMOND TELLER
(of Penn + Teller)

Appropriate "contracting" may include being careful with your budget and choosing a library book over purchasing a book. You may decide to watch a video at home instead of taking family members to a movie theater.

Contracting is natural. But we must pay attention: Contracting can lead us to resent our current circumstances and limitations. And we feel pain. So contracting can actually disrupt any chance you have at getting to calm. And contracting cannot be your sole stance in life. You need some "expansion" in your life.

How can you have some "expansion" in your life?

Here is a crucial distinction: Often, when people complain about how their lives are contracting, they indulge in a cycle of feeling pain, complaining and suffering. Instead, you need to break this cycle so that you can ride out any crisis and get yourself to calm. Find an inexpensive way to have some "expansion" in your life.

The purpose of existence is growth [and] expression.

ROBERT COLLIER

The truth is – we feel happy when we feel hope and we express ourselves creatively. Some people protest that they are not creative. These people need to expand their perception of what creativity truly is. It is creative to help out at a soup kitchen like my friend Linda does. During numerous holiday seasons, she has created good feelings in the people she has helped and, as a by-product, she lifts her own spirits.

> *Happiness is not a goal, it is a by-product.*
>
> ELEANOR ROOSEVELT

Also, many of us find happiness is doing some activity that expresses our unique creativity. I am happy in this moment as I type out these words; I feel expansion occurring in my life experience. No matter what difficulty you may be experiencing in your life, I invite you to find ways to experience expansion on some level. My clients report these activities help them to feel expansion:

- Painting a picture (or another hobby)

- Meditating

- Praying

- Visiting a museum on the "free day" of each month

- Taking a class at a community college or continuing education center

- Taking a yoga, tai chi or cooking class

- Reading a book

These activities can help your heart feel fulfilled. You may discover that you feel *calm-in-the-moment* while doing the activity.

> *Our purpose is to look deeply into our*
> *hearts and share what we love.*
>
> SONIA CHOQUETTE

Sonia's quote gives us a springboard to finding ways to have expansion in our lives. For example, if writing and selectively sharing your poetry expresses what you love, then that can brighten and energize your day. My client Valerie writes as she commutes to work on a subway train.

Nothing pays better interest than judicious reading.

ROBERT COLLIER

For example, Rhonda Byrne turned her life around after receiving a book from her daughter. The book, *The Science of Getting Rich*, inspired Rhonda to produce the phenomenal bestselling video *The Secret*, which in turn has influenced millions of people.

ENGAGE

According to *The American Heritage Dictionary*, "engage" is defined (in part) as:

1. "To win over or attract: *His smile engages everyone he meets.*"

2. "To draw into; involve: *Engage a shy person in conversation.*"

One of the most important ways to gain a new job is to hone your personal brand. Your well-developed personal brand will engage the interviewer with whom you're seeking a job. A personal brand is the shortest distance to trust. Imagine which person stands out in a job interview. It's the one with a clear personal brand. A personal brand is your answer to the question: What are you best known for? For those seeking a new job, the personal brand process shows you how to be effective, which can inspire feelings of calm.

The personal brand process

Here are six elements of your personal brand:

1. What are you best known for?

2. Ideally, what do you want to be best known for?

3. What high visibility details of your job are important to your boss, the supervisor above her or him, to the company, CEO or shareholders?

4. Identify two anecdotes.

5. Use a sound bite.

6. Develop a moniker.

What are you best known for?

When I was invited to speak to the Silicon Valley Chapter of the Project Management Institute (a.k.a., PMI Silicon Valley), I asked the meeting planner what the members needed. Here is what I wrote for the announcement to introduce my presentation "Empower Your Personal Brand: Align Yourself for Promotions and Raises."

> Who are you? What extraordinary benefits do you provide for your team and your company? If your supervisor, co-workers and direct reports don't have a concise answer on the tip of their tongues, you're in trouble! Your Personal Brand is the shortest distance to trust, promotions and raises. In this tough economic climate,

no project manager can risk being a "vague cloud" in the minds of his or her business associates.

This presentation/workshop will give you the opportunity to craft your Personal Brand so people get your strengths fast and remember them. This can translate directly into more income for you!

The top project managers communicate so effectively that people trust them and feel good in cooperating with them. What are their secrets? This workshop by "the Personal Branding Instructor" (reported in the *San Francisco Examiner*) reveals the techniques and mindset of people who gain success with ease.

By attending this event, professionals will be able to:

- Learn to be heard and be trusted.

- Discover how to get a self-absorbed boss to listen to you and your ideas.

- Get resistance out of the way and get colleagues to buy into what you're proposing.

- Communicate powerfully in high stress situations.

Make your Personal Brand clear, concise and memorable, and career opportunities come to you. Take this vital step forward and align yourself for promotions and raises.

My point is that you need to work on your personal brand over a span of time. It is like feeding a baby. You can't go for a day without taking care of that little one. Similarly, you need to take daily action by keeping a Job Diary and updating your résumé if you have a job right now. Also, pull out your personal journal (for your thoughts and feelings) and write down your best guess to the question: What are you best known for?

Ideally, what do you want to be best known for?

My client Sarah told me that she is known as a *just-in-time project manager*. She later realized that she truly wants to be known as the *ahead-of-the-game project manager*. This is better for Sarah's career because people who are heroes, the ones who get things done just in time, may fail when a team member falls ill. The house of cards tumbles if a project manager fails to put in buffer days and fails to guide team members to get ahead of the game. So write in your personal journal what you really want to be known for.

Which high visibility details matter to your superiors?

The supervisor over Sarah's boss says, "During this recession, everything is about budget. Watch your costs, people!" Sarah took note and started strategizing how she could save funds on the budget for her new project.

Let's face this together. Who will a boss hold on to and choose *last* for any lay off? The person who makes the boss look good to her or his supervisor! Pay close attention to what is most important to the influential people at your workplace – your boss, their supervisor, the company, CEO, and shareholders. You can discover the high visibility details of your job by asking this question: What's most important to you about _____?

Identify two anecdotes

An anecdote is a story with a point. Here is a crucial distinction: *It's not real until you tell a story*. How is this true? A story inspires an *experience* for the listener.

We tell stories all the time. Here's a story a client told in one sentence: "Using one of Tom's methods, I got more done in two weeks than in six months." Apparently, she learned to streamline her process. I have posted this endorsement in many places including different Web sites.

Be careful about what stories you tell about yourself and your performance. Tell stories in which your skills and capabilities are clear. I guide clients and graduate students in preparing for job interviews, and I encourage them to have at least two anecdotes per each skill or positive trait they want to highlight when interviewed. An anecdote can include something like: "My client Sarah's face lit up at how fast I turned around the bid. She said that she could always trust me to come through."

Use a sound bite

During a news broadcast, an interviewee may say, "We're looking into the problem now." Then the program cuts back to the announcer. Those six words form a sound bite.

Here's another example of a sound bite: "When a tech problem needs solving – who can? Jan can."

It's true that some people may find this phrase trite. But it is memorable. To this day, I still remember "Coke adds life."

The best sound bite includes words of praise from a supervisor, co-worker, or client. To capture these words keep all e-mails that praise your work. The plan is to be able to say in a job interview: "My supervisor at Acme Company said, 'Joe, I can always count on you to plan ahead for possible delays. You always make sure that we finish products ahead of schedule and with quality.' " Such a sound bite sounds true because someone else (your boss) had said it.

Make sure your sound bite is connected to something that you are both good at and enjoy doing. Write three possible sound bites now:

1. "My supervisor at Acme Company said ______." (A positive comment about you and your work.)

2. "One of my clients said ______."

3. "My co-workers said ______."

Develop a moniker

Have you heard a label like "America's favorite financial adviser"? That's a moniker. Monikers sound like:

- The go-to person for software

- The Tech Wizard of Department M2

- The results coach

- The big jobs manager

A moniker can be a positive nickname. Thirty years later, I still remember the moniker "Superfoot Wallace" that described martial artist Bill Wallace's skill with fast kicks. A moniker can be helpful for your personal brand.

To align ourselves for promotions and raises, we need to be careful about what moniker we get stuck with. We need to come up with a moniker before someone else applies a nickname to us. For example, author Robin Fisher Roffer nearly dropped her drink at a networking event when one of her clients introduced her as "The Coupon Queen of Cable." Robin's client wanted to help her with his introduction. This proves the point that if you are not proactive in placing your personal brand in other people's minds, they'll make their own label (or moniker) for you.

To develop your moniker, listen carefully to how people describe you. For example, my father has often said, "Tom, nothing can stop you [this contributed to my book *Nothing Can Stop You This Year*]." Others have said, "You're unstoppable." At this point, I could incorporate the word "unstoppable" into a moniker.

Once you have a moniker, you can use it in various forms. For example, my client Martha said at a networking event: "My clients often call me The Self-Promotion Master. Now I help people do ..." It takes practice to smoothly incorporate your moniker into your conversations.

Remember, one of the most powerful ways you can engage with a new person is to have your personal brand in fine order.

Act

"You must take action," many of us have heard over our lifetime. But the question is: What action?

> *Power based on love is a thousand times*
> *more effective and permanent than the*
> *one derived from fear of punishment.*
>
> MAHATMA GANDHI

Focus on actions that are positive or expressions of love and kindness.

In this section I provide a number of methods for people to protect their current job or shine in a job interview. People tend to emphasize an outside occurrence like a job loss. *The real crisis is fear* – whether someone is going through employment trouble or a divorce. It's true that we need to take care of ourselves as we grieve over the loss of a job, retirement funds or something else. But we must focus on: *Where do I want to go from here?* That's why we need to concentrate on positive actions as we remember Gandhi's quote.

As this is being written, the current extreme recession is giving people *punishment* 24/7. I noticed for many days in a row that the headlines on my Yahoo.com page included discouraging comments like: "Stock market falls 777 points, 800 points … Asian markets take a beating …" This is not a breakfast of champions. In fact, the most effective Olympic athletes train themselves to focus on positive direction even during the most pressure-filled moments. It is reported that they tell themselves things like, "Run down the track like a gazelle. Explode off the springboard. Glide. Spin. Stick the landing."

Every command is a positive one. In essence, the top Olympic athlete takes action twice: First in her mind, then with her body.

One of the most powerful actions you can take is to bring yourself or someone else to calm. Take these following steps to guide someone to be more cooperative.

The Bring Calm Steps

1. Release your own disquiet.

2. Breathe deeply before seeing or calling the person.

3. Match tone, volume and pacing.

4. In graduated steps, lower your tone and volume … and in graduated steps, slow down your pacing.

Release your own disquiet

As we go through our days, some things happen that disrupt our inner peace. And, unfortunately, we carry them like baggage. The idea is to release this baggage. The *Write Down, Rip Up Method* begins when you write down the truth about what is bothering you. Then rip up the sheet of paper and place it in your pocket. Do not re-read your agitated comments – that would be like picking up the baggage all over again. Once the upsetting thoughts are down on paper and then ripped up, you will likely discover that you feel lighter and better.

Breathe deeply before seeing or calling the person

If you are scheduled to meet with a troublesome client or an upset manager, make sure that you personally calm down. Many of us find that deep breathing brings calm feelings. Breathe in and allow your stomach area to get "fat." Then breathe out, allowing your stomach area to deflate. This is called belly breathing. You can breathe in for four counts and hold your breath for two counts – and finally breathe out again to four counts. My clients often like to use an affirmation in place of counting. A number of them breathe in with an affirmation like: "Higher Power relaxes me" or "God holds me safe." They then repeat the affirmation while they hold their breath and breathe out again.

Match tone, volume and pacing

As we speak the sound of our voice can have a pleasing tone like a violin or a grating tone like grinding car gears. To bring another person to calm, we need to meet him or her on the same level. If that person is intense, we can sound intense, too – but we are careful with our words. A salesperson can say with a matching, intense tone: "Yes, you're right, sir. It is an important problem. I'm going to focus on helping you."

We also need to match volume. Replying to a customer's barking voice with syrupy-soft volume and tone will often cause the barking customer to get more agitated. It is better to start by matching tone, volume and pacing. About pacing: Often we see that someone from New York can do better when talking to someone from the southern United States by slowing down her pace of talking.

In graduated steps, lower your tone, volume, & pacing

According to cognitive and neuro-scientists, we have mirror-neurons in our brain. These are the cells that match the energy of someone who is talking to us. As you gradually lower your tone, volume and speed of talking – through mirror-neurons – the other person will often quiet down, too. In this way you bring the other person to calm.

~~~~~~~~~~~~~~~~~~~~

The secret about Act is to focus on actions that provide *leverage*. Leverage is when you strategically apply a small amount of effort for a big result.

You take effective action when you:

1. Know what you want.

2. Know how to tell when you have what you want.

Knowing these two details makes it easier to decide on a good action – in this moment. This will bring feelings of calm. How? You start to see that you're on track and that you have hope that you can influence your life situation for the better.
~~~~~~~~~~~~~~~~~~~~

Here are guiding ideas for taking action:

You will only get paid *by taking action.*

MIKE COLLINS

*Your best work is not the triumph of
technique but the purity of purpose.*

TOM MARCOUX

Imperfect action is better than perfect inaction.

HARRY TRUMAN

*Start by doing what's necessary;
then do what's possible;
and suddenly you are doing the impossible.*

ST. FRANCIS OF ASSISI

DECREASE DOWNERS

"Downers" are things, activities or people that drain your energy. We *confront the myth*: One should be strong enough to put up with a lot of stress. *The truth is*: No one has time or energy for all things.

We must pick our battles and conserve our energy for what we can truly influence.

Write down what drains your energy. For example, I had to tell a close friend to stop sending me certain cartoons. These cartoons were clever but they brought down my energy. They were filled with complaints. So I told my friend, "Please stop sending me these cartoons. They do not empower me to be good to my clients, my family, nor my students." In this way I decreased (or shut off the flow) of one type of downer.

Reduce the impact of downers in your life and you increase your moments of calm. You will actually feel stronger.

SHIFT TO INNER SOURCES OF HAPPINESS

A crisis is often something outside of our control that knocks us down. It can be a job layoff, a divorce, the loss of a loved one, a severe illness or something else that drains energy and brings great pain. Truly, it's when external sources of happiness are snatched away. Now is the time to build and use internal resources. When the world appears to be crashing down on the outside, we need to shift to inner sources of happiness. In a crisis, two things happen: First, we've lost something so we're grieving. Second, our energy is drained. This tough spot causes many of us to find that we can't implement a life-improving shift of perception because we don't have the energy. Here's a solution: Use a *Low Mood First-Aid Kit* to recover energy. Your kit is a list of activities that you can do on your own to comfort yourself. My clients have reported using:

- A warm bath

- Knitting

- Listening to music

- Playing with pets

- Walking in nature

- Reading a good book

- Writing in a personal journal

- Quiet time for meditation or prayer

Do an activity that makes you feel alive! Focus on the moment. If you're walking in nature with a friend, avoid talking about soaking your aching feet when you get back home. Instead, stay in the moment and focus on the new sights, new aromas and new sounds. Shift to what you can control: your effort. I guide my clients to separate Effort Goals and Result Goals. You can control your own efforts like making ten marketing phone calls. You cannot control the results. But you can have an inner source of happiness or satisfaction by setting a goal (Effort Goal) and fulfilling it.

My clients report new feelings of calm when they can see that they're making true incremental progress. That's what logging Effort Goal activities provides for you.

Happiness is something to do,
someone to love,
and something to hope for.

CHINESE PROVERB

Effort Goals provide the feelings of hope and calm. My clients log their actions related to attending networking events, sending out résumés, taking quiet time away from cell phones and e-mail, and doing something to enhance personal health.

How to shift to inner sources of happiness

To improve your mood, what is often the most effective thing to do? – Focus on a question.

> *The answer is in the question. Ask better*
> *questions. What am I learning here?*
> *How can we make this better?*

TOM MARCOUX

Try this question: What am I grateful for? Write down your answers.

> *Happiness cannot be traveled to, owned, earned, worn,*
> *or consumed. Happiness is the spiritual experience of*
> *living every minute with love, grace, and gratitude.*

DENIS WAITLEY

What are your sources of grace? Prayer? Quiet time? A phone call with a supportive friend? Focusing on inner sources of happiness is really about devoting time to your personal spiritual path.

> *The only true security is in Spirit ... if our inner*
> *world is lit by love, we are unshakably secure.*

ALAN COHEN

> *Choose faith, not fear.*

JOEL OSTEEN

To choose faith is to focus on things that empower you. Make a plan and take action. Hold on to the thoughts and intentions that you are moving forward and *through* the crisis. Winston Churchill said, "If you are going through hell, keep going." Researchers have noted that people who press onward often exclaim, "I didn't know I could be that strong" and "I learned to have better priorities."

The Truth No One Will Tell You is … You set up your own rules about your own happiness. If you set up conditions, then you will be unhappy more moments of each day. Some people set up the condition: "When I get a new job, I'll be happy" or "When I have a romantic relationship, I'll be happy." Researchers note that human beings adapt to any new situation. It is not about setting conditions; it is about finding the good in the present moment. If you set up expansive opportunities for happiness, then you can enjoy more happy moments.

> *If you want others to be happy, practice compassion.*
> *If you want to be happy, practice compassion.*

THE DALAI LAMA

> *Treat yourself kindly and with compassion.*
> *Happiness is not a destination.*
> *It is a method of life.*

AUSTIN O'MALLEY

So choose to find ways to enjoy this moment. It's up to you.

> *I don't know what your destiny will be, but one thing I do know: the only ones among you who will be really happy are those who have sought and found how to serve.*

ALBERT SCHWEITZER

> *Life is to be fortified by many friendships.*
> *To love and to be loved is the greatest happiness.*

SYDNEY SMITH

Be flexible like a dancer – poised to move in any direction. Dancers are at their best with rest, sleep, good nutrition, time with friends, and opportunities for laughter. Remember, shift to an inner source. Live in this moment.

How to Improve Your Financial Situation

At one point, an interviewer asked me, "What are some secrets of making money?" I replied that I have personally used a set of principles that I created for my clients and myself. I'm so concerned about misinformation in general use that I streamlined the principles into the T.R.U.T.H. process for making money.

T – Transform to "Yes."

R – Run in better races.

U – Untangle from the money-for-time trade.

T – Take on risk.

H – Hone your persuasion skills.

A great source of feeling calm in turbulent financial times is to have hope. See which of the T.R.U.T.H. process methods seize your attention and then make an action plan. In this way you will have the hope you need to rise out of any financial rut. As you take baby steps forward, you will begin to feel more hopeful.

Action is the antidote to despair.

JOAN BAEZ

Let's get started …

Transform to "Yes"

Have you noticed that people often have an automatic "no" response to new ideas or new actions? When some new opportunity to earn money comes along, many of us find that "no" rises up. "No, I won't be good enough." "No, they'll reject me and that will feel bad."

Instead, I invite you to transform that "no" to a big "Yes."

- "Yes, I'm going to give this a chance."

- "Yes, I can handle a possible rejection. Instead, I'll call it 'we didn't have a match.'"

As a teenager, I began my work life at a fast food restaurant making minimum wage. I was 15 years old and I washed everything, including floors, windows and toilets. The first time I earned $400 an hour, *I stepped significantly out of my comfort zone.* I earned that $400 modeling for an advertisement for a software company.

I was afraid during that photo shoot. For one thing, the position called for an Asian person born and raised in another country. That was not me. I was born and raised in the United States.

In fact, when I walked into the building, the photographer said, "You were born in the U.S., weren't you?" At that point my jangled nerves felt like I wanted to escape out a window.

To make the photo work, I placed my hands together in a reverent manner like I had seen Asian monks do. The photographer took a photo of my head and shoulders. He said, "That's better." Evidently my posture had changed from the hard-charging energy that I usually walked around with. I was playing the role of someone raised in an Asian country.

Here is an important part of Transform to "Yes": *Step out of your comfort zone and make the best of a situation.*

I remember the first time that I made thousands of dollars through the Internet. I was seized with an idea. At the time I was on a train en route to teaching a graduate level class. I took quick notes. Upon arriving, I got off the train and walked quickly to the university. I went into a side room and quickly typed out two thousand words on my laptop.

My point here is that I said "Yes!" to the idea. I took action and ultimately completed writing a new e-book. People in 12 countries purchased that e-book through the Internet.

When I wrote the first two thousand words of the e-book, I had no idea if what I wrote would work. But I had another "Yes" response.

"Yes, it's all good practice. I'll get better as a writer."

"Yes, I can probably adapt this writing to something else in the future."

Let's move to the second strategy …

RUN IN BETTER RACES

Years ago I was feeling overwhelmed. I told my sweetheart, "I'm like a racehorse."

"Run in better races," she replied, encouraging me to be more selective.

Good point.

This led to my idea: I need to be in an area where a big payday is possible.

This proved to be true the first time I earned $1,000 in one hour. At the time I was earning $14 an hour as a marketing assistant.

My question was: Is there something I can do that comes easy to me, but is hard for other people?

Write down your own possible answers to this question, which I will repeat: *Is there something I can do that comes easy to me, but is hard for other people?*

I knew I could study, synthesize information, and convey it in an entertaining way.

Acclaimed Television Host Johnny Carson said, "People will pay more to be entertained than to be educated." So I earned $1000 in one hour by speaking to a group on a topic which I had never presented before.

An interviewer commented, "It sounds like it takes chutzpah and courage to try new things and put yourself at risk."

Often, one needs to act with courage. My audiences like my phrase, *Courage is easier when I'm prepared.* The point is that I prepare every day for my next speech, interview or book that I write. In recent years, I have read 108 and 109 books per year, respectively. I prepare by keeping up with my fields of interest.

How does one get into a better race?

It's about your skills in building relationships. And the essence of effective networking (for jobs and more) is building good relationships. So often opportunities that I have enjoyed have come from building business and personal relationships. My first opportunity to be marketed by a speaker bureau at the $5,000 level came from years of building a relationship with the bureau's team members. *This is how you get in a better race. You are friendly, trustworthy and helpful in all your dealings with people. Then people bring you opportunities.*

The truth about dealing with a financial crisis

Let me tell you about someone I truly admire. Linda had trained as a graphic designer for the hi-tech industry. But when the Silicon Valley Dot-Com Bubble burst, she went through some pain and had to shift gears. Through the years she gained training in a number of fields so that she has *multiple ways* to bring value to the marketplace. Currently she is one of my editors. She is also a personal chef, author and weight loss counselor. Formerly she was a hair stylist and hair salon owner. Let's learn from Linda's example: *Make sure that you can earn money in many ways.* This is called having *multiple streams of income.* I invite you to follow Linda's example and look for possibilities to use your hidden talents and gain new training for when a crisis arrives.

An interviewer asked: "Does a person need to be assertive?"

It depends on the situation. Would you like to know *four sentences* that meant $171,543 to me?

After I gave a speech an audience member walked up to me and said, "You should speak for Acme Company." I replied, "Thank you. Who do I talk with? [He told me.] Oh, you have your cell phone? How about we leave her a message now?" *Those were the four sentences.* The person immediately left a voicemail message and I ultimately closed the deal (that resulted in a number of presentations).

The point here is that I needed to be assertive. First I needed to notice if I had enough rapport with the person who praised me and said, "You should speak for Acme Company." Also, the reason why the four sentences were important is because the man who gave me the compliment was at a peak in his emotional approval of my speaking. That's the reason I wanted him to immediately leave a voicemail message. I knew his enthusiasm would appear on that message.

Let's explore the next technique …

Untangle from the Money-for-Time Trade

Many of us are caught in a real trap: Trading one hour of our time for a certain amount of money. Do you know how I first earned $225 per hour? I asked for it! I realized, though, that there was an upper limit on the hourly wage. But if I could write books … I would do the work once and get paid again and again.

For example, I wrote material for actors and was paid multiple times, including:

- Fees paid for teaching classes.

- Fees paid by students at the classes who chose to purchase the workbook at a cost of $25 each.

- Fees paid in recent years by people who purchased the same material as an e-book entitled *101 Acting Secrets: Tips from A Director for Your Acting, Auditions, Movie Roles, and Self-Promotion.**

Another example: Author Joel Osteen is not in the trap of trading time for money. Joel reportedly earned a $13 million advance fee for his second book. As a pastor he speaks to his in-person congregation of around 40,000 people each Sunday. And millions more view his television broadcasts. As I men-

---

* To get your copy of *101 Acting Secrets: Tips from A Director for Your Acting, Auditions, Movie Roles, and Self-Promotion*, please visit www.TomSuperCoach.com/SpecialOffer.htm.

tioned earlier: *You need to be in an area where a big payday is possible.* Joel lives this secret.

An interviewer commented: "Well, that's good for Joel. He has a whole team. His father had built the congregation up to 8,000 people before Joel Osteen took over."

Excellent points! This reminds us that there are no self-made millionaires. Everyone rises to a higher level with the cooperation, help, and guidance of others.

Five ways to stop trading time for money

Write something

If you have some writing talent and you enjoy writing to some measure, consider writing a book, a novel, a screenplay, an audio program or graphic novel. With writing, a secret is to continually make progress. If you write an article, the material can later appear in an audio program, speech or book. I write some material every day. Some of my clients choose self-publishing and sell their material on the Internet; and other clients go the traditional route of agents and getting a book deal with a major publisher.

This is an "and" universe; that is, you can do one thing *and* another. A writer can pursue *both* routes. Some people hesitate because they do not feel like an expert. I alert my clients to the empowering idea that *an expert is someone who has devised a system that people like and use.* To become an expert may be a lower hurdle than many of us think. Many people start with a personal problem, learn how to solve it, and then train others to solve that problem.

Invent something

Some of us remember the Pet Rock, which was merely a rock with brilliantly witty packaging. Gary Dahl, the man with the idea, offered his graphic designer $50,000 to sell his share of the project. So Gary went on to take the risks and gain the benefits solo. Soon Gary earned $1 million with the Pet Rock.

To find your inspiration, you might read books or watch television shows like "American Inventor." For example, viewers were enthralled when they saw a fireman, Gregg Chavez, propose an idea for a fire safety device called *The Guardian Angel*. Chavez described his Guardian Angel invention as, "A small, pressurized tank of water, disguised as a Christmas package that is placed under the Christmas tree and attached to a small hose leading to the top of the tree where a fusible link is disguised as an angel. The heat from a fire pops the link and water suppresses the fire."

Close real estate deals

As this is being written, a number of real estate agents express their concerns about how the real estate market has faltered. Let's realize that the real estate business, like a number of other industries, cycles back. For example, a friend recently told me that his real estate agent made $6,000 on the sale of a home. When I mentioned this in an interview, the host said, "Wait a minute. That still sounds like trading time for money." I replied, "I see your point. And, we realize that once a real estate agent acquires the knowledge for closing deals, she can be working on multiple deals at the same time. A number of effective real estate agents have an assistant that does much of the routine office work. This is all about *multiplying one's ability to earn large sums in less time.* This process is still different from making a set fee of $20 per hour or even $300 per hour."

Sell through the Internet

Millions of people sell items through eBay. Others sell information-related products. For example, my friend author David Barron teamed up with another author (with a large e-subscribers list). David had written and put together a system that guides people to become powerful influencers, and David's share of the profits was $6,000! I have coached clients on how to interview top people in a field, write an article and place it on Web sites. This is how you begin relationships with other authors that can lead to joint, mutually beneficial ventures.

Author and Internet entrepreneur Randy Gage mentions these popular topics that can be written about and sold as an expert's opinion on the Internet: marketing strategies, home-based business, health and wellness, weight loss, sales, crafts, art, wealth building, spiritual enlightenment, finding good employees, relationships, Web site design, gardening, raising a family, nutrition, travel and presentation skills. I would add: ways to live well on a small budget, humor and pets.

Team up

Some of my audience members say, "I'm not a writer." Don't let that stop you. Years ago, as a ghostwriter, I wrote a speech for a millionaire. And this millionaire had previously sold 1.4 million copies of a (probably ghostwritten) book. Sometimes my clients ask me, "How did you write and publish six books in three years?" I reply that I have a system:

- I write the material.

- I read it out loud to a team member. I revise the material as I hear the spoken words and watch my team member's responses.

- Then I have two editors (one in California and one in Canada) work on the material.

You do *not* need to be a writer. A client, Marcy, talks into an audio recorder. She has a nephew type up the material. Then she hands the material to a part-time college instructor for revision.

Teaming up is a powerful strategy. For example, I have produced ten audio programs that have all generated income. But I did *not* purchase a sound-editing program for my office computer. Why? Because it is more cost effective for me in terms of time and money to go to a veteran sound engineer. He can perform a refinement on the program in 20 seconds when it would take me 20 minutes (of frustration) to do the same function. He has devoted 17 years of his life to his craft of sound engineering and editing. I can walk into his studio, record my material, and step out with a completed master recording within hours! Also, my sound engineer gives me guidance on how I can improve the program as we edit it. This guidance raises the level of quality. *Remember to team up.*

Constantly prepare for the home run.

TOM MARCOUX

The major principle for gaining sudden profits is to constantly prepare for the home run. That is, on a daily basis, practice and prepare so that when you're *in the game* you can gain a big, life-improving result. Being in the game may occur when someone says, "You should speak for Acme Company" (an experience I mentioned earlier). Being in the game can also be when you're meeting a friend's sister at a party and it turns out that she needs an employee like you. By the way, use a number of methods of this section so that you feel calm when you're meeting people. A person who experiences some calm and some happiness each day is the person who radiates charisma. People offer charismatic individuals new opportunities. And remember that people tend to like others who listen to them. When you experience calm and some happiness each day, you have more energy to listen to new people you meet.

The point is this – a number of successful people who seem to become an overnight success have been devoting effort over a number of years. They have been continually improving their craft. That is, *they constantly prepare for the home run.* For example, Jon Stewart (star of "The Daily Show" on Comedy Central) said, "I can't believe how lucky I have been already. And it's not in 'Aw, shucks' … *I have worked really hard. And I've tried to get better.*"

I learned something about success when bestselling author Richard Carlson told me his journey when we appeared on a radio show together. Richard said, "*Don't Sweat the Small Stuff* was my tenth book." Richard loved to write and he kept going through nine previous books, each with varying degrees of success.

Richard was perfecting his writing style with every book he wrote. In this way he was constantly preparing for the home run, which became his bestselling book *Don't Sweat the Small Stuff.* Soon, Richard had a bestselling series, including *Don't Sweat the Small Stuff in Love, Don't Sweat the Small Stuff with Money* and others.

TAKE ON RISK

In Part II, Section One, *Reduce Risk*, I describe the R.E.D.U.C.E. process. Here I want to emphasize that life does not only reward hard work. Big profits often result when someone takes on appropriate risk. A number of people shy away from appropriate risk. That's because they do not have a strategy for risk-taking. Please see Part II, Section One, *Reduce Risk* for methods that can brighten your life.

> *I will do what others will not do, so in the*
> *future I can do what others cannot do.*
>
> RANDY GAGE

HONE YOUR PERSUASION SKILLS

In Part XI of this book, I discuss the P.E.R.S.U.A.D.E. process. Here I want to emphasize that we truly can open the floodgates of financial abundance when we learn and practice positive persuasion skills. My life changed when I learned that persuasion can have positive outcomes – when I start focusing on how I can benefit the listener.

> *Win-win or no deal.*
>
> STEPHEN COVEY

Positive persuasion is about making sure that a transaction results in benefits for both people – a win-win result. True success is built on positive business and personal relationships. Learn the skills of positive persuasion and gain a whole new world of opportunities.

Comfort can be desirable, *but opportunities are fun!*

This section, *Truth No One Will Tell You*, has been an overview of highlights from my audio programs and presentations. I invite you to read the rest of this book and to seek out my other products for in-depth methods and support in your journey to thrive and empower yourself through any crisis.

Principles:

About the L.E.A.D.S. process: To thrive during a crisis, you need to lead yourself and others to calm.

About the T.R.U.T.H. process: In order to do better financially, you need to stretch and take appropriate risks.

Power Questions:

Which loved one or friend can you invite to practice the Bring Calm Steps? How can you have expansion in your life? Is there something you can do (to earn money) that comes easy to you, but is hard for other people? Where or how can you get additional training so you can have multiple streams of income?*

CONCLUSION TO PART IV, SECTION 2

In any crisis the truth is: we need to lead ourselves – our thinking, our feelings, and our actions. We cannot wait for anyone else to provide leadership. Fortunately, you will gain cooperation when you begin by focusing on benefits for all involved.

• •
* Here! Get your copy of the *Ultimate Make Money While You Sleep via the Internet System* at www.TomSuperCoach.com/SpecialOffer.htm.

In Part V, *Great Communicators Win with Job Interviews*, you will learn how to convince a job interviewer that you have the skills and can-do attitude that would most benefit his or her company.

Let's move forward. You will strengthen yourself for your next job interview.

Part V

Great Communicators Win with Job Interviews

"AN ELECTION is a grand job interview," former President Bill Clinton said at a private luncheon I attended. "Have a 20-minute talk, a 15-minute one, and a one-minute talk. If you can't express it in one minute, you don't know why you want it."

When Bill Clinton gave his secrets of public speaking, I listened with rapt attention. He said, "The microphone is your friend. It enables everyone to relax. Relax, overcome fears and speak plainly. Strip things down to straight talk..."

President Clinton also said, "The mechanics of leadership in any public endeavor is a team sport. It's very important to focus on teamwork. It is important to have people on your team that are different from you."

President Ronald Reagan has often been called the Great Communicator. In 1984, in their first televised presidential election debate, his opponent, Walter Mondale, put in an unexpectedly strong performance. Mondale questioned Reagan's age and capacity to endure the intense demands of the presidency.

But then in the next debate, on October 21, 1984, Reagan effectively neutralized the issue when he said, "I will not make age an issue of this campaign. I am not going to exploit for political purposes my opponent's youth and inexperience."

The media dropped the topic of age, and Ronald Reagan went on to gain the office of President of the United States.

We began this section with Bill Clinton's comment about an election campaign as a job interview. What we see from both former Presidents is the ability to make a warm, human connection.

Being heard and trusted depends on your ability to make a warm, human connection.

The Bottom Line About Job Interviews

In a new employee, employers want the following:

1. High productivity

2. Low maintenance (getting along well with team members, and more)

3. A "bargain" (top value without having to pay top dollar)

In a job interview, you need to convey that you're going to be a good team player. Part of making a warm, human connection is being perceived as credible. Here are Craig Harrison's comments on credibility.

Be a Credible Communicator, Make Honesty Your Policy!

CRAIG HARRISON

Credibility in the workplace means believability. Simply put, do customers, clients and colleagues believe what you say? Is your track record one of telling the truth? Are your estimates accurate, your forecasts realistic and your word solid? Or are you a big talker, a storyteller, or a spin doctor? Become a credible communicator.

The Right Way to Write and Speak

From the moment you initiate contact with a prospect or co-worker the credibility counter is activated. Are your statements accurate, assertions factual and your references, degrees and awards correct? Whether spoken or written, your communication must withstand the truthfulness test.

From football coaches to Pulitzer-winning authors to high-level accounting executives to politicians we've seen many a professional undone by a lack of credibility. Don't end up the butt of Jay Leno's jokes! Donald Trump isn't the only executive who can tell you "you're fired!"

Your Word is Your Bond

People listen to what you say and how you say it. In every communication you can become known as a person of his or her word. Conversely, you can become known for shading the truth, telling people what they want to hear, or parsing words as a defendant might do under courthouse cross examination. Little boys who've lost credibility get eaten by wolves. Big boys and girls get fired when they lack credibility.

Words are Sticks and Stones

Beyond misrepresenting your own accomplishments or capabilities, be cautious of making assertions about others. Character assassination is fatal to careers, and not just the person you're slandering. Your words carry a weight to them that affects others. Gossiping, spreading falsehoods or even half-truths about your competitors or colleagues flags you as dangerous, untrustworthy and unprofessional.

Marketplace success requires trust from your colleagues. Gossiping or betraying confidences destroys your own credibility – as an honorable colleague, a safe confidante, and an ally.

Take the High Road

The workplace affords you ample opportunities to earn credibility. Every time you make a deadline, do what you say you'll do or are there in a time of need for others your credibility rises.

When you defend the honor of absent co-workers, refuse to engage in gossip, or caution others to give colleagues the benefit of the doubt, you are showing class, wisdom and professionalism, raising your credibility quotient.

Similarly, when you "say the right thing" or "do the right thing" in ethical situations your credibility is enhanced.

Earning Your Stripes

Don't fall down when it comes to admitting mistakes. The credible communicator can admit errors or mistakes in a forthright and direct manner. Address and then go about rectifying errors, restoring confidence in yourself. Those lacking in credibility might try to cover up, ignore or minimize their folly, often compounding the error of their ways. Ultimately, it's less important that you made a mistake, than that you fixed it and can assure others it won't happen again.

Know When to Say No

The credible communicator doesn't just tell people what they want to hear. Life would be easy if we could say "yes" to every request we received. Realistically, agreeing to something you ultimately can't deliver on is detrimental to your reputation. Develop the fortitude to say "no" when it's the right answer, through it may not be the popular one. Over the long term, you will be respected for the accuracy of your assessments, decisions and determinations, even if the news isn't music to the ears of all who listen. Sometimes the truth isn't popular or pretty, but a person who is a "straight shooter" is respected by all.

The Power of Your Platform – For Better and Worse

Public speaking magnifies the importance of your credibility. Misstatements, misrepresentations and inaccuracies are multiplied tenfold or more when issued in a public setting: speech, public statement or PowerPoint-styled presentation. Whether you speak inaccurately, misuse language or misrepresent the truth, it's like putting feathers back into a ruptured pillow … in a wind tunnel! Once you've misspoken publicly it's on record for all to hear, read and reread!

The Simple Truth about The Truth

Strive to boost your credibility rating in your professional relationships. Don't be in-credible … strive to be incredible!

Craig Harrison, author of *Cultivating the Leader in You* and *The Voice of Customer Service. Expressions of Excellence!*™ provides sales and service solutions through speaking. For information on keynotes, training, coaching, curriculum for licensing, and more.

(510) 547-0664
craig@expressionsofexcellence.com
www.ExpressionsOfExcellence.com

To be effective in job interviews, we use the I.M.P. R.E.S.S. process:

I – Inquire

M – Mention how you fulfill criteria

P – Prepare for questions

R – Review just before

E – Engage connection

S – Send scarcity messages

S – Save money for last

Let's take the next step …

INQUIRE

A prudent question is one-half of wisdom.

FRANCIS BACON
(philosopher & scientist)

How do you help someone easily decide to hire you? Ask questions. This means *inquire* as to what they really want in a new employee. It takes some finesse to ask an appropriate question at an appropriate time.

To influence anyone to make a decision that is in your favor, you need to know what the person wants and how the person wants it. The crucial method is to *uncover the interviewer's preferred input style.*

We receive input all day long. There's some input we like, some we don't, and some we are indifferent to. But your new job is on the line here. So it is best to learn how to identify the interviewer's preferred input style.

First, be prepared for when the interviewer asks, "Do you have any questions?"

Here are three useful questions:

1. "What is most important to you in a candidate for your team?"

2. "What has to happen for you to feel that a candidate is ideal for this position?"

3. "What else do you need to know from a candidate?"

Choose just one of these questions. Avoid using more than one. Let's look at question "2" in detail. We use the phrase "what has to happen" to discover the person's preferred input style. Her preferred input style is *how she prefers to receive information.* There are three primary input styles: visual, auditory, and kinesthetic (touch).

Preferred input style: *The clue that identifies the input style*

Visual: *"I need to see some sample work."*

Auditory: *"I'd like to hear comments from your references."*

Kinesthetic *(touch)*: *"We need to find out if you'd work smoothly with the other team members. The next step is* *for you to have interviews with team members."*

About the person with the kinesthetic-input style

People who prefer kinesthetic input often say,

- It didn't feel right to me.

- That feels like a good fit.

- I'm just not comfortable with that detail.

- I hope your presentation went smoothly.

An interviewer asked me how these comments specifically offer the clue that the person prefers kinesthetic input. Note how each sentence *deals with touch.* We see key words, such as, "feel right," "good fit," "not comfortable," and "smoothly."

Each interviewer is a unique individual with a preferred input style. The good news is that when you listen carefully, you can often discover what the preferred input style is. Then you can supply the right information in an *effective* way. That's when you can be heard and be trusted.

Principle:

Ask appropriate questions to discover what is really important to the person, so that he or she will decide in your favor.

Power Questions:

Practice asking questions that can help you learn vital information during your job interview. Which words flow easily from your mouth? How can you modify a particular question so that you get the information you need *and* still feel at ease?

MENTION HOW YOU FULFILL CRITERIA

Once you have the answers to your questions, you can provide comments that connect with what the interviewer wants (the interviewer's criteria).

Here are some examples:

1. "As you see on my resume, I have worked in a fast-paced, multi-tasking environment. For example, I was working with a client I'll call Sarah and … "

2. "Yes, I thrive under pressure. I completed a project report plus a prototype in a two-week period. It was and still is a company record."

When I work with graduate students to help them prepare to perform well in job interviews, I mention *the employer's favorite three.* (We covered a version of this earlier.)

The employer's favorite three:

1. High productivity

2. Low maintenance

3. A bargain

Employers like it when a $60,000 employee brings in four times that revenue. That would be a bargain.*

> *The world belongs to the energetic.*
>
> RALPH WALDO EMERSON

---

* The precise ratio of salary to revenue that an employer would find amenable varies by industry, or more particularly the associated profit margin of the revenue stream.

Have at least *three* prepared anecdotes. The best way to alert the interviewer to how you fulfill the job criteria is through anecdotes.

Examples of anecdotes

- "Doing well in a multi-tasking environment is one of my strengths. I learned how to do this while working at Acme Company … "

- "Thinking fast is a skill I developed when I worked …"

Principle:

Provide compelling anecdotes so that you let the interviewer experience how you've done whatever the job requires.

Power Questions:

What are examples of your shining moments with past jobs? How can you talk about those moments in brief anecdotes?

PREPARE FOR QUESTIONS

Ever been hit in an interview by a question that knocked you for a loop? Imagine being prepared for some of the toughest questions.

Prepare for the standard questions:

1. I see a gap in your resume. What were you doing then?

2. Why did you leave your last position?

3. What do you want to be doing in five years?

4. Describe your ideal job.

5. What are your weaknesses?

In my class on *Professional Presentation and Communication Development*, the graduate students prepare by having two anecdotes ready to answer these questions:

- Tell me about yourself (your strengths)

- Tell me about your weaknesses

- What are you best known for? (your personal brand)

Facts go in our brains. Stories go in our hearts.

SANDRA BLOCH

People don't buy with their head but with their heart.
The heart is closer to the wallet than the head.

MARK VICTOR HANSEN

The *weaknesses* question in particular gets job applicants in trouble. In the past, some *misguided* advice stated, "Cleverly say things to make the weakness actually sound like a hidden strength." *Stop!* Interviewers can see through that antiquated tactic.

Avoid the phony answer. A *better approach* is to say something such as, "In the past, I tended to be overly focused on details. To counter that tendency, I took a course in project management. In that workshop, I had an experience in which I used the 80/20 Principle to set priorities. Now I continue to practice what I learned by having a note posted on my day planner page that reads '80/20.'"

Know your tendencies and compensate for them.

TOM MARCOUX

You can't expect to win unless you know why you lose.

BENJAMIN LIPSON

At a luncheon I attended, Bill Clinton was asked a tough question about his mistakes during his presidency. He replied that one of his mistakes was answering all the allegations of the Whitewater scandal. "I worried about this for about two years. [But then I realized] what you know is from the two minutes on the evening news. If I answered something about Whitewater, you would think I wasn't doing my job [about education, the environment and more]." Subsequently, Clinton made sure that the television sound bites were about something that was of value to his administration.

Bill Clinton also said, "The people who are most disappointed and beaten down have not known colossal failures. I've known colossal failures … " He smiled, and the audience chuckled *with* him.

We see from this comment that it's important to admit an event or tendency that has inspired you to learn to modify your behavior.

It is helpful to avoid trying to seem to be all things to all people. Focus on being the right person for the right job. For example, I have a extremely detail-conscious person do the typesetting of my books. I have artistic people work on the illustrations of my children's books. And I have an intuitive person, who has not read all the books I've read, who listens to a first draft of my writing. She can point out details that may need expansion.

Everyone has weaknesses. Not all weaknesses can be eliminated. The effective person makes good choices and finds ways to compensate for weaknesses.

> *Talent is cheaper than table salt. What separates the talented individual from the successful one is a lot of hard work.*
>
> STEPHEN KING

What is the hard work? Rehearsal! Rehearse before the job interview.

Prepare anecdotes of actions you've taken in previous jobs, to highlight what a great team player you are. Avoid the self-aggrandizing, self-absorbed comments that smart but arrogant people say during job interviews. Mention a few appropriate details about how your team members did well and how you supported their efforts and initiatives. In this way, you *can* give the impression that you are a personable and competent team player.

Prepare for tough questions. My graduate students learn to gain "think-space," so that they can think *before* they answer. Here are some phrases you can use to give yourself some think-space:

1. "When you ask that question, it reminds me of … "

2. "I can see you are concerned about that, and I'll need to pause (think) for a moment. I want to make sure that I give you a valuable answer … "

3. "I haven't looked at it this way before. *I'm* interested in that, too. I'll need to look into it over the next one or two days."

Principle:

Prepare for the tough questions and rehearse.

Power Question:

What are the questions that make you squirm? Write these questions down and note three possible answers to each one. Rehearse with friends to see what responses feel real and appropriate to you.

REVIEW JUST BEFORE

"Every little bit of studying helps," my father used to say during my high school years. At St. Ignatius College Preparatory, my friends and I would sit on the rug in the hallway before class and before exams. I would study right up to the last minute. Each time, something that I saw in those final minutes would be on the test, and I would get it right.

Just before you go into an interview, review the annual report. Take a look at the firm's Web site. Review the company's press releases. Review your notes from people in the organization whom you've interviewed on your own. With all the details fresh in your mind, you will come across as a confident person who has the firm's interests at heart.

Use a mnemonic device to help you remember crucial details. For example, you can use the letters of N.E.W. to remember key words, such as **N**ew product; **E**arly adopters; and **W**hy I want to work here. You can also hold a 3-by-5 card of key notes in your hand.

Some of my clients hesitate to use the 3-by-5 card during an interview. To handle this situation, I encourage them to have a phrase like this ready: "I just have a couple of notes here, because there are a few details that I know can be helpful during our discussion." In this way, they are ready for the interviewer's quizzical look at their 3-by-5 card.

Principle:

Review just before the interview.

Power Questions:

What areas of your preparation feel fuzzy at the moment? How can you "get solid" about those details? Can you create a mnemonic device?

ENGAGE CONNECTION

How important is a resume? Often, it is simply a tool to get the interview. During the interview, you *must* use excellent first-impression skills. In my workshop entitled *First Impressions Are Everything: Break the Four-Second Barrier and Influence People,* I emphasize the Power-Three of Influence.

The Power-Three of Influence:

1. Show how much you care.

2. Show that you and your interviewer have common concerns, traits and feelings.

3. Demonstrate that you're a trusted advisor.

A journalist asked, "Trusted advisor?"

I replied, "Yes. Every good co-worker is called upon to voice a hypothesis or learned opinion as the team solves problems."

To influence the interviewer to give you a job, you want to do things that help create the *Power-Three of Influence.* You are seeking a "me, too" moment. For example, if two people find that they are both parents, they might make a connection, a moment of understanding. But avoid "me, too" – one up. If the interviewer says that she has one son, avoid mentioning that you have *three* sons.

To help you prepare in advance for the interview, draw up a list of possible ways to connect with a new person. To construct this list, you need to reflect about various facets of your life and your own preferences. Also, see if you can get some information about the interviewer (through Google, for example) *before* your meeting.

Principle:

Connection is crucial.

Power Questions:

How can you feel comfortable about connecting? Have you identified 20 possible ways that you can connect with a new person?

SEND SCARCITY MESSAGES

Imagine a method so powerful that it is like fire. At the right time, you could use that method well and you'd really be cooking – or you could *burn yourself*. Be careful! This method is to be used carefully *or not at all*.

People often want something more when it appears that they cannot have it. So if an appropriate moment comes up, you might share a vague detail about how you're looking at a number of opportunities at this time. This sends a scarcity message: you may not be available.

Be sure to consider mentioning this only after you are *certain* that you have a rapport with the interviewer, and after the interviewer has already expressed significant interest in your joining the company. Someone asked me, "How do you know if the interviewer has expressed significant interest?" I replied, "You listen carefully for phrases such as,

1. "Oh, when you're working here … "

2. "How soon can you start?"

Be prepared for an interviewer who asks, "Which companies have an interest in you?" You can reply,

1. "As you know, in this industry it's more appropriate that I not to go into that."

2. "You know, I'd rather discuss how I can be an asset to your team."

There is a way to send a powerful message *without* sending a scarcity message. This way is to support yourself, to feel your own value, which you contribute wherever you go. Now Dr. JoAnn Dahlkoetter will share some methods to empower yourself.

Enhance Your Confidence and Self-Image

DR. JOANN DAHLKOETTER

Here are three powerful ways to enhance your confidence and self-image:

1. Separate who you are from what you have achieved.

Athletes frequently use their stopwatch, their scores or their performances to define their self-worth. A disappointing race performance does not indicate that you are a poor athlete. You need to begin with a firm foundation, a secure sense of self. Consciously light up on harsh self-judgments. Come to accept yourself as a valuable person regardless of the outcome.

2. Become aware of subtle, degrading self-statements.

Diminish the intensity of your negative self-attacks while nourishing more healthy self-talk. When someone gives you a compliment, rather than dismissing it, take it in and let it enhance your self-esteem.

3. Choose a positive quality you want to develop.

Let's say you want to train more efficiently, with a sense of confidence, lightness, and power. Select another athlete who possesses these qualities and visualize that person's style during your workout. Imagine that you are that athlete, floating effortlessly, with endless amounts of energy and self-assuredness.

As your self-image becomes more positive, the degree of excellence will correspondingly rise in all areas of your life.

Dr. JoAnn Dahlkoetter is the coach to CEOs and Olympic Gold Medalists. She is the author of the bestselling book *Your Performing Edge*. She won the San Francisco Marathon and achieved 2nd in the Hawaii Ironman Triathlon. She has been a frequent expert commentator on ABC Television. For your Free Teleseminar Training, visit her at

www.DrJoAnn.com

Dr. JoAnn's comments apply to both athletes and "corporate athletes" (people who compete in business).

Remember, when you nurture yourself and take good care of yourself, you radiate charisma, confidence and good will.

Principle:

People often want what they apparently cannot have. In certain circumstances, a scarcity message can help you.

Power Questions:

When would you feel that the risk of sending a scarcity message might be worthwhile? When would you be better off to *avoid* sending a scarcity message?

Save Money for Last

When George Takei (Sulu of *Star Trek*) first met Gene Roddenberry (the creator of *Star Trek*) in an informal meeting, Gene was late.

> "I hope it wasn't too long," Gene said.
>
> "Oh no, not at all," George replied politely.
>
> "How do you pronounce that last name of yours?" Gene asked, just after he'd mispronounced the name as "Tah-K-eye."
>
> George replied that it rhymes with okay.
>
> "Oh, okay. Takei as in okay. Takei is okay." Gene laughed.
>
> George flowed in the moment and mentioned that the *other* way Gene pronounced his name was a "legitimate Japanese word."
>
> "Really? What does it mean?" Gene asked.
>
> "Well, it translates into English as 'expensive.'"

"Oh, my God! I'd better make sure I call you Takei. Takei is definitely okay," Gene laughed.

In this conversation, George demonstrated a lighthearted way to create a connection and help the other person feel comfortable.

Talking about money often makes people uncomfortable. In a job interview, it is best to discuss salary *after* you have proved your value to the company.*

If the interviewer starts the meeting with, "What are your salary requirements?" you need to have some effective possible responses ready. You could reply, "Oh, you're offering me the position?"

At that point, the interviewer usually backs off and says, "Not yet. Let's continue with the interview."

Another response to the early "salary requirements" question is, "My salary requirements are in line with the market rates connected to my experience and skills. How about we continue talking about how I fit in with this team and how I can be of service?"

The interviewer is looking for ways to screen you out. You need to first *prove* your value to the firm. Researchers report that firms will often create a new or modified position when they know the special skills of a particular candidate. The point is, avoid discussing salary until you know that the firm wants you.

. . . .

*As a sidenote, years ago, George Takei taught me something about filmmaking. I showed him some feature film storyboards, and he saw a shot in which a character's tear flowed down and splashed in his teacup. George said gently, "Uh, Tom, isn't that a bit melodramatic?" Yes, George, I never filmed it. Thanks.

The secret to making $1,000 a minute in a job interview

A number of authors have discussed this powerful method to help you gain a higher salary. Practice this pattern with a friend before you have a job interview in which salary will be discussed.

The $1,000-a-minute pattern

Interviewer: "We're prepared to offer you $40,000."

Janet: "Hmmm. $40,000."

> (Then Janet is silent. She waits – even if she's just thinking of her phone number backwards. Her facial expression gives the impression that she is thinking about the offer.)

Interviewer: "Um … uh … Perhaps we could go to $45,000."

Janet: "$45,000 … "

(Janet is silent again. She waits.)

Interviewer: "Okay, okay. $50,000 is the best we can do. It really is our last offer."

> (Janet notices all the clues in the situation and decides that this truly is the last offer.)

Janet: "Great! I'm really looking forward to working here."

Janet has just made $10,000 in three minutes.

The important keys to the $1,000-a-minute pattern:

1. Repeat the figure so the interviewer knows you heard it.

2. Be silent. Let the silence push the interviewer to the next step.

3. In many first-impression situations, you can show your good character by listening. During a salary negotiation, the prospective employee creates the first impression that the employer receives. She shows confidence, poise and knowledge of her own value (and the effort she'll devote to the job). The interviewer thinks, "She must be good. Her confidence shows it. She held out for nearly the top of our salary range."

Let's remember, the interviewer is looking for a bargain – a valuable worker for a reasonable salary. This pattern of silent waiting is gentle enough so that you do not appear unreasonable in your salary demands. Rehearse the pattern.

Important warning: Sometimes it is best to avoid negotiating. No method is appropriate for all situations. Sometimes, it is best to *avoid* negotiating. If you are going into a *new* field, you might be better off to take a modest salary for the chance to get started in the industry. There are times when we have a deep intuitive feeling ("I had this gut feeling") that we should be working at a particular company. It might be important for you to just get in the door and take a modest position with a modest salary. Numerous case studies show how successful people started in the mailroom or as an assistant, and then made sure that they were in the right place at the right time.

Remember to prepare and rehearse for your job interview.

Principle:

Save the money discussion for last, after you've proved what a terrific asset you would be to the team.

Power Questions:

Are you willing to risk losing the position just to gain some more money? Are you at the point in your career at which you're aiming to "trade up"? Be brutally honest with yourself. Do you have the skills and finesse to be *highly desirable* to a new employer? If not, what can you do this week to improve your skills and gain relevant experience?

CONCLUSION TO PART V

In Part V, we explored the I.M.P.R.E.S.S. process to being effective in job interviews:

I – Inquire

M – Mention how you fulfill criteria

P – Prepare for questions

R – Review just before

E – Engage connection

S – Send scarcity messages

S – Save money for last

> *Do unto others as they would like done unto them*
> *[the Platinum Rule].*

DR. TONY ALESSANDRA & MICHAEL J. O'CONNOR

The main idea is to find out how the interviewer prefers to take in information.

In Part VI, *Win When Dealmaking and Negotiating,* you will learn how to make money and get better deals.

Let's get started …

Part VI

Win When Dealmaking and Negotiating*

WHAT IF just by knowing one of Donald Trump's favorite words, you could put $100,000 in your pocket? Donald Trump talks about *leverage*. His use of leverage has put millions of dollars in his pocket.

"Leverage," Donald Trump says, "is having something the other guy wants … needs … or best of all, simply can't do without." Donald says that you need imagination and salesmanship. For example, when he wanted New York City to approve his deal to buy the Commodore Hotel on East 42nd Street, he convinced the owners to tell the press that they planned to close it down. Donald used this leverage to influence the city, saying that a boarded-up hotel would be a disaster for the Grand Central area and all of New York.

In another use of leverage, Donald Trump was trying to close a deal to purchase a huge hotel casino in Atlantic City that was owned by the Hilton Hotels Corporation. Trump bid $320 mil-

* Formerly titled *Communicate to Win*.

lion. Toward the end of the negotiation, he had the intuition that the Hilton negotiating team probably had received a better bid and was trying to kill the deal. When the Hilton team came back to the table two hours late from a break, Trump was convinced. He decided that the only way to close the deal was to "shame them" into it. He used a hurt tone and said things like, "How could you shake my hand and then not stand by the commitment? How could you negotiate for three days and then walk away? How could you force me to spend hundreds of thousands of dollars on lawyers and not follow through?" Trump told them, "It is a disgrace … It is immoral … It is dishonorable."

He decided that since much of the deal had been negotiated, the Hilton team would find it "hard psychologically for them to walk away" if he did not give them an excuse to do so. In this way, Donald Trump used *negative* leverage to achieve his objective. He renamed the property Trump's Castle. In the first year, Trump's Castle earned $226 million gross.

Here is another example of leverage – *positive leverage* in this case. When my friend Linda was searching for an apartment in San Francisco, she arrived early and well-dressed at the apartment building. She created a rapport with her potential landlord, asking him about the building, parking, neighbors and how things were going for him generally. In this way, she made herself stand out from the crowd of people who merely filled in an application and left. A few days later, the landlord called and offered her the apartment.

Behind every negotiation is a relationship between people. As Linda's story demonstrates, creating a rapport is crucial.

To effectively make deals and negotiate well, there are three other vital things you need to do:

1. Know your Maximum Supportable Position (MSP)*

2. Know your Least Acceptable Result (LAR)*

3. Flinch at the first offer

The Maximum Supportable Position (MSP) is the best deal you believe you can make. Your MSP is not a crazy offer. It is something you can support with good reasons. For example, a first-time screenwriter with an effective agent may set up a bidding situation that raises the screenplay fee to $1 million. The agent can refer to similar first screenplays that earned that level of compensation, demonstrating that $1 million is a reasonable fee.

Now Mike Robbins shares his thoughts about asking for what you want.

Ask For What You Want

MIKE ROBBINS

This quote from Tony Robbins is one of my favorites: "The answer is always 'no' if you don't ask." Isn't that the truth?! So often we know exactly what we want, but for a myriad of reasons we are unwilling to ask for it. Usually we're scared we'll get rejected or we're worried about what others will think of us. We let these concerns (and others) stop us from asking for what we really want. Erroneously, we think that if we work hard enough or are a "good" enough person, people will reward us by giving us exactly what we want. Unfortunately, as most of us know, this often leads to disappointment and frustration.

* Author Herb Cohen writes about MSP and LAR.

We can't expect other people to read our minds and know what we want if we don't tell them. One of the best things we can do to appreciate ourselves and get what we want in life, while at the same time empower the people around us, is to make specific requests.

Many of us, however, aren't all that good at making requests. Because of our insecurity about all of this, we either don't make requests at all or the ones we do make are actually demands. A true request can be accepted, declined, or negotiated – without any consequence. When we ask for something, don't get it, and then get upset about it, chances are it was not really a true request to begin with; it was a demand disguised as a request or simply a manipulation.

Asking for what we want does take courage. Many of us have been taught not to make too many requests. Requesting exactly what we want is not arrogant, self-absorbed, pushy, or any of the other negative things people have told us. When we remember the difference between a request and a demand, we can give ourselves permission to simply ask for the things that we want in life. As simple as it may seem, people who have an ability to ask for what they want are more likely to get what they want.

By asking for exactly what you want you are setting yourself up for success and reminding yourself that you deserve whatever you desire. In addition, making specific requests empowers you to take responsibility for your life and it gives people around you the opportunity to support you and contribute to your happiness. When we have the courage to ask for what we want in life, without attachment, we create a sense of freedom, peace, and gratitude within us that can transform our lives and help us create anything.

Action – What You Can Do:

Take out a piece of paper and write down at least five things you really want but have been unwilling or too scared to ask for. With each item, figure out exactly who you can ask and what you can ask them for. Challenge yourself to make these specific requests in the next three days. Remember, "The answer is always 'no' if you don't ask."

Mike Robbins , author of *Focus On the Good Stuff*, Mike helps individuals and companies to be more successful, fulfilled and grateful.

www.Mike-Robbins.com

Let's remember to be kind to ourselves, as we would be kind to a friend. Do you remember a time when you asked a friend, "What do you want?" When your friend replied, "tea," or anything else, you were happy to help. So pull out your personal journal and ask yourself, "What do you want?" Then go one step deeper. Ask yourself, "What do you want to feel?"

Your *Least Acceptable Result* (LAR) is the minimal deal that you will accept. As long as you do better than your LAR, you know you're successful. For example, a speaker whose regular fee is $9,000 may agree to accept $6,000 when she wants to enter a new market. If her LAR was $4,000, then she's still done well.

When you *flinch at the first offer*, you are likely to get a better result for yourself, and the other person will feel better in the long run. How is this possible?

Here is an example: Trudy considers purchasing a used car that is advertised at $3,000. She offers $1,000. The car owner immediately accepts. Does Trudy feel good?

No. She thinks, (a) "what's wrong with the car?" and (b) "I could have done better." It would have been better for the car owner to flinch at the first offer and express discomfort.

Negotiation, sales, and many forms of business relations depend on rapport. The *Merriam-Webster's Medical Dictionary* defines "rapport" as (1) relation characterized by harmony, conformity, accord, or affinity; (2) confidence of a subject in the operator (as in hypnotism, psychotherapy, or mental testing) with willingness to cooperate.

Here are Michael Soon Lee's comments on rapport in various cultures:

Building Rapport with Multicultural Customers

MICHAEL SOON LEE, MBA

Building rapport with culturally diverse customers is not the same as with Anglo Americans. In this country we assume everyone wants to be greeted with a firm handshake, a broad smile and direct eye contact but this is not necessarily true for people from outside the United States.

For instance, touching some customers in any way can be extremely offensive. Simply shaking the hand or touching the shoulder of traditional Middle Eastern, Asian Indian or Japanese women can be the equivalent of assault in their country. This is why it's crucial to let the customer take the lead rather than assuming how anyone wants to be greeted.

When meeting a new customer, hesitate for a moment after introducing yourself and see what kind of greeting the customer offers you. Most multicultural men will give you a handshake but may also bow to you at the same time and you should do likewise. Others may hug you and even kiss you on both cheeks so again, let the customer do what comes naturally to them rather than assuming they want to be greeted with a handshake.

American men, in particular, are not used to being hugged by strangers. We are especially uncomfortable having other men kiss us on the cheeks but you should never turn away. If you do, there is a strong likelihood that one of those kisses could land on your lips! This would be exceedingly embarrassing for both parties.

Next, when meeting a couple for the first time, be aware of how you greet the female. If you shake the hand of the male then drop you hand to your side before turning to the woman so you don't force her to shake her hand which may be against her culture or religion. If she extends a hand then by all means shake it, but more likely she will just nod at you and you should do likewise.

While this seems like a small adjustment, it speaks volumes about your sensitivity to people from other cultures. By letting customers do what comes naturally to them your relationship will develop much more quickly and comfortably for all concerned.

Smiles convey different things in different cultures. In America we interpret the gesture as being friendly while in many parts of the world people smile to cover over grief, hide embarrassment or conceal the fact that they don't know the answer to some question. Too much smiling by you can imply that you are engaged in one or all of these behaviors.

Direct eye contact is assumed to be a sign of honesty and sincerity in America. However, in many other cultures around the world, direct eye contact is rude and intrusive. To show respect for others, these people avert their eyes by looking down. Unfortunately, many people in this country interpret this as a sign of disrespect which is obviously the opposite of what was intended.

Learning about cultural differences cannot only be interesting but profitable as well. Think about how many salespeople are silently turning away business by not being sensitive to other people's cultural beliefs. By simply adjusting the way you behave to be more comfortable for them you will find people from diverse cultures to be very loyal and interesting customers.

> Michael Soon Lee, MBA, is a diversity consultant and speaker who helps companies increase sales to multicultural customers. His clients include: Coca-Cola, General Motors, State Farm Insurance and hundreds of other companies. He is the author of the book *Black Belt Negotiating* (Amacom Books, 2007) and four books on marketing and selling to diverse customers. Michael can be reached by phone at

> (800) 417-7325

In my seminars and keynote addresses on how to *Communicate to Win* and *Be Heard and Be Trusted*, we use the A.C.T.I.O.N. process:

A – Approach them in ways they prefer

C – Communicate vividly

T – Touch them five times

I – Invite action

O – Open to personal value

N – Note value and gratitude

Let's go into action …

Approach Them in Ways They Prefer

How do you know how a person prefers to be approached? Now, that is a powerful question.

First, let's notice that every person has a preferred way to be approached. We take in new information through different modalities: audio, visual, and kinesthetic (touch).

Some people prefer to –

1. Hear a phone call

2. See someone face to face

3. Read an e-mail message

4. Read a postcard

How do you find out how a person prefers a first contact? You observe and listen. At a networking event, you can hear people's preferences in their offhand comments:

- "I get about 90 e-mail messages a day. It takes so much time to go through them … "

- "I hate those awful faxes that are just advertisements. What a waste of paper!"

We have just learned that approaching these individuals through e-mail or a fax might cause hard feelings. So we can seek another way to create connection.

We need to focus on two crucial details when approaching someone:

1. Be respectful, and

2. Approach the person with something that can help him or her.

Be respectful

At a number of my speeches, audience members can enter a drawing for one of my products. Even if they do not win the product, they can choose to receive an e-newsletter, *Success Secrets*, and an e-book. Audience members fill out a rating sheet that respectfully offers them the options to choose to receive the e-newsletter and e-book. The whole interaction is about my giving them continued value. This is respectful.

Approach the person with something that can help him or her

If you have any hesitation in approaching someone, get clear on the benefit you are offering. Let this be your central question: "How can I help this person (so the by-product is that she will take the action I prefer)?" What value do you offer? You know that you will work hard, be on time, and avoid complaining. You will give great value for the opportunity to perform. This reminds me of an idea that relates to manifesting wealth: "I am here only to be truly helpful."

Give the person "permission"

We often see people hesitate even when they truly want something. We can help the person by providing the atmosphere of permission. The way we subtly help things flow along is to use such language as, "When you are using this (product) … " With such a statement, you are basically assuming that the sale has been made. You are demonstrating your confidence that the person will close the deal with you.

Finally, there are times when we do not know what the best approach to someone will be. Then we look for a good approach, one that involves both being respectful and offering something helpful.

Principle:

People have a preferred way to receive information: visual, auditory, or kinesthetic (touch).

Power Questions:

How can you discover the person's preferred way of taking in information? Can you participate in a group discussion so you can hear her comments? Can you talk with her assistant? Can you read a book or interview she's done? (Use Google.com to find any articles posted on the Internet.)

COMMUNICATE VIVIDLY

> *If a [person] would move the world,*
> *he must first move himself.*
>
> SOCRATES

In order to communicate powerfully with people, you need to communicate clearly with yourself.

Ask yourself:

- What do I really want?

- How important is this to me?

- What do I need to learn here?

Armed with the answers to these questions, you are ready to communicate vividly. Use the following general principles:

Use word pictures

Use word pictures, a personal story, and an appeal to the emotions. Remember that people tend to buy on emotion and then justify their decision on fact. Word pictures create an image. For example, a friend can say, "When I was waiting for you, I felt like a puppy cast adrift in a tiny raft in the middle of the huge ocean."

Here's an example of how a personal story invited people to give to a foundation. A friend sent me and many others an e-mail message about how a certain foundation had sent his loved one a monthly stipend to help with her rent and living expenses when she was incapacitated by a disease. This story was effective because we all knew the person and appreciated how the foundation had helped during her time of need.

Use the salted oats process

Another way to communicate vividly is based on the salted oats process. Author Stephen Scott, in his book *Simple Steps to Impossible Dreams*, tells the story of how to lead a horse to water and ensure that he drinks. You put salt into his oats, to make him thirsty.

In conversation, one sets the stage so that the listener eagerly awaits certain details. Here's an example:

Susan: "This reminds me of something Lynda Obst (producer of *Sleepless in Seattle*) said about going into meetings with film finance people. She had a special strategy that she learned from Peter Guber. Would you like to hear about it?"

Deanna: "Yes. This sounds interesting."

Use the Principles of Influence

In his book *Influence,* researcher/author Robert Cialdini noted the principles of influence, including:

1. Reciprocity

2. Commitment and consistency

3. Social proof

4. Perception of scarcity

5. Liking

6. Authority

Let's look at these in more detail...

Strategy 1: Create reciprocity

Reciprocity occurs when one person gives something and the other person feels compelled to return the favor. Bestselling author Roger Dawson tells the story of asking someone at an airport for change so he could make a 25 cent phone call. The man gave Roger a quarter, and Roger gave him one dollar and then had to run for his plane. The man and his family followed Roger across the airport, trying to give him his change. Their feelings of fairness were pronounced.

The principle of reciprocity is the basis of my encouraging you throughout this book to help someone first. You will stand out as a helpful and genuinely kind human being.

Strategy 2: Use the commitment & consistency principle

When people commit to something small, they are likely to follow through because they want to feel and appear to be consistent in their actions. This is like the flow of the martial art aikido. The aikido master gently leads the opponent in the direction in which the opponent is already going.

Notice these options:

Question: *"Susan, how can we stay in contact?"*

Person's Reply: *"I'm sorry – I'm out of cards."*

Answer: *"Oh, I'll make one for you." (You pull out one of your business cards and write the person's contact information on the back.)*

Question: *"Do you have e-mail at Yahoo.com or Hotmail. com?"*

All these questions flow forward to the goal of getting an e-mail address. This idea is to invite someone to do something small; the anonymous e-mail of Yahoo.com or Hotmail.com is a small commitment. Most of the time, the person will give a personal e-mail address. He or she was already flowing in that direction.

Strategy 3: Demonstrate social proof

When bestselling author Anthony Robbins bought a large mansion ("a castle"), he created social proof that his methods yield tremendous rewards. I encourage my students who are actors to place photos of their television and film appearances on their Web sites. In the minds of casting decision-makers, such photos create the impression, "She must be good. All these other professionals have cast her. She's always working."

Strategy 4: Enhance the perception of scarcity

People often want what they can't have. In sales, it's called the *take-away close.* For example, a real estate person selling a house might say, "Oh no! I just saw something in my notes. I may not be able to offer this house to you. I have a note here that says the owner was talking with another buyer. I'm sorry." Suddenly, the buyer finds that she wants the house more. She has the perception of scarcity. (By the way, if you are concerned that this method may be manipulative, please see my book *Darkest Secrets of Persuasion and Seduction Masters: How to Protect Yourself and Turn the Power to Good.*)

Create an impression that you're not waiting by the phone. People want to work with those professionals who are highly sought after by others.

Strategy 5: Set the stage for you to be liked

People will do a lot for a friend. In directing a feature film, I expanded the part of the little girl who portrayed the daughter of the main character because I liked her and her parents. They were a joy to work with. I had no hesitation in rewriting the script to expand her part.

On the other hand, I have worked with people who were disruptive. I arranged the schedules so that they were off my movie set quickly.

Being likeable is a big component in getting a job, a movie role and other opportunities. (You can call this the *liking factor*.) How can you encourage someone new to like you?

Use the L.I.K.E.–M.E.–N.O.W. process:

L – Listen

I – Interview

K – Kindle similarity

E – Express gratitude

M – Monitor time

E – Engage the person's concerns

N – Note ideal clients

O – Open to humor

W – Watch and help

Listen

Listen first. Ask a gentle question such as, "So, how do you know our host, Matt?"

Interview

You can easily start a conversation and put the person at ease. I often ask, "What are your hobbies?" This is a valuable question because people frequently enjoy their hobbies more than their current jobs. Or you can ask, "What are you looking forward to?"

Kindle similarity

A conversation warms up when people have a "Me, too!" moment. You often you hear this kind of comment: "Oh, you like skiing, too? What's your favorite resort?"

Express gratitude

You can say, "Thanks for your time," or "Thank you for your efforts on this one." In an e-mail, it often helps to begin with "Thank you for … "

Monitor time

Respect the person's time. Say things like, "This will be quick. I know you're busy."

Engage the person's concerns

Ask gentle questions to find out what is causing pain or inconvenience for the person. Then you can show how you hold similar concerns. This creates connection.

Note ideal clients

You can ask, "Who's your ideal client?" or "Are you looking for specific types of people? Perhaps I can help send some folks your way."

Open to humor

Humor is something to be careful about. In fact, in my book *Wake Up Your Spirit to Prosperity*, I cover 30 Secrets of Humor. I emphasize that it is helpful to observe what the person finds funny and flow with it if possible. One author states that the people he loves are the ones he laughs with.

Watch and help

You can ask, "How can I support what you're doing?" This is a better question than "How can I help you?" because many of us recoil when hearing a salesperson ask that question in a store.

Strategy 6: Inspire compliance with authority

A number of people are conditioned to comply with requests by an authority figure. For example, years ago at a certain training weekend, a seminar leader required that people not leave the room to use the restroom. Then the seminar leader said, "So, we have agreed on our rules." Because the leader was the authority figure, many people automatically nodded their heads. But one man stood up and said, "No. Those are *your* rules. I have not agreed." With that, he left the auditorium. The other people remained.

Researchers note that many people still react through the conditioning they have received since childhood to comply with an authority figure's demands. Let's look at two points. First, we can make sure to pay attention so that we do not respond to unreasonable demands solely because of our conditioning. Second, if we are in a position of authority, we can do things to strengthen that position of influence.

A number of authors noted that President Jimmy Carter did certain things that seemed to undermine the authority of the Presidency during his term in office. He was seen carrying his own baggage into the White House. On the other hand, President Ronald Reagan did many things to strengthen the image of the presidency. He always wore his suit jacket, unlike previous presidents, who had been more casual in the Oval Office.

We have explored the Principles of Influence emphasized by researcher/author Robert Cialdini. Once again, they are:

1. Reciprocity

2. Commitment and consistency

3. Social proof

4. Perception of scarcity

5. Liking

6. Authority

Principle:

To influence someone, focus on helping her in some way.

Power Question:

What gentle questions do you feel comfortable asking? How can you gently discover ways that you can help the person?

TOUCH THEM FIVE TIMES

> *Be like water making its way through cracks ... You put water into a bottle and it becomes the bottle. You put it in a teapot; it becomes the teapot. Now, water can flow or it can crash. Be water, my friend.*
>
> BRUCE LEE

Water can touch an object in many places. Similarly, researchers have noted that in order to close a transaction, it's necessary to ask an average of five times.

Have at least five ways to *ask for the sale*:

1. So, you're ready to go forward with this?

2. This will work for you, right?

3. Would you okay this? (instead of: Sign here)

4. How about we take care of the paperwork now?

5. You'd like delivery when?

Part of the *five touches* can be just staying in touch. That is, you demonstrate that you are a nice, helpful person. People tend to do business with people they like.

Principle:

Ask for the sale five times, gently.

Power Question:

What are five different ways to ask for the sale (or agreement) that are comfortable for you?

INVITE ACTION

How can you avoid a person's resistance? Gently invite her to act. As you hand her a pen to sign the agreement, say, "Would you okay this?" Avoid the phrase "please sign this." To *okay* something is gentle. On the other hand, to "sign this" is scary.

> *The answer is always 'no' if you don't ask.*
>
> PATRICIA FRIPP & ANTHONY ROBBINS
> noted by both

Again, the strategy is to pre-plan five methods or ways to ask to close the sale.

> *If you don't ask, you don't get.*
>
> MAHATMA GANDHI

Some novice salespersons hesitate to ask because they are afraid of being intrusive. If you are a salesperson in a store, the people there have already placed themselves where they can buy something, so you are being helpful. In fact, years ago when I was trained in retail sales, I learned to say, "So, what brings you into the store today?" This was better than the annoying "May I help you?"

You can invite action gently by asking, "How would this product improve your daily life?" Then follow up with a minor detail such as, "Would you like it in blue?" This is a subtle way to invite action.

Principle:

If you don't ask, you don't get.

Power Question:

Which friend or family member can help you rehearse ways to smoothly and comfortably invite the buyer to take action?

OPEN TO PERSONAL VALUE

Imagine if I could give *you* a method that would ensure that you could get what you *really* want. Interested?

I have just demonstrated the power of zeroing in on what someone wants on a personal level. People buy on emotion. ("What's in it for me?") Then they justify their purchase based on facts.

When you help someone to *open his or her perspective* to a personal gain with your product, you can be doing that person a favor.

> *All the money in the world is spent on feeling good.*
>
> RY COODER

Researchers note that people make decisions for reasons related to *personal* gain. Superstar salespeople do not ask solely how the buyer's company will profit. These superstars help the prospective buyer *imagine the personal benefit* of a "yes" answer. To do this, ask a question like, "If the product does just what you need it to do, how do you benefit personally?"

If the buyer responds, "My boss will like the fact that I handled the problem," you have the fuel to move toward the next step. The personal gain may be a happy boss who retains the employee during layoffs, or who will be inclined to offer the employee a raise or promotion.

If you are talking with a sole proprietor, you can say, "When you use (the product), you'll save $3,000 in the first two weeks."

Remember to discover what is most important to the prospective customer on a *personal level.*

Principle:

To get the person to say *yes*, create an experience of how he or she will *personally* benefit.

Power Questions:

How can you ask gentle questions so that you identify how the person will *personally* benefit from saying *yes*? How can you help the person experience (imagine) a personal benefit?

Note Value and Gratitude

Remind the person of the value and benefits she will enjoy now that she has agreed to your proposal. This helps the sale or negotiated agreement stay solid. Remember, each sale or negotiated agreement is ideally part of a good long-term business relationship.

The second point is to effectively *thank* the person for working with you. People appreciate a heartfelt "thank you." The crucial thing to remember is that each individual has a *preferred way* to receive appreciation and gratitude.

Along this line, while researching how people build healthy relationships, I discovered Dr. Gary Chapman's book, *The Five Love Languages.* In this book, Gary Chapman points out that each person has a personal "love language." If you speak the person's language, he or she will truly *experience* your gratitude.

The five love languages:

1. Words of affirmation

2. Gifts

3. Quality time

4. Acts of service

5. Physical touch

Our goal is to appropriately and effectively express gratitude and create positive feelings.

You want to express your gratitude in a way the person can *readily accept and feel*. Here are examples related to the love languages:

Words of affirmation

"Joe, thanks for all your efforts. You were really effective in finding solutions to help our two teams work together. Thank you."

Gifts

A small, appropriate gift that relates to the person's hobby can be helpful. It's great when we honor people this way.

Quality time

When meeting with a new customer, turn off your cell phone. When someone acts as though taking a cell phone call is more important than talking to us, it hurts. Don't let this happen with your new customer.

Acts of service

Often, a customer will appreciate receiving an article that relates to the hobby of her son or daughter. In this way, you can enrich your business relationship with the customer. The idea of service is that you extend an extra effort for the other person's well-being.

Physical touch

Each person needs to be *careful* about this detail of touching. If the new customer has extended his or her hand for a good handshake, then you can shake hands. (Please see the article about cultural differences by Michael Soon Lee, quoted earlier in this book.)

Remember, the idea is to effectively express gratitude and create good, friendly feelings.

Principle:

Develop business relationships. Help the person feel good by showing the value gained through your presence and by expressing your gratitude.

Power Questions:

How can you gently remind the person of the value he or she has gained? How can you express your gratitude?

CONCLUSION TO PART VI:

In Part VI, we explored the A.C.T.I.O.N. process:

> A – Approach in ways they prefer
>
> C – Communicate vividly
>
> T – Touch them five times
>
> I – Invite action
>
> O – Open to personal value
>
> N – Note value and gratitude

Energy and persistence conquer all things.

BENJAMIN FRANKLIN

The A.C.T.I.O.N. process helps you strategically put energy into preparation. Prepare questions that help you learn what someone truly values. From there, you can build a good relationship.

In Part VII, *Be Heard and Be Trusted on the Telephone*, we will cover powerful techniques to let the person be at ease and receptive to what you're talking about.

Learn how to skillfully connect via the telephone.

Part VII

Be Heard and Be Trusted on the Telephone

WHAT IF you could change your life with one phone call? And what if you had the skills to make that phone call go extremely well?

One phone call changed the life of Michael Eisner, former CEO of the Walt Disney Company. Years ago, Frank Wells, who would become the president and COO of the Walt Disney Company, said to Michael, "It's over. Sid [Bass] isn't buying," referring to the largest shareholder in the Disney Company. Michael Eisner had been Frank Wells' choice for the job of CEO – the top leadership position in the company – but he and Frank both knew that without Sid's backing, Michael did not have a chance.

Michael wanted to take another shot at the job. He made a call to Sid, who was at his Fort Worth office. On the speaker-phone, Michael said, "I think you're making a mistake, Sid. It's going to take a creative person to run this company. Look at the history of America's companies. They have always gotten into trouble when the creative people at the top are replaced by managers."

Sid hesitated. Then he realized that the Disney Company needed someone who would have the decisiveness and the freedom to choose those projects he thought best for the company. Sid later recalled, "Michael has to have the final word. That's when I first thought Michael was CEO material."

Michael became the top leader, Chairman and Chief Executive. It was a dream come true for him, because Walt Disney had been Michael's personal hero. What we learn from Michael's effort is that he persisted in the face of apparent defeat, and he effectively communicated his passion for the job.

Successful people are great communicators. All of us can make efforts to improve our communication skills.

The challenge with the telephone is that you have *fewer tools* – only your voice, with no facial expression or body language.

These ideas are from my presentation "Telephone Power: Sell More and Convert Irate Customers into Customers Referring Business."

We will use the P.H.O.N.E. process:

P – Practice smiling

H – Honor personality styles

O – Own your energy level

N – Note timing

E – Earn her trust

Let's get started …

PRACTICE SMILING

Researchers have demonstrated that people can hear a smile on the phone. So, smile! And stand up; you will sound confident and energetic. Use a mirror. It will remind you to lighten up before you pick up the phone receiver.

One day, I called a company to register myself and my team member for a seminar. That's it. All I wanted to do was register two people. But before a minute went by, I found myself purchasing a book and asking if there were any other products I should know about.

As soon as the salesperson answered the phone, her tone of voice told me, "I'm happy to be talking with you. Your call is the most important one of my day. I'm here to help you take your business to the next level." She immediately put me at ease and gently guided me to purchase more; that is, she let me see how I could gain more benefits from the company's products. It was a good thing for me that she wasn't selling houses!

> *If you have zest and enthusiasm you attract zest and enthusiasm. Life does give back in kind.*
>
> DR. NORMAN VINCENT PEALE

When you practice smiling, you practice placing yourself in a better state of being.

Principle:

A smile can be heard on the phone.

Power Questions:

How will you place a mirror near your phone? Will you use a Post-It Note with the word "smile," too?

Honor Personality Styles

If your caller talks quietly, talk quietly. Match her tone. A person who talks loudly may feel that someone who speaks softly is untrustworthy. People tend to trust people who talk in a similar fashion as they do.

> *By agreeing that whatever [the person is] experiencing is valid, you create rapport ... It's this rapport that melts resistance. People don't like to feel alone. They want someone on their side. A friend is easier to buy from than a salesperson or marketer. Be a friend.*
>
> JOE VITALE

Researchers have identified four personality styles. Over the years, I have seen that audience members find it easier to remember the styles when I give them animal labels:

- Lion

- Beaver

- Dog

- Peacock

Below are descriptions of these personality styles, which I revealed in my book *Darkest Secrets of Persuasion and Seduction Masters: How to Protect Yourself and Turn the Power to Good.*

Lion: *A hard-charging leader, who may be considered abrupt or bossy.*

Beaver: *An analytical person, who likes tables, graphs and lots of details. This person wants to appear intelligent* *and makes decisions slowly due to a great fear of making a mistake.*

Dog: *A supporter, who likes routine and cares about the feelings of others. This person may be slow to accept change.*

Peacock: *An extrovert, who loves to stand out in a crowd and gain approval. This person may be ineffective when it comes to follow-up.*

The solution is to identify what your personality style is.

Then you can get your own preoccupations out of the way and speak in a way that will immediately make the other person feel comfortable. For example, if you are a hard-charging person and are talking with someone who has a Dog personality style, it helps to ask how he or she is *first*, before launching into the conversation.

The following will help you adapt to your listener's personality style, it lists what you should tone down in different circumstances.

Lion addressing Dog: *Ask how the Dog is* first. *Tone down your fast-paced, intense talking style.*

Dog addressing Lion: *Go directly to the point and talk about the bottom line. Tone down any of your comments that may reveal "weakness" in the Lion's eyes.*

Lion addressing Beaver: *Let the Beaver give you some details, or identify which topics you would welcome details about. Tone down your need to talk quickly and move on.*

Beaver addressing Lion: *Identify three possible solutions and ask the Lion if she wants any particular details. Tone down your need to provide all the details.*

Beaver addressing Peacock: *Provide details that help the Peacock "look good." Tone down your disdain for "flashy people" or "hype."*

This is a first look at how you can relate to a personality style that contrasts with your own style.

Apply the elements of personality styles so that you can match the person's tone, volume and pacing. Each personality style has a distinctive sound. Furthermore, many people feel that tone is related to attitude.

Here is a table of how tone, volume, and pacing (speed of speech) relate to personality styles.

Personality Styles			
Style	Tone	Volume	Pacing
Lion	Intense	Loud	Fast
Dog	Soft	Soft	Slower
Beaver	Precise	Medium	Slower
Peacock	Energetic	Loud	Might be fast

Practicing with friends or a coach can help you make the transitions to different tones and pacing. The idea is to rehearse so that you can easily adapt to the sound of the new person. Then you can be heard and be trusted.

Principle:

Match the person's tone, volume and pacing.

Power Questions:

How will you arrange times and ways to rehearse matching a caller's tone, volume and pacing? Which friends can help you?

Own Your Energy Level

When do people change a habit? They change when they own a problem. Owning a problem means acknowledging that they have a problem and that they can do something to make things better.

Each individual needs to identify what brings his or her energy level up or down. If a customer brings your energy down, then do what works for you: take a walk to the water cooler, step outside and walk around the block, or close your eyes briefly and take a few deep breaths.

The ancestor of every action is thought.

RALPH WALDO EMERSON

The idea is for us to have useful thoughts that come to our minds by reflex. Here are two helpful *thoughts*:

1. *Next!* (if you are selling something and the person shows absolutely no interest). This is a powerful word because it reminds us that there are other people to connect with, and it is likely that they will be a better match for what we're offering.

2. *Oh, you're the one in 100! I have 99 nice people to talk with next.* This helps avoid letting one negative interaction slow you down.

If you notice that you're craving a candy bar, you can assess what helpful thought can relate to that. Perhaps you need a change of pace. You can energize yourself by walking to the water cooler and taking a drink – and you'll avoid the after-candy-bar crash in energy.

Principle:

Discover your own healthy ways to raise your tone and energy level.

Power Questions:

What raises your tone and energy level? How can you make sure to put in breaks and short transition times during your workday?

Note Timing

> *Timing in life is everything.*
>
> LEONARD MALTIN

"Is this a good time to talk?" can be a crucial question to begin a phone call. When we call, we have no idea what state of being the person is in.

Throughout the phone conversation, note how the person sounds. Is she tired? Is she too busy to take this call? Is she distracted? If so, ask what would be a good time for you to call back.

> *It is the mark of an educated [person] to be able to evaluate a thought without accepting it.*
>
> ARISTOTLE

Similarly, it is the mark of the educated person to note a personal feeling and be able to flow past it. That is, you can note the urgent feeling, "I must get a meeting with this person." Then you can reply to yourself, "Okay. I hear you (you acknowledge your feeling). And I'm *more likely* to get the meeting by respecting her and accommodating her feelings."

This internal dialogue can occur in seconds, and it can shift how you feel. This is crucial because how you feel affects how you sound (your tonality). So it is helpful to practice asking a prospective customer, "Is this a good time to talk?" *before* you call the person.

Principle:

Find out whether the timing of your call is agreeable.

Power Question:

Which ways of asking whether it's a good time to talk feel appropriate to you?

Earn Her Trust

> *I long to accomplish a great and noble task,*
> *but it is my chief duty to accomplish small*
> *tasks as if they were great and noble.*
>
> HELEN KELLER

Do the correct small tasks and do them in a respectful manner, and you can earn someone's trust. You can follow this pattern even when you cold-call someone:

"Hello, Susan. Janet Smith said that it would be great for us to connect. My firm provides training to help salespeople double their sales. I'm Carol Wilson, and I'm the president of Wilson & Associates. Is this a good time to talk?"

Carol earned trust in these ways: (a) She began with a personal referral. (b) She expressed a benefit: doubling Susan's sales. (c) She asked, "Is this a good time to talk?" (expressing respect for the person's time and comfort).

The friendly person is

1. Respectful

2. A good listener

3. Helpful

If you get an intuitive feeling that you would do well to call a particular customer or prospective customer, make the call *as soon as possible*. You may be calling at just the right time to be a friend. Perhaps a business transaction has gone south for her, and your solution is just what she needs.

> *A real friend is one who walks in*
> *when the rest of the world walks out.*
>
> WALTER WINCHELL

Remember, earn your listener's trust.

Principle:

Without trust, nothing can move forward.

Power Question:

How can you immediately establish that you are caring and trustworthy?

CONCLUSION TO PART VII

In Part VII, we explored the P.H.O.N.E. process:

P – Practice smiling

H – Honor personality styles

O – Own your energy level

N – Note timing

E – Earn her trust

All that we are is a result of what we have thought.

BUDDHA

As a man thinks in his heart, so is he.

PROVERBS 23:7

Approach your next phone interaction in ways that will make the process enjoyable for all involved. Fill your mind with positive thoughts:

- We're both going to enjoy this call.

- I'll listen well, and the person will feel good.

People can hear your smile in your voice. So create a genuine smile by telling yourself, "Smile! This is good for all involved." Your intention will color the experience.

In Part VIII, *How to Use Your Brand as Your Shortcut to Trust*, you will learn to create credibility.

Learn the secrets of creating and expressing a brand.

Part VIII

How to Use Your Brand as Your Shortcut to Trust

DO YOU EVER buy the brand-name product? Why? Perhaps you feel that you can trust the product.

When you want to expand your firm's prosperity, you will be interested in the process of making a brand name. Researchers point out that there are certain actions that create a well-received brand.

In Walt Disney World, a little girl was eating an ice cream cone while standing in line for an attraction. Just before she stepped aboard the ride, one of the attendants said, "I'm sorry. You can't bring the ice cream on the ride." The little girl cried. Her parents looked on with concern. Then the attendant said, "I can hold the ice cream cone for you until you come back from the ride." The little girl stopped crying and said, "Okay." After the ride, the girl retrieved the ice cream cone from the attendant.

The important detail here is that the parents knew the original ice cream cone had melted in the hot Florida sun. They realized that while they were enjoying the ride, the attendant had run over to the ice cream stand for another cone. This story creates powerful positive feelings toward Walt Disney World and the Disney organization. What a vivid example of a trust-worthy brand!

Now we will use the P.O.W.E.R.–B.R.A.N.D. process:

P – Point out warranty

O – Open with USP

W – Wring out feelings

E – Energize a category

R – Ramp up "the first"

B – Bring one message

R – Repeat the "one word"

A – Arrange to lead

N – Nominate one person

D – Duck the "spreading brand" tendency

Let's effectively create sales through the process of creating a brand …

POINT OUT THE WARRANTY

What is an effective shortcut to the buyer's trust? A brand name. With a brand-name product, you expect a certain level of performance.

The warranty guarantees the level of performance. When someone considers buying a product, natural buying anxieties arise. The warranty is an important part of reducing the buyer's level of anxiety.

People are slow to make decisions when they feel they are at risk. You can counter this feeling. The way you return phone calls, your sales literature, how customers with complaints are treated – everything about you, your product or service, and your firm – must convey trustworthiness. Word-of-mouth begins your road to brand status. Help your buyers feel comfortable with you. Make every act demonstrate your trustworthiness.

> *Sow an act, reap a habit;*
> *Sow a habit, reap a character;*
> *Sow a character, reap a destiny.*
>
> G.D. BOARDMAN

When someone's firm is not a brand name, follow-up meetings with the buyer's colleagues are necessary. This reminds us that there are three powerful words for closing a sale: *money back guarantee.*

Marketing experts talk about *risk reversal,* so that customers feel all the risk is on the side of the vendor. Here's an example of an offer with no risk to the buyer:

"This is your exclusive 30-day FREE trial invitation! 'Please send me this product. If I'm not amazed and delighted with the information I receive, I'll return the program to you at your expense.' "

Be certain of the value you offer, and do *not* hide your money back guarantee.

Principle:

Make your warranty visible and reduce the buyer's perception of risk.

Power Questions:

What is your warranty? Are you hiding it? How can you smoothly mention it in conversations?

OPEN WITH USP

Have you heard the phrase, "Fresh, hot pizza to your door in 30 minutes or less, guaranteed!"?

This is a USP, or Unique Selling Proposition. With this message, Tom Monahan and Dominos Pizza captured a 50% share of the saturated pizza industry. You'll notice that they did not even promise good pizza. They did not say gourmet pizza, either. They focused on a specific detail: when people call for pizza delivery, they are *hungry*.

Another powerful USP comes from marketing consultant Dan Kennedy: "Within 45 days or less, I will help you be the dominant presence in your category for $2 or less per prospect. I will help your sales force increase their productivity by 100%."

You know that your USP is working when you mention it during a networking event, and someone responds, "Really? How do you do that?"

> *Our deeds determine us,*
> *as much as we determine our deeds.*
>
> GEORGE ELIOT
> (pen name of Mary Ann Evans)

Identifying your USP is an important action that can determine your success. What do you do that is unique and provides an exceptional benefit to your customer? Write your answer(s) in your personal journal. Then craft effective ways to speak about your USP.

Principle:

Make your USP compelling, brief and memorable.

Power Questions:

What is most compelling about your product or service? How can you make the USP brief? How can you pump up the ways your product is memorable?

WRING OUT FEELINGS

If they don't feel it, they won't buy it! You need to inspire appropriate feelings in the buyer. Prospective customers want to feel that they can trust you and count on you, and that you will treat them respectfully.

Stories sell! Facts just tell. Help your delighted clients give you powerful mini-stories as testimonials, such as, "Joe's product helped me save $10,000 last month." Include client testimonials and partial client lists in all your marketing materials.

People go with their first impressions, so ensure that the first impression is favorable. Director James Cameron faced a big decision: who would he choose as the male lead for his blockbuster $200 million feature film *Titanic*? At first, Leonardo DiCaprio refused to audition for James. That could have been a real mistake, destroying Leo's opportunity to play Jack Dawson, the lead role in the film. But Leo had a second chance; he finally agreed to audition. James said, "Leo read the scene once, and then he got up and started goofing around ... but for one split second, *a shaft of light came down from the heavens and lit up the forest.*" Even big mistakes can be overcome when you are known to perform at a high level prompting someone like James Cameron to offer a second chance.

Leo had other things going for him. For example, when Jim arrived late for their first, informal meeting at Jim's Lightstorm offices, he discovered that almost every female Lightstorm team member was in the conference room with Leo. Jim said, "Leo must be used to this, because he charmed everyone in the room." One week later, right after Kate Winslet (who played Rose) auditioned with Leo, she pulled Cameron aside and told him, "Even if you don't hire me, you have to hire Leo."

James Cameron found Leo "incredibly mercurial," able to run ten different emotions through a scene. The 20th Century Fox executives were not sold on Leo to star in the film, even though they were seeing dailies of *Romeo + Juliet*. But James Cameron said, "*I always trust my first impression.* It sounds corny, but that's what the audience does."

Principle:

Inspire powerful feelings in the buyer. This will help the person buy easily.

Power Questions:

What are the powerful positive feelings associated with your product? What are the buyer's negative feelings that your product can eliminate?

Energize a Category

When the software ACT! was created, the company told the marketing team, "We have a program that does everything. It keeps your notes about all your contacts, it ties in with e-mail, and it reminds you of your appointments."

The marketing team created a new category for ACT!: *contact management*. It was reported that ACT! owned 70% of the contact management market.* Creating your own category is about emphasizing the *unique element*.

Christopher Reeve was a *unique* individual who transformed the tragedy of his paralysis into a springboard to a new and meaningful phase of his life. He wrote,

> *A hero is an ordinary individual who finds the strength to persevere and endure in spite of overwhelming obstacles.*
>
> CHRISTOPHER REEVE

We, too, are tasked with finding our *uniqueness*. Creating your own category can be a breakthrough task for the success of your business. Find a way to be a *hero* to the customer.

Imagine that finding your unique category is a heroic quest. How? Answer these questions:

1. How can you serve people in a unique manner?

2. What do you bring to the marketplace that improves people's lives?

Principle:

Stand out in the marketplace. Create a new category for your product.

---

* The claim of market dominance might be said to be wholly dependent on their definition of contact management. Microsoft's Outlook, commonly classified as a personal information management (PIM) tool, had far wider distribution. It too managed contacts, e-mail, and appointments, as did scores of other software titles. ACT!'s claim was premised on the implicit claim that contact management was a distinct subspecies of the PIM marketplace.

Power Questions:

What is unique about your product or service? How can you describe it as being in a whole new category?

RAMP UP "THE FIRST"

> *What would excite you?*
> *[is a better question than]*
> *What do you want?*
>
> TIMOTHY FERRIS

I have included this quote to prompt you to identify what your leading product or service *can* be. Focus on something that excites you. Then you have the possibility of exciting potential customers.

Whenever possible, be the first company to do something. 3M was the first company to offer Post-It notes. Wouldn't it be great to offer something unique, something incredibly helpful?

> *The biggest adventure you can ever take*
> *is to live the life of your dreams.*
>
> OPRAH WINFREY

Pull out your personal journal and answer these questions:

1. What would excite you?

2. How would you like to help people?

3. How could you act like a hero with your product?

See if you can be *the first* to offer some terrific benefit.

Principle:

Find a way to be first in offering some unique product or service.

Power Questions:

What is unusual about your product or service? Is there an appropriate way to claim that your company is the first to offer something unique in this area? (It often helps to develop new language. For example, for my book *Nothing Can Stop You This Year*, I forged a new concept: the *Ease-Through*™.)

BRING ONE MESSAGE

If you say three things, you don't say anything.

CHIP HEATH & DAN HEATH

What *one* idea is associated with Disney? Family entertainment.

Years ago, when the Disney organization branched into entertainment targeted at adults, they effectively avoided confusing people by creating a new brand name, Touchstone Pictures. Walt Disney Pictures releases *Meet the Robinsons*, *Aladdin*, and *Tarzan*, while Touchstone Pictures releases *Down and Out in Beverly Hills* and *Ruthless People*. You get the idea.

It helps when a company (or person) emphasizes *one message*. Another example of the importance of the message is the "Coke Adds Life" ad campaign for Coca-Cola. This campaign included healthy young people enjoying energetic activities. The single, powerful message was brief and emotional. (As a sidenote, a Chinese translator* wrote this: "Coke brings your ancestors back from the dead." Use one powerful message and *more than one translator*.)

Principle:

Boil your marketing efforts down to one solid, compelling message.

Power Questions:

What is the most important thing about your product or service? How can you convey this in one compelling message? What is the *best* benefit offered by your product or service?

REPEAT THE "ONE WORD"

Look at these products and the words they own:

1. Coca-Cola (cola)

2. Kleenex (tissues)

3. Xerox (photocopying)

4. Kodak (photographic paper)

5. Volvo (safe cars)

6. Mercedes-Benz (prestige cars)

My team reinforces this connection: Tom Marcoux (communication). That is the reason for my moniker, America's Communication Coach.

•••••••••••••••••••••••••••••••••••••

*This story is likely apocryphal and sometimes refers to a similar catchphrase used by Pepsi, but the point is still valid.

You have to come as an original. If you come in and you're imitating everyone else, you get swept away in the game. But if you're coming as one unto yourself, they can't replace you; they can only try to get somebody who's like you.

WHOOPI GOLDBERG

Having one word for a brand name has power. Let's look at Nike. In 1962, Nike began as Blue Ribbon Sports, founded by Phil Knight who sold shoes out of his trunk. Knight, a dedicated runner felt that shoes designed by athletes for athletes filled a true market niche. "Nike" is the name of the Greek goddess of victory. This company name was mirrored in what Phil Knight called the "Pyramid of Influence," which relates to Knight's observation of how many people were greatly influenced by what top athletes were wearing.

Ultimately, Nike added two powerful details to the mix: their swoosh logo and the advertising slogan: "Just do it."

Here are three powerful elements we notice from the Nike story:

1. A company founder who was the consumer – a runner

2. An understanding of the primary influencers of the behavior of potential customers

3. The emphasis on simplicity in both a logo and advertising slogan

In an informal survey, I noted that Nike – the one golden word – was the *first word* that came up for people when asked about athletic shoes and clothing.

Principle:

Seek to *own one word* in your prospective customer's mind.

Power Questions:

What is unique about your product? Describe the extraordinary benefit about your product or service. How can you boil it down to one compelling word?

ARRANGE TO LEAD

Become the leading brand. Given a choice, consumers want the leading brand. They tend to think, "It's the bestselling brand; it must be good."

> *We're here for a reason. I believe a bit of the reason is to throw little torches out to lead people through the dark.*
>
> WHOOPI GOLDBERG

People often feel stuck in pain, almost as if they are in the dark. Then a terrific leading brand serves them in the best way possible. For example, when it comes to Theme Parks, Walt Disney World holds the number one position and Disneyland is in the top five, so Disney is the leading brand. People *trust* that they will have a good time in the Disney Theme Parks!

Principle:

Become the leading brand.

Power Questions:

In what ways does your product or service pull ahead of competing products or services? How can you be the leading brand?

NOMINATE ONE PERSON

We are what we repeatedly do. Excellence then, is not an act, but a habit.

ARISTOTLE

Think of a company with a front person. Whom do you recall? Perhaps you thought of:

- Walt Disney, for the Disney organization

- Lee Iaccoca, for Chrysler (at one time)

- Mary Kay, for Mary Kay Cosmetics, or

- Colonel Sanders, for Kentucky Fried Chicken

Having one person who embodies the message is powerful and memorable. Once he bought Gillette Razors, Victor Kiam declared that he could never go outside without shaving his face. He had to embody the product.

Carefully decide who embodies your product. If a company makes clothing for working women and its owner is a working woman, there is a natural match. Be careful to avoid a mis-match, because the all-pervasive media can shoot your brand down with one Internet image or one sound bite. For example, Olympic gold medalist Michael Phelps lost his Kellog's contract over one unfortunate photo.

Principle:

Identify one person who can be the front person.

Power Questions:

What characteristics do you want people to associate with your brand? How can one person be the spokesperson for the brand?

Duck the "Spreading Brand" Tendency

Think of Chevrolet. Now, what kind of car are you thinking of? That's the question. According to researchers, Chevrolet has too many types of cars and no clear image. On the other hand, think of Mercedes-Benz. Boom! A prestige car comes to mind.

Researchers emphasize that in a society in which people are bombarded with thousands of advertising messages a day,* you need to have *one* clear, memorable message.

> *If you desire many things,*
> *many things will seem but a few.*
>
> BENJAMIN FRANKLIN

Benjamin Franklin is talking about over-desiring. Some executives appear to *over*-desire: they want to have many products under one brand, to increase profits. It is better to slow down. It may be wiser to start a separate brand.

Certain authors assert that Kodak misfired by trying to spread its brand into Kodak Digital. They believe it would have

---

* Research on this subject predates the digital information explosion, dating from 1972 and earlier. That research found exposure to no more than 300 ads daily, with attention being paid to less than a third of those. Nonetheless, 3,000 is a number commonly circulated without citation to authority.

been more effective if Kodak, which has long been associated with film, had developed a new brand for the digital market.*

Principle:

Avoid spreading your brand too thin.

Power Questions:

What is the essence of your brand? Would it be better to start a new, different brand for your new product?

CONCLUSION TO PART VIII

In Part VIII, we explored the P.O.W.E.R.–B.R.A.N.D. process:

P – Point out warranty

O – Open with USP

W – Wring out feelings

E – Energize a category

R – Ramp up "the first"

B – Bring one message

R – Repeat the "one word"

A – Arrange to lead

* *

* On the other hand, as previously noted, Kodak was known not only for film, but for photographic paper. Their transition to digital photographic paper involved marketing specialized paper to consumers rather than to film processors (owing to digital film's ability to be printed at home), but the products were substantially similar. As for film, while that transition was profound, from emulsion coated polyester to plastic coated memory chips, the need being answered was the same – image storage – and the customer base identical – photographers.

N – Nominate one person

D – Duck the "spreading brand" tendency

Branding gives you the opportunity to become brand-new ... Those things you're passionate about give you the best possible chance for success ... What words come to mind when people say your name?

ROBIN FISHER ROFFER

Form your brand strategically and communicate the benefits you offer.

In Part IX, *Great Communicators Make Good Luck*, you'll learn how to open the flow of good opportunities.

Let's move forward to more joyful times ...

Part IX

Great Communicators Make Good Luck

HOW DO great communicators create good luck?

> *Great Communicators put people at ease, create connection, and then are offered more opportunities.*
>
> TOM MARCOUX

Think of lucky people you know and have heard about in the news or from other sources. You'll notice that lucky people are offered more opportunities than others are.

> *Anyone who is successful in any business who doesn't use the word 'luck' is a liar. Luck played a part in it.*
>
> PAUL NEWMAN to LARRY KING

> *Happiness often sneaks in through a door you didn't know you left open.*
>
> JOHN BARRYMORE

By creating an atmosphere of good will, the great communicator leaves many doors open. People like to work with great communicators. They call them to offer projects. They give referrals.

The more valuable you become to more people, *the more opportunities will open for you.*

We will use the M.A.K.E.–L.U.C.K. process:

M – Make yourself prepared

A – Align your persuasion skills

K – Keep searching

E – Excel on another horse

L – Look to help

U – Use everything for networking

C – Course-correct constantly

K – Keep going for what you really want

Open the door to enjoyable opportunities!

MAKE YOURSELF PREPARED

*Spectacular achievement is always preceded
by unspectacular preparation.*

ROBERT H. SCHULLER

Would you like to know how Bill Gates took a few thousand dollars and translated them into a multi-billion dollar business? He used the power of information.

At a pivotal moment in PC history, Bill Gates knew three vital details:

1. IBM was looking for an operating system for its original computer,

2. Seattle Computer had created an operating system that it called Q-DOS,

3. Seattle Computer did not know of IBM's need and IBM did not know of Seattle Computer.

Bill took action. He borrowed $50,000 from his father, bought Q-DOS, renamed it MS-DOS, and licensed it to IBM. These actions started the ball rolling toward a gain of billions of dollars.

Bill Gates has repeatedly demonstrated his attention to detail and preparation. This reminds us to prepare ourselves.

Similarly, Oprah Winfrey prepared herself to make the most of opportunities as they arrived. At age 19, Oprah became the first woman and first African-American to join Nashville's WTVF-TV as an anchor. Three years in that position became a springboard to a larger market, WJZ-TV in Baltimore. Then Oprah received a big disappointment: the 6 o'clock news producers decided that she reported news with too much emotion. The producers demoted her to the morning show, *People Are Talking.*

Some people might have labeled her dismissal from the evening news as a failure. Then something extraordinary happened. Oprah later said, "The minute the first show [*People Are Talking*] was over, I thought, 'Thank God, I've found what I was meant to do.' It's like breathing to me."

Oprah had found her niche. Within five years and after a personal crisis in Baltimore, Oprah had *The Oprah Winfrey*

Show and was grossing $30 million. She was 30 years old with millions of fans.

> *Think like a queen. A queen is not afraid to fail. Failure is another steppingstone to greatness ... I do not believe in failure. It is not failure if you enjoyed the process.*
>
> OPRAH WINFREY

Yes, Oprah has found her niche. But she was always active. On the way to her niche, she kept looking for a way to contribute.

> *I think education is power. I think that being able to communicate with people is power. One of my main goals on the planet is to encourage people to empower themselves.*
>
> OPRAH WINFREY

Everything counts. The events of our life often add up to surprising benefits. Anna began playing the piano at age six. She went on to play the church organ.

Her parents had instilled in her a strong practical streak, so she graduated from college and went into computer programming. Yet music remained a powerful part of her life.

Anna also loved movies. She went to the movie theater at least once a week. One year, she teamed up with Maxine, a documentary filmmaker. Anna took the right risk and invested her money in computer equipment and synthesizers, which simulate the sounds of an entire orchestra. With this equipment, Anna created the music soundtrack for Maxine's documentary film. Now Anna is a motion picture soundtrack composer.

I've come to believe that each of us has a personal calling that's as unique as a fingerprint – and that the best way to succeed is to discover what you love and then find a way to offer it to others in the form of service, working hard, and also allowing the energy of the universe to lead you.

OPRAH WINFREY

If you don't know exactly what you truly want to do, be comforted. It took around 35 years for Anna to discover her destiny. Anna went from the piano to computers, and then to composing with computers.

Everything you've done and everything you've learned contributes to your destiny.

TOM MARCOUX

Do what you want to do on a small scale *now*. Practice your craft. Let's say an editor at a top publishing company calls me tomorrow and asks, "Can you write a 246-page book in three months?" I can reply "Yes!" because I've prepared for opportunities. I've practiced the art of writing for years. I also have experience in pushing myself to write on demand, which is a crucial skill. Having written 10 books, I can adapt my information to fit a new situation.

Many people say, "I could write a book." That may be true, but if they don't take action, they will never know. Training *overcomes* fear.

Continually prepare for the home run.

TOM MARCOUX

A vital part of preparation is identifying what you *truly* want. Here are Marc Allen's comments on his startling discoveries about creating a life you truly love:

Move Beyond Abundance to a Life of True Fulfillment

MARC ALLEN

The first step to discovering the secret of manifestation is to write your *ideal scene* on paper, your dream life five years in the future. Begin with the end in mind, and keep it in mind. The day I turned thirty, I sat down and took a sheet of paper and wrote *Ideal Scene* at the top. I imagined everything had gone as well as I could possibly imagine and somehow, over the next five years, I was able to create the ideal life for me. What would it look like? What would I do and have, and who would I be?

I was surprised, even shocked in a strange way, at what came spilling out on paper. I imagined I had a publishing company, successfully publishing books and music, including my own books and music. Before I sat down and wrote out my ideal scene, I had absolutely no interest in business. I had never taken a business course. I had never written a book or recorded my music. The words that spilled out when I wrote my ideal scene surprised me as much as they were to surprise just about everyone else I knew.

I imagined I wrote successful books and recorded beautiful music as well. I imagined I had a lovely white house on a hill in northern California, one of my favorite places on earth. I imagined I had a wonderfully loving relationship. I dared to imagine my *ideal*, so I imagined I had plenty of time for it all: creativity, a successful business, friends and family, and plenty of time alone for myself as well

… That was my ideal: success with ease, and success without compromising the other things that were important to me in life …

The second step to discovering the secret of manifestation is to write your goals as affirmations, beginning with "In an easy and relaxed manner, in a healthy and positive way … " Years later, looking back, I realized how powerful those words were – so powerful, in fact, that by repeating them daily, I overcame many of my doubts and fears …

The next step to discovering the secret of manifestation is to write a one page plan for every major goal …

The final step to discovering the secret of manifestation is to take action …

We know the secret, deep in our hearts. We've always known the secret. *To love one another and all of creation, is the greatest secret of all. Love overcomes fear, and transforms our lives and our world.*

Marc Allen, publisher, author of *The Greatest Secret of All: Moving Beyond Abundance to a Life of True Fulfillment,* and cofounder of New World Library.

www.MarcAllen.com

Talking with and listening to Marc Allen has transformed my life. I have brought happy moments into my life by holding the idea of " … success with ease … in an easy and relaxed manner, in a healthy and positive way … " I invite you to re-read Marc's comments and implement his suggestions. Your possibilities will expand.

Principle:

Devote time and effort daily to preparing for upcoming opportunities.

Power Question:

What might be a terrific opportunity that you need to prepare for now – *before* such an opportunity is offered?

ALIGN YOUR PERSUASION SKILLS

What if you could get what you want without needing to persuade anyone? You'd be living in Fantasyland.

Our modern life is noisy and filled with distractions. Researchers estimate that we are bombarded with thousands advertising messages a day. For anyone to cooperate with you, they need to hear you. *To make good luck,* we need to be heard and to persuade.

> *The most important persuasion tool you have*
> *in your entire arsenal is integrity.*
>
> ZIG ZIGLAR

"I don't like selling!" many people proclaim, almost like a badge of honor. To align yourself with persuasion skills is to let go of your limiting beliefs and empower yourself. For many people, the dislike of selling is really about three things:

- The dislike of rejection

- The dislike of manipulating someone

- The dislike of being seen as a manipulator

There *is* a solution. You can view positive selling as coaching someone. Let's remember what a coach does: she encourages you to do something for *your* benefit. A coach persuades you that it is worth your effort to make a change, take a risk, or stretch yourself. In a sense, Mahatma Gandhi coached or persuaded the British Empire to release its hold on the people of India. He succeeded.

Our focus here is on persuading with integrity. Integrity implies wholeness. In order to persuade with integrity, your heart and good will must be included.

To make your luck, you need to be able to help other people experience the value of participating in what you're offering. So let's replace "I don't like selling" with "*I like coaching* people to action."

The best salesperson is a trusted advisor. Let's say that Sam wants to make his luck by making a small, independent feature film. He persuades actors to work with him by emphasizing the benefits they will enjoy: an excellent demo reel and valuable work experience. He tells them that when established producers see the finished film, the actors will be more likely to gain other roles. For example, it was after Robert De Niro saw the actor Joe Pesci in a small feature film that Pesci gained the part of De Niro's brother in the film *Raging Bull*.

The key to successful persuasion is this:

> *Only speak of details that you know will definitely benefit and appeal to the person you're persuading.*

Persuasion is most important when you're persuading *yourself*. When you want good luck, more money and feelings of fulfillment, who is the most important person you need to persuade? You!

Many of us truly feel that there are elements in life more important than money. Love, health and friendship come to mind. Furthermore, it is possible to earn money with integrity.

You can put your heart into activities that earn money *and* align with your talents and interests.

Sometimes, it takes a couple of years of free-lance or part-time work to make the transition into doing what you love as your livelihood. From a place of integrity, one can choose to find methods of creating significant benefits for other people. As a by-product, these methods can bring financial abundance.

Some years ago, I was feeling overwhelmed. As I mentioned earlier, I told my sweetheart, "I'm like a racehorse." She replied, "Run in better races." Her comment got me thinking about how I could multiply the benefits I have to offer. This led me to realize,

> *You've got to be in the game where*
> *a big payday is possible.*
>
> TOM MARCOUX

If you want to make a leap forward and bring financial abundance into your life, you need to *persuade yourself* that you can gain new skills. For example, Jolene, a dishwasher, has a physical limit on how many dishes she can wash per hour. However, if she learns entrepreneurial skills and opens one restaurant, then another, she can greatly expand the financial abundance that flows into her life.

The process of persuading yourself often requires that you look for breakthrough ideas. Bestselling author and high-paid speaker David Bach offers:

> *The market doesn't pay you what you're worth – it*
> *pays you what it has to … and what you're willing to*
> *accept!*
>
> DAVID BACH

The bottom-line real reason I am able to charge 10 times more today for virtually the exact same speech I gave five years ago is simply I decided to charge more … I kept stretching my comfort level and raising my fee …

DAVID BACH

To make good luck happen, learn to persuade positively. Persuade yourself that what you offer is of tremendous value to your customer. Become a *coach-to-action* for yourself.

Principle:

Convert the idea of "selling" into "coaching to action."

Power Questions:

How can you change the story you tell yourself so that you focus on benefits for the other person? How can you feel good about your efforts to help someone?

Keep Searching

What is one crucial way to create good luck? Aim for something and take action.

I have had many lucky breaks because I was aiming for something. One of my screenplays was passed from one software engineer to another, then to a real estate developer, and finally to the California Motion Picture Commissioner. Three years later, the same Commissioner secured the San Luis Obispo Airport and an American Eagle airplane – for free – for a motion picture I was directing. (The finished film went to the Cannes Film Festival market.) This lucky break happened because I was searching for help and connections in the film industry. So keep searching for better ways.

Without heroes, we are all plain people,
and don't know how far we can go.

BERNARD MALAMUD

The principle is to keep searching and be open to all positive possibilities. Then you will find what you're looking for. Make your dreams come true. "Knowing what you know now, what would you have done differently?" I asked Marcia Wieder, best-selling author of *Making Your Dreams Come True.*

Marcia replied, "I would have done more research about expanding the multimedia creative services agency I had … I expanded too fast. I didn't really have a full understanding of what that meant in terms of time, effort and commitment. Based on the things I really value like flexibility, freedom and friendship – the two just didn't line up."

Marcia had lived in Washington, DC for 10 years and was president of a company employing up to 15 people. Although she appeared successful, she was not passionate about her work, her clientele and where she lived.

Then she envisioned a new dream, in which she was free to travel anywhere at anytime, live with a view of water and mountains, create her work as play, and live a life filled with self-expression. She moved to San Francisco and started a whole new life. Marcia now says, "I've become a successful dream coach, speaker and author. I have been paid to travel to Hawaii, Rome, Greece, and Indonesia to inspire people to dream."

"What's the best question that anyone ever asked you, and how did you respond?" I asked.

Marcia replied, "On her television show, Oprah asked me what my dream was – after I asked her first. She said her dream was to create a company where people could have fun. And then she asked me, 'What's your dream?' I said, 'My dream is that people will have dreams. That we will open our calendars and schedule the date that we're going to do them.'"

(Marcia Wieder is the author of *Making Your Dreams Come True* and founder of My Dream Circle and Dream Coach University, visible at MyDreamCoach.com)

While you *keep searching*, it is important to discover how to improve your job performance. Use questions that help you focus on career-enhancing actions.

Many of us hold positions that require us to work on multiple projects at one time. The following section outlines a process you can use to identify the vital elements in each project.

1. **Ask your supervisor what she feels is crucial to the success of the project.** Knowing the crucial details (your supervisor's preferences) will help you perform to her expectations.

2. **Ask your supervisor what excellent outcomes she wants from the completion of the project.** When you know what outcomes your supervisor wants, you have more possibilities to meet and perhaps exceed her expectations.

3. **Ask your supervisor what can be left out of the project.** There is rarely enough time to make everything perfect. However, you can excel on the tasks that your supervisor feels are important. To do this, you must know what she feels can be left out of the project. One of the worst things is to hear your supervisor say, "That's nice, but it

really doesn't matter." Asking a question about what can be left out helps you avoid sweating the small stuff.

4. **Send a confirming e-mail.** It's important to discover whether you clearly understand your supervisor's priorities. Some supervisors like e-mail, others do not. Discover your supervisor's preferences. If she is okay with e-mail, follow up on your discussion with a confirming e-mail. If your supervisor does not like e-mail, take good notes and then ask follow-up questions.

5. **Briefly ask, "Did I leave anything out of the e-mail?"** If you use e-mail, make sure to ask this question. This is an opportunity to help your supervisor elaborate on what she really needs you to do.

6. **Ask your supervisor what she feels are your strengths.** It's helpful to know what your supervisor feels you are doing right.

7. **Ask your supervisor what specific steps she thinks you should take to capitalize on your strengths.** Your supervisor's specific instructions will give you a road map to a great performance evaluation.

8. **Ask your supervisor what steps you could de-emphasize, so that you can concentrate on your strengths.** This can help your supervisor expand her awareness so that she'll be able to direct you in ways that provide more value for the company.

9. **Ask your supervisor what skills she feels you need to refine.** This is a hard question for many of us. We'd rather not hear bad news. However, find out early. Then

you can take action toward creating a great performance review. If you wait until review time, it could be too late.

10. **Ask your supervisor what specific steps she feels she'd like you to take during this quarter toward improving your skills and earning a great performance evaluation.** You can follow up with questions like, "And if I do these steps, I'll earn a five on my next evaluation in the initiative category?"

11. **Listen to your supervisor's speech patterns.** To discover what's important to your supervisor, listen to her speech patterns. In another section of this book, I discuss the four personality styles: Lion, Beaver, Dog, and Peacock. Here is how you can spot each one:

   a) The Lion (hard-charger) says, "What's the bottom-line here?" "What's taking so long?" "Spare me the details. What's the point?"

   b) The Beaver (engineer type) says, "Can I be available for a cup of coffee after work? Well, that depends on the Acme account, Joe's letter on the widget issue, Susan's laryngitis, …"

   c) The Dog (relater) says, "Well … I … I just … well, they're pressuring me into a decision on this and I …"

   d) The Peacock (socializer) says, "The answer is yes. No, I don't need more data. I've got a feeling about this one. We're going to look good with this one."

Note some of your supervisor's favorite phrases. What personality type do they imply? When you know your supervisor's personality style, you can communicate in ways that help her feel good about you and your work. (For more information on this topic, see the later chapter entitled *Emphasize Personality Styles*.)

12. **Ask your supervisor, "Ideally, what would you like to see happen?"** Sometimes, supervisors are not sure what they really want to see happen. This question helps you and your supervisor discover the ideal outcomes to the project. When you can help the desired outcomes occur, you demonstrate your value. In your personal journal, write a question like, "Ideally, what would you like to see happen with this project?"

13. **Ask, "How can I better serve (the team, the project, what you're doing …)?"** This question helps you get to the point. You're asking your supervisor exactly how you can do better. In your journal, write this question in a form you'd be comfortable with, perhaps something like, "How can I better serve the project?"

14. **After your supervisor responds to a question, ask a *confirming question*.** For example, once I asked a team leader, "Mirnah, what's the next thing you need me to do for the team?" She replied, "Write an article for Acme magazine." Then I reflected on our other deadlines and asked a confirming question: "Oh, so you'd like me to make writing that article my first priority?" Then Mirnah was free to clarify what she preferred me to focus on. In your personal journal, write a confirming question.

Remember to ask questions that clarify your supervisor's expectations. Take notes based on her answers. Finally, follow up to understand your supervisor's expectations.

To form your team, *keep searching* for people who have similar goals and a similar commitment to excellence.

> *[Composer] John Williams has made the biggest contribution to my movies, and they reach the heart universally, in every country, on every continent of this planet. John Williams speaks to people. And John rewrites my movies musically. At the end [of ET, the Extraterrestrial] ILM and I can make those bicycles lift off the ground. We can do that. But John Williams is the only one who can make them truly airborne. Because the audience lifts off the ground on John Williams' violins.*
>
> STEVEN SPIELBERG

When an entrepreneur hits a plateau, it often means that it's time to expand his or her personal network of contacts. Find ways to be helpful to others, and gently let people know what you do. My client Tarena said, "You're welcome. I was glad to find that lead for you. Oh, speaking of leads, please let me know if you know someone who is seeking to *gain clients quickly*. That's my specialty as a sales coach. Thanks."

Principle:

Identify what you truly want and keep searching for ways to make it happen.

Power Questions:

What do you truly want? First, what do you want to eliminate in your current life? What don't you like about your current life?

Now turn it around. (*Example:* If you don't like your current boring job, the *turnaround* is, "I want meaningful work that I enjoy.")

EXCEL ON ANOTHER HORSE

When the horse my father was riding ran straight for the barn, my father had one idea: survive! Good thing, too, because if he hadn't ducked, his head would have slammed into the barn door frame. We often hear the phrase, "Get back on the horse," but my father realized that this errant horse was stuck in its mood. Instead of getting back on that unruly horse, he chose to ride a *different* horse.

Similarly, years ago I learned to excel *on another horse.* At that time, as a result of seeing my demo reel, an international seminar company invited me to fly to another state to audition as a speaker. The company was paying for the ticket, so I said, "Sure!" At the audition, I saw two other hopefuls, one of them a young blonde woman who seemed to glow.

Later, the company informed me that I had not been selected. I was extremely disappointed. It was as if I had fallen off a horse. So I decided to get on another horse: I rented a space and held my own seminar.

Before this, the seminar company had had control of the decision-making. This time, I took control and created my own opportunity. I made my luck with another horse.

To achieve our goals, *we often need to be flexible* and select a new method. Earl Nightingale, bestselling author and cofounder of Nightingale-Conant, the leading educational audio program company in the world, said, "Success is the progressive realization of worthy goals." Everyone feels moments of happiness when they achieve a goal or fulfill a desire, but many of us find joyful moments simply by traveling in the direction of our personal goals.

Happiness is how you travel. The crucial thing is to feel happy on the path. We experience more time on the path than at the lofty plateaus of successfully completed projects. When we have methods to experience joy in small daily achievements, we feel better and are more productive.

To experience happiness, *it helps to know what is important* to you. For example, when Johnny Carson interviewed Jimmy Stewart, star of the Holiday Season movie favorite *It's a Wonderful Life*, Johnny asked, "How would you like to be remembered?" Jimmy thought for a moment and replied, "[As] a guy who believed in hard work and decent values and love of country, love of family, love of community, love of God."

> *It comes down to the story you tell yourself.*
>
> TOM MARCOUX

My client Serena was telling herself a story that made her feel bad about a failed project. With my coaching, Serena learned to tell herself a new version of the story: "With this project, I had three goals: (a) serve people, (b) help our careers, and (c) make money. I got two out of three. That was good. And I'm learning how to do better next time."

The detail that helps you excel on another horse

Lynda Obst, producer of *Contact*, starring Jodie Foster, and *Sleepless in Seattle*, starring Tom Hanks and Meg Ryan, was telling me about the early days of her film-industry career, when she used to wear a good-luck outfit to every meeting. I asked, "What brings you fulfillment?"

She replied, "Writing." This is a *crucial* detail: if you know what brings you fulfillment, you can be flexible and excel on another horse.

Dr. Bernie Siegel, bestselling author of *Love, Medicine and Miracles*, reported a list of steps for healing and staying well, as written by Steven James. Here are a few of Steven's suggestions:

> *Do things that bring a sense of fulfillment, joy and purpose that validate your worth ... Take care of yourself – nourishing, supporting and encouraging yourself ... Release all negative emotions, resentment, envy, sadness, anger. Express your feelings appropriately. Don't hold onto them. Forgive yourself ... Accept yourself and everything in your life as an opportunity for growth and learning. Be grateful. When you screw up, forgive yourself. Learn what you can from the experience and move on ... And keep a sense of humor.*
>
> STEVEN JAMES

To excel on another horse:

1. Observe what is *not* working.

2. Reconnect with your real goal (what brings you fulfillment).

3. Seek another method ("another horse").

4. Take a new action.

Principle:

Be observant and discover if you would do better on another horse.

Power Question:

What are your criteria to decide if it is better to cut your losses and choose *another horse* (a more viable opportunity)?

Look to Help

> *You will get all you want in life if you help*
> *enough other people get what they want.*
>
> ZIG ZIGLAR

I often ask friends and colleagues, "How can I be supportive of what you're doing?" Once, a video producer responded, "I'm looking for Human Resources managers to participate in a video program." I went to my database of colleagues and connected her with a manager. The video producer later turned around and connected me with an association that engaged me as a speaker. This new speaking lead was a lucky break, which began with my act of kindness.

Make your luck by sowing seeds of help for many people. Some people hesitate to ask if someone needs help. This hesitation arises from fear that the person will ask for too much. The solution is to have prepared responses that follow your offer, so if someone accepts your offer and asks for help, you can give yourself time to think. You can respond, "Hmmm. Let me think about that one. I might be able to connect you with someone who can do that better than I can."

The value of connection is so great that it is worth the effort of asking people what they need. There are hidden pearls of luck waiting for you. You can discover them *by helping others.*

Great communicators are visible in helping the team effort. Look for ways to help a team effort, and unexpected benefits result. Tom Hanks, wanting the feature film *Saving Private Ryan* to be excellent, suggested that one-third of his own lines be cut. "That's the first time I ever saw an actor cut his own lines," Steven Spielberg said.

Even from the beginning of the production of *Saving Private Ryan*, Tom Hanks was helpful. A crisis arose when Tom and the other actors were in boot camp to train for the film, while Steven Spielberg was busy editing *The Lost World: Jurassic Park II*. Tom called Steven and told him with concern that the actors were fading under the training and they all wanted to quit. Steven said, "Tom, I'm here, and you're there. See what you can do." Tom went back to the other actors, encouraged them and lifted their spirits. The actors stayed with the film. Tom demonstrated that he was a great team player.

Steven trusts Tom. In fact, they later teamed up to co-produce the $120 million HBO mini-series *Band of Brothers*, and Tom directed the fifth episode. Connections of trust with others create opportunities.

> *I love what I do for a living, it's the greatest job in the world, but you have to survive an awful lot of attention that you don't truly deserve and you have to live up to your professional responsibilities and I'm always trying to balance that with what is really important.*

TOM HANKS

Yes, amazing opportunities happen when we focus on *looking to help.* Authors Linda and Charlie Bloom focus on service.

Life-Changing Moments

LINDA & CHARLIE BLOOM

Sometimes a moment can be enough time to create a permanent life change. Fourteen years ago, I (Charlie) had such an experience. It occurred quite unexpectedly in India. I was on my way to Bangladesh on a two month work assignment for the World Health Organization. I had a thirteen-hour layover on my itinerary between New Delhi and Dakka, the capital of Bangladesh. Rather than spend the day in the airport I decided to see the sights of the city and I hired a driver to take me around town. The last stop that I asked him to make before returning to the airport was at one of the hospitals run by Mother Teresa's Order, the Sisters of Charity.

When we got there, the driver explained in Hindi to the sister that greeted us as we entered the building that I wanted to see the hospital. At least that is what I asked him to say. Something must have gotten lost (or found) in the translation because the next thing I knew, I was being shown into a large empty room and offered a bench to sit on. After about 15 minutes Mother Teresa herself came into the room. She headed straight towards me, took my hands in hers, and with a smile as big as the sun said in English, "Hello! How are you? It's so good to see you!"

"Shocked" would be too mild a word to describe what I experienced as the tiny woman looked into my eyes in a way that made me feel like I was the most important person in the world to her. I was literally speechless.

Mother Teresa sat down on the bench next to me and began asking me questions about myself, about what I was doing in India and where I had come from. I eventually regained my ability to speak and within a few minutes I was feeling like I was with a friend that I had known all of my life. Throughout the conversation there was another background conversation going on simultaneously in my mind in which the words "I can't believe that this is actually happening" kept getting repeated.

Towards the end of my visit, as if to provide me with concrete proof that what I had experienced was real and not an apparition, Mother Teresa gave me a small card. "My business card," she said. On the card was written the words:

> *The fruit of silence is prayer.*
> *The fruit of prayer is faith.*
> *The fruit of faith is love.*
> *The fruit of love is service.*
> *The truth of service is peace.*

Still somewhat stunned but feeling blessed and blissed simultaneously, I left clutching the card which contained the life-changing words that would have a profound impact not only on my two months in Bangladesh, but on the rest of my life as well. What's different is that it is no longer possible for me to deny that my highest priority is to create peace within myself and to promote it through my relationships with others.

What's different is that it's no longer possible for me to deny that I have the power to influence the degree to which peace exists within my world. It's no longer possible to pretend that peace is someone else's responsibility. What's no longer possible is to believe that I am unworthy of being a peacemaker.

When I connected to Mother Teresa, I connected to the vision of me that she reflected back through her eyes. In her eyes, I saw the beauty, the strength, the love, and the power that she saw in me, and I simultaneously saw that it is in every one of us. Since that time, it has been impossible for me to continue to live the lie that who I am does not really matter in the great scheme of things. I know that it does.

For me, one of the things that being in service involves is the reflection back to others of the basic goodness that I know is in their heart and the power that each of us has to touch others in a truly meaningful way. This is only one of an infinite variety of ways to be in service. Notice the words: BE in service. That is, embodying a spirit of service, of caring, of contribution simply by being genuinely who you are, and touching others with that presence.

Being In Service

The recurring theme of our (Linda and Charlie's) work in Scandinavia, Japan, Brazil, Bangladesh, China, America and other countries and cultures throughout the world, has to do with identifying, answering, and taking action from the question "What is my work in this situation?" Is it to learn to set effective boundaries? To listen non-reactively? To take a clear stand for what is really important to me? To speak my truth?

To resist the temptation to criticize? To only give feedback when it is solicited and not when I feel like it? Is it to cultivate the qualities that will make me a more loving and conscious human being, such as courage, integrity, compassion, patience, commitment and discernment? Is it to learn how to ask myself the hard questions like "What is my intention in this moment?" Why am I reacting so strongly right now? What am I really needing in this moment? "What is it that my partner really needs right now?" or "What am I really afraid of right now?"

If it is in fact love that makes the world go round, then it is the lack of it that causes suffering and can compel us to find the courage, inspiration and motivation to do our own work. In so doing we may, like the boy in the Nat King Cole standard "Nature Boy" find that "the greatest thing you'll ever learn is just to love and be loved in return."

Linda and Charlie Bloom, coauthors of *101 Things I Wish I Knew When I Got Married: Simple Lessons to Make Love Last*

www.BloomWork.com

From the above comments from Linda and Charlie Bloom we are inspired to focus on service and as a dividend terrific opportunities come to us.

Principle:

Approach new people, seeking to be helpful, and your opportunities will multiply.

Power Questions:

Would you feel comfortable asking, "How can I be supportive of what you're doing?" (If you are hesitating, how would you rephrase this question so that you can ask more easily?)

USE EVERYTHING FOR NETWORKING

Move out of your comfort zone. You can only grow if
you are willing to feel awkward and uncomfortable
when you try something new.

BRIAN TRACY

"Are you going to call that person back?" I asked a business owner when I happened to visit while he was playing back a message on his answering machine.

"No," he replied – because the caller had dialed a wrong number. But the business owner could have called back and informed the caller that she needed to try a different phone number. That would have been a kind gesture. Unfortunately, this business owner didn't realize …

> *You make your luck by honoring every gift*
> *of connection that the universe offers.*
>
> TOM MARCOUX

Every person we meet can connect us with others. Help people as they appear in your life. You never know when a seed of kindness you plant will later blossom into an opportunity.

> *Don't be the smartest one in your group.*
> *Get a bigger circle … You have to have people*
> *who inspire you, who are further along than you.*
>
> JOEL OSTEEN

How to respond to a request for feedback

Sometimes, a person in our network requests feedback. This can be a minefield. A fumble here can create an enemy. First, realize that a number of people asking for a critique are really hoping for your agreement. Here is a process to help you provide nurturing feedback when someone truly asks for your opinion:

1. Ask these questions in this order:

   a) Who is it for?

   b) What were you aiming for?

   c) What were you hoping I'd talk about?

2. Start talking about "what works." (Talk about the elements of the project that are praiseworthy).

3. If the person insists that she wants help to make improvements, ask: "Is there an area you're concerned about?"

4. If possible, refer to a *straw person*. Here's an example: "I was wondering how the average person who goes into a video store will compare your DVD's cover with the other DVDs on the shelf ..." (By referring to the average person you are speaking of a straw person, that is, a fictional person.)

5. Close your comments with a summary of the praiseworthy elements of the project.

I prefer to talk about "What works ... and Areas to Improve." And I tend to avoid the label, *critique*.

Avoid gushing advice. In fact, don't offer unsolicited advice. People's ears will be closed. And if you are pressed to give feedback to someone in your network, make sure that the process is truly a supportive *dialogue*.

Principle:

Welcome surprise opportunities to expand your circle of contacts. Be gracious to everyone.

Power Questions:

What are unusual (and safe) ways to meet new people? Can a return call be a possible opening to expand your circle of contacts?

COURSE-CORRECT CONSTANTLY

Did you know that on any airplane flight bound for Hawaii, the plane is off course about 90% of the time? How does the pilot ensure that you arrive safely and on time? She has the plane make constant adjustments; that is, she course-corrects constantly.

How do you know if you're on target? You put in an evaluation processes. A new screenwriter can make sure that her work is reviewed by seasoned screenwriters who have sold screenplays. The new screenwriter does *not* need to implement all their suggestions, but their input gives her tools for improvement. One idea can spark the crucial idea that makes your project outstanding.

The author Steve Alten sold his used car to gain funds so that he could hire an excellent editor for his first book, *Meg*. With the editor's revisions, *Meg* attracted a publisher and proved successful. Steve Alten went on to write many novels that have been published.

You get what you inspect. Develop ways of monitoring your progress. This allows you to identify what to continue doing and what to modify.

Course-Correct through *Choice-Market Testing*™.

Imagine that you are considering creating a new product. So many choices arise. How would you pick a catchy title or hook (one-line description)? How would you choose attractive packaging?

To market test a title, use my process of *Choice-Market Testing*. For example, for a film I was producing and directing, I had two poster concepts created.

Then I asked people, "Which movie would you pay to see?" It's crucial to give people a choice, because many prefer to be polite and thus avoid providing critical feedback. If you show them only one cover or title, they say, "That's nice." For real feedback, I always give two choices. I ask, "I have two titles for my new book. If you were in a bookstore looking for a book for yourself or a friend, which title would you buy?" I watch their faces. They pause and give a useful answer. Then I gently ask, "I see that you prefer title number two. What do you think that title is about? What about it grabs your interest?" In your personal journal, note two items that can serve for your first use of *Choice-Market Testing*.

Course-Correcting is vital at work. Let's look at three methods to help you protect your job and earn raises:

1. Get credit with progress reports

2. Peform high-visibility tasks

3. Do what you were hired to do

Method 1: Get credit with progress reports

Discover your supervisor's preferences. Once I was hired to be part of a major organization's team. I needed to understand quickly which methods of staying in contact my new supervisor preferred. I asked his assistant, who informed me, "He hardly looks at e-mail. Voicemail is good, but he gets so many calls that he is slow to return them. But he does look at his faxes." Later, I followed up by asking my supervisor directly how he preferred that I stay in contact. When I had some time-urgent information, I left a voicemail message and also sent a fax.

Be effective and help others (including your supervisor) *see* that you are doing a great job. Get credit for everything you do right. Use your day planner like a job diary. Note all achievements daily so that you can send periodic progress reports to your supervisor. It helps to ask your supervisor, "Would you like me to keep you posted via e-mail?" If she says no, you can give verbal reports and keep notes in your job diary.

Here is a progress report e-mail message:

From: Michelle
To: Nadia
Re: Progress Report

Nadia,
Just to keep you posted. On September 2nd, I began telemarketing with 20 minutes of phone calls each day. To date I have acquired 10 new customers.

Keep all progress reports and e-mails praising your work in a progress file. Bring this file and a summary memo with you when you go in for your review and when you ask for a raise. It is easier to get a raise when you demonstrate that you are a valuable employee.

Lou Heckler, a national speaker and former executive for ABC television, mentions that he found exact quotes from his own written progress reports (submitted as e-mail messages) in the performance evaluation his supervisor wrote. Lou's supervisor only knew of Lou's actions based on Lou's reports; so in essence, Lou had written his own performance evaluation!

In your personal journal, note specific facts and figures that you can put in your progress report.

Method 2: Perform high-visibility tasks

High-visibility tasks help you do a great job, and they help others *see* that you're doing well for the company.

Which tasks will make you look good? Jennifer focuses on having her weekly sales figures done one day early, and routinely sending new invoices out in the mail on the same day.

Which tasks will cause trouble if any errors occur? Jennifer makes sure that all dollar amounts on invoices are accurate and all collection letters are sent at specific intervals (noted in her day planner). These items are vital because if any errors were present, customer complaint letters would go to Jennifer's supervisor. Jennifer devotes significant attention and time to these tasks and protects her job.

In your personal journal, note high-visibility tasks that help you do a great job and help others see your progress. List high-visibility tasks that need to be done carefully.

Method 3: Do what you were hired to do

Remember, your job description is likely to evolve over time, so you need to take time frequently to review which tasks are the most important for you to accomplish. It also helps to have a meeting with your supervisor to clarify the current priorities for your position, taking into account your supervisor's priorities, the good of the department, and the company's mission and objectives.

In your personal journal, write notes on these topics:

a) I was hired to do these specific tasks …

b) Am I completing these tasks efficiently and effectively? If not, how can I improve?

By reviewing these tasks, you are preparing yourself to excel at your job. *Remember to focus on high-visibility tasks.*

Principle:

Make course-corrections constantly.

Power Question:

How can you monitor your progress so you can correct your course?

KEEP GOING FOR WHAT YOU REALLY WANT

Once you make a decision,
the universe conspires to make it happen.

RALPH WALDO EMERSON

Identify what you really want, and the universe moves to help you. Sylvester Stallone was certain that he wanted to portray a boxer in the film *Rocky*, based on his own screenplay.

Early in my acting career I realized the only way I would ever prove myself was to create my own role in my own script. On my 29th birthday, I had $106 in the bank. My best birthday present was a sudden revelation that I had to write the kind of screenplay that I personally enjoyed seeing. I relished stories of heroism, great love, dignity, and courage, dramas of people rising above their stations, taking life by the throat and not letting go until they succeeded … To cheer myself up, I took the last of my entertainment money and went to see the Ali–Wepner fight on closed circuit TV. Chuck Wepner, a battling, bruising club fighter who had never made the big time, was having his shot. It wasn't at all regarded as a serious battle. But as the fight progressed, this miracle unfolded. He hung in there. People went absolutely crazy. Wepner was knocked out in the 15th and final round, almost lasting the distance. We had witnessed an incredible triumph of the human spirit and we loved it. That night, Rocky Balboa *was born.*

SYLVESTER STALLONE

The producer offered Stallone $130,000 if he would just accept a screenwriting fee and give up his desire to act in the film. Stallone had been living at a subsistence level for years, and the offer was incredibly tempting. But Stallone decided to go for what he really wanted: *to perform the lead role.* He emphasized his true desire, and his attorney made sure the contract contained a clause requiring that if Stallone needed to be removed as lead actor, it couldn't happen until midway through the filming. This strategy was highly effective because the producers would be reluctant to throw away half their production budget and start over.

It was Stallone's clarity of purpose that led to his lucky break. The role of Rocky turned him into a box office superstar and led to four sequels. After the disappointment of *Rocky V*, Stallone wanted to do another film. Six years went by …

> *The people in the studios that really green light films today are Marketing Department people … Can they sell the film of a 59 year old has-been boxer? Doesn't exactly inspire confidence … But you know what? I said, 'Everyone feels like a has-been when they are not. That is the whole point. That is the whole premise of the story. That we all still have this thing burning inside of us and if we nurture it, it can revitalize us.' This time it almost didn't happen. It was almost an accident. They had turned it down for nearly seven years and then the studio head was replaced. The new studio head happened to walk into a small Mexican restaurant at a few minutes to midnight on New Years Eve in Mexico when he bumped into me at a table. 'Hi Sylvester, how're you doing?' 'Oh, hi Joe. I'm finishing up Rocky Balboa.' 'Can I see it?' … [The new studio head] takes it home. His wife reads it – she cries and the movie was green-lit. So don't ever underestimate women in boxing.*

SYLVESTER STALLONE

Finally, in 2006, when Stallone was 59 years old – thirty years after the first *Rocky* film – he wrote and directed *Rocky Balboa*. It proved to be a critical and commercial success.

> *Never give up. And never stop believing.*
>
> tag line for the film ROCKY BALBOA

Whoopi Goldberg has also demonstrated the power of persistence. She dealt with dyslexia and supported herself by working as a bricklayer and a funeral parlor make-up artist. (By the way, both Sean Connery and Jackie Chan also supported themselves for a time as bricklayers.)

Eventually, Whoopi created a one-woman satirical production in which she played several characters. Her show originated in San Francisco and toured the U.S. and Europe. The show earned acclaim and the attention of director Mike Nichols. Mike directed a 1984 Broadway version of the show, which earned Whoopi a Drama Desk Award and Theatre World Award, as well as a Grammy for the album recording.

Whoopi's breakthrough in film came when she portrayed the lead character in Steven Spielberg's movie of the Alice Walker novel, *The Color Purple*. Whoopi's performance was rewarded with an Oscar nomination and Best Actress Golden Globe, providing the actress with instant stardom. Then it looked as though Whoopi made some big mistakes. She had a number of roles in movies that were box office duds.

> *I don't believe that there is any 'good career move'*
> *or 'bad career move'. I believe there are*
> *only the things that make me happy.*
>
> WHOOPI GOLDBERG

> *I am where I am because I believe in all possibilities …*
> *I am the American Dream. I am the epitome of what*
> *the American Dream basically said. It said, you could*
> *come from anywhere and be anything you want in this*
> *country. That's exactly what I've done.*
>
> WHOOPI GOLDBERG

Principle:

Keep going for what you *really* want.

Power Questions:

What would you do if Aladdin's kind genie offered you exactly what you truly desire – if you only wrote it down? Another version: If you knew that you could not fail, what would you do? What is your pie-in-the-sky desire?

CONCLUSION TO PART IX

In Part IX, we explored the M.A.K.E.–L.U.C.K. process:

M – Make yourself prepared

A – Align persuasion skills

K – Keep searching

E – Excel on another horse

L – Look to help

U – Use everything for networking

C – Course-correct constantly

K – Keep going for what you really want

I will see it when I believe it.

DR. WAYNE DYER

To make good luck, first imagine terrific outcomes. Then take appropriate action:

1. Prepare before the interaction

2. Have poise and endurance during the interaction

3. Assess your results, and

4. Choose the next effective action.

You will see good results when you believe you can influence situations and you take appropriate action.

In Part X, *Great Communicators Give Compelling Speeches*, we will cover how to seize the audience's attention and guide them to take action.

Learn to be truly persuasive.

Part X

Great Communicators Give Compelling Speeches

What would you do if you were terrified of speaking before a group? Would you become a professional speaker? That's what I did.

How did I make the transition? When I was in grammar school, I was pushed to play the piano for thirty-two elderly people living in a senior-care facility. I sat down and my leg began to shake. I was sure they could see my terror. My foot shook so hard that I was afraid it would fall off the pedal with an embarrassing *thud*. I was focused on the thoughts, "How am I doing? They've heard these songs before. My playing is not that good. They'll wince at all the wrong notes."

My fear of public performance has been part of my path to being a public speaker who entertains thousands of people all across the United States. I had to learn techniques to handle my fears. When I speak now, my focus is, "How may I serve?" I let go of the thought, "How am I doing?"

To make things better, it is crucial that you take action. To give good speeches, here's my action: I rehearse. Anytime I feel uneasy about an upcoming speech, I rehearse for a few moments.

Jay Conrad Levinson shares similar insights about taking action:

Instantly

JAY CONRAD LEVINSON

I make tough situations better by eliminating them ASAP each time. One of life's greatest satisfactions for me seems to be throwing things away. Although you'd never know it to look around my home, I seem to be dedicated to removing stuff from my files, computer desktop, real desktop, in-basket, and to-do list. At the end of every workday, which means Monday through Wednesday to me, I delight in crossing the final task off the list in my datebook.

At the end of every year, I cross the line into true ecstasy when I fill several full-sized garbage cans with paper no longer needed. I feel pretty much the same when I relieve my hard drive of data nobody on earth will ever need again. I've learned that by dealing with work assignments only one time, I am able to gain a lot more precious free time for myself. Instead of putting the work aside for a later date, I deal with it at the moment it comes in, so that I won't have to be involved with it ever again. People say that I'm a good e-mail correspondent. I answer that it's mainly because I don't like having e-mail to answer. That's why I'm getting back to you instantly.

Jay Conrad Levinson, is the author of the bestselling marketing series in history, *Guerrilla Marketing*, plus 56 other business books. His books have sold 15 million copies worldwide. And his guerrilla concepts have influenced marketing so much that his books appear in 43 languages and are required reading in MBA programs worldwide. Jay taught guerrilla marketing for ten years at the extension division of the University of California in Berkeley. He was a practitioner of it in the United States – as Senior VP at J. Walter Thompson, and in Europe, as Creative Director of Leo Burnett Advertising. A winner of first prizes in all the media, he has been part of the creative teams that made household names of many of the most famous brands in history: The Marlboro Man, The Pillsbury Doughboy, Charlie the Tuna, Morris the Cat, Allstate's Good Hands, United's Friendly Skies, and the Sears Diehard Battery. Jay is the Chairman of Guerrilla Marketing International. His *Guerrilla Marketing* is a series of books, workshops, CDs, videos, a CD-ROM, a radio show, a series of podcasts, an Internet landmark, and The Guerrilla Marketing Association – a support system for small business. Guerrilla Marketing is a way for business owners to spend less, get more, and achieve substantial profits. To transform you into a marketing guerrilla, there is no better person than The Father of Guerrilla Marketing – Jay Conrad Levinson.*

(415) 452-2162
jayview@aol.com
www.gMarketing.com

If you are called on to give a speech, it helps to follow Jay's example and take action instantly.

If you are confronted with the situation of needing to give a speech within one week, or even within five minutes, you can use the following S.P.E.E.C.H. process:

S – Summarize

P – Prepare your first sentence and last sentence

E – Express an anecdote

E – Enter with a benefit

....

* When Jay sent me the above information, I realized that including it here would be an opportunity to show you how he tells the story of his experiences. Many of us would benefit greatly from posting something this clear on our personal Web sites.

C – Conclude with "Thank you"

H – Honor three memorable points

Let's get started with the first method ...

SUMMARIZE

What is the most important point, which you want your audience to remember for weeks after your speech?

Imagine how great you would feel if someone came up to you one year later and said, "I heard your speech, and I will always remember that you said ... " This is what happened for speaker/author Hyrum Smith, CEO and cofounder of Franklin Quest Company (prior to a later merger). Hyrum gave a speech, and one year later he received this letter:

> Hyrum, I went to your seminar a year ago in Princeton. It never occurred to me that what I do on a daily basis ought to be based on my governing values ... the things that really matter most to me ... I decided to dedicate my life to making a good life for my son [here he describes several activities shared with his son] ... Hyrum, last week my son, eight years old, was killed in an automobile accident. I have experienced some real pain at the loss of my son. But I have to tell you that I have experienced no guilt ... Hyrum, thank you.

Inspired by Hyrum's speech, this father had taken action to make a good life for his son. To make a powerful impact such as this, we must know our most important point. That point will be a highlight of the summary at the end of the speech.

Your summary creates the *powerful ending* you desire. I emphasize to my graduate students that a good speech ends with the speaker in control. Avoid ending with a question-and-answer period; it has a puttering-out effect.

Instead, prepare for your ending by writing down three memorable points. At the end of your speech, say something like: "And now I will summarize. First, remember to … Second, we do better when we … And finally, you make a great impact by … Thank you."

> *Speak properly, and in as few words as you can, but always plainly; for the end of speech is not ostentation, but to be understood.*
>
> WILLIAM PENN

> *A proverb is much matter distilled into few words.*
>
> BUCKMINSTER FULLER

> *Do not say a little in many words, but a great deal in a few.*
>
> PYTHAGORAS

Principle:

End with strength. Summarize your points.

Power Question:

What are your three main points? Write down a strong way to repeat those points in a summary.

PREPARE YOUR FIRST SENTENCE AND YOUR LAST SENTENCE

Did you ever attend a speech that the speaker simply read? Have you endured watching a speaker stare at the back wall as he spoke, as if his speech was plastered on that wall?

I advise my graduate students to avoid memorizing each word of a speech. Instead, we want the presentation to have a rapport-creating naturalness. It helps to start strongly with a memorized first sentence and end powerfully with a memorized last sentence.

For your first sentence, you can begin with:

- A question

- A powerful fact

- A detail that moves emotions

Be sincere; be brief; be seated.

PRESIDENT FRANKLIN D. ROOSEVELT

Principle:

People remember the beginning and end of your speech. Start and finish with strength.

Power Questions:

What is a strong first sentence for your speech? Note three possibilities. What is a memorable last sentence for your speech? Note three possibilities.

Express an Anecdote

How do you get past a person's natural resistance? Tell a story. An anecdote is a story with a point. In fact, a powerful way to state clearly the value of a story is to end it with "And so, my point is …" or to conclude with "What I learned that day was … "

What we observe is not nature itself,
but nature exposed to our method of questioning.

WERNER HEISENBERG
(physicist)

Related to Heisenberg's comment, we see that our story is like a "method of questioning." When questioning something we are actually forming our own version of a story. Choose your questions well to set the direction of your story. The anecdote touches the hearts of your audience in ways that logic and rational arguments cannot.

We're not seeing what's real; we just see our story.

TOM MARCOUX

A good, heartfelt story helps you give the audience a new view of reality. The story provides an experience in which the audience can invest their emotions. Carefully select three anecdotes and try them with friends and family. Find out which anecdote reaches people's hearts.

Principle:

Express an anecdote to seize attention and change lives.

Power Question:

How can you make your point with an anecdote that inspires minds and moves emotions?

ENTER WITH A BENEFIT

"Would you like me to show you how to have an extra $364 for your next vacation with no work, ethically and legally?"*

Our ears and thoughts tend to be tuned to: "What's in it for me?" So begin with a benefit for the listener. Another way to begin a speech is, "Imagine if I could show you how to make $1,000 a minute in a job interview. That's what we're going to discuss today."

When you start a speech, the listener subconsciously asks the *Three Ws*:

1. Who are you?

2. Why should I listen to you?

3. What's in it for me?

Answer these questions. You seize the listeners' attention and are on the path to be heard and be trusted.

Researchers report that people will *put out more effort to avoid a loss* than to gain joy. When addressing my graduate students, I illustrate this point by placing a $10 bill on my left knee and a $20 bill on my right knee. I mime having the $10 snatched away. I then ask, "What will people put more effort into, avoiding the loss of $10 or gaining $20?" The students reply, "Not losing the

----

* At one point, I placed the minimal down payment to hold a reservation at a resort. Then, I placed the balance of vacation savings in a Certificate of Deposit account to earn interest.

$10." They are correct. My students tell me that this illustration makes a visceral impact, driving home the point that we're all interested in avoiding loss.

Hard-charging people are concerned about the loss of time. They fear things that "waste their time."

> *Focus on being productive rather than being busy*
> *– your life depends on it.*
>
> TIMOTHY FERRIS

Show people how they will save time, gain leverage, and get more done, and you have their attention. When you focus your speech on *the vital few*, your audience will bless you. By "the vital few," I mean the three major points that provide compelling benefits for your audience. I emphasize three benefits because that gives you *three* chances that any given audience member will find one of the benefits to be compelling.

Place benefits in your pitch. A pitch is a brief presentation usually designed to get someone (in the film or publishing industry) to read something. A pitch is also used in sales.

The idea of putting a benefit into your pitch is to give the listener an *experience of the benefit you're offering.*

When I guide my students in the art of pitching, I include these ideas to improve the pitch:

1. Avoid beginning with the best idea.

2. Warm them up.

3. Often, you can begin by explaining how you came up with the idea.

4. Introduce suspense (tension, suspense and release).

5. End in a big, memorable way.

6. Ask for the order. ("And so, I hope you will please say *yes to publishing my book.*")

If you are pitching a screenplay or novel, the benefit you're giving is the experience of anticipation or curiosity. That's the reason I said "introduce suspense." Your target is to get the listener to feel, "This story has potential. I wonder how it works out!"

Ask for the order. To ask for the order is to request clearly and gently what you want. For your closing, use this pattern: "Because of [first reason] and [second reason], I hope you please say yes to my project."

By providing two powerful reasons for saying yes, you are guiding the listener to respond favorably. Also, by saying the word *yes*, you have put the idea of *yes* into the room. Then *yes* will echo in the thoughts of the decision-makers.

Principle:

Begin with a benefit.

Power Questions:

What is the most compelling benefit that you offer with your speech? How will you make the audience members' lives better, easier, more profitable or more fulfilling?

Conclude with "Thank You"

Imagine you have just heard one of the most inspiring speeches in your life. Your blood is pumping. You feel a *zing* of energy. You know in your heart that amazing possibilities are in store for you. Then the speech ends, "That's it," like a deflated balloon.

One of the best speakers I have heard ends her speeches with "That's it," smiling and rocking back on her heels. This deflates the life-changing, uplifting power of her message.

On the other hand, a great communicator pauses after her final statement and simply says, "Thank you." Those are two powerful words. You have just participated in something important. You and the audience have had a dialogue, even if you did all the talking and they did the nodding. They gave you their attention. You gave them words to grow on.

Helen Keller said something that truly opened my eyes. Scarlet Fever in her infancy had left her blind and deaf, and no one thought she would ever be able to talk. Her teacher, Anne Sullivan, helped Helen learn to speak. Helen wrote,

> *I thank God for my handicaps for, through them,*
> *I have found myself, my work, and my God.*
>
> HELEN KELLER

The idea of "thank you" is not merely for the end of the speech. Numerous scholars and authors talk about what you attract in your life.

> *The enlightened give thanks for what most people take for granted. As you begin to be grateful for what most people take for granted, that vibration of gratitude makes you more receptive to good in your life.*
>
> DR. MICHAEL BERNARD BECKWITH

> *What this power is, I cannot say. All I know is that it exists and it becomes available only when you are in that state of mind in which you know exactly what you want.*
>
> ALEXANDER GRAHAM BELL

Ask, and it will be given you; Seek, and you will find;
Knock, and it will be opened to you.

JESUS OF NAZARETH

Be thankful toward your audience before you give the speech. Reach out to audience members as they come in the door. I have seen top speaker Zig Ziglar shake hands with everyone as they enter the auditorium.

Principle:

Conclude your speech with a heartfelt "Thank you."

Power Questions:

What are the gifts you are giving with your speech? What can you feel proud of bringing to your audience? (Remember a time when you were grateful for someone's kindness. Focus on that feeling. Then connect with feeling grateful to audience members for their respectful attention.)

HONOR THREE MEMORABLE POINTS

What do you remember from the last speech or workshop you attended? Researchers have noted that people tend to remember only about three points from a speech. So choose your points with care. Make them memorable.

If you have an important point to make, don't try to be
subtle or clever. Use the pile driver. Hit the point once.
Then come back and hit it again. Then hit it a third time
– a tremendous whack!

WINSTON CHURCHILL

In his speech to a graduating class at Stanford University, Steve Jobs said,

> *Today I want to tell you three stories from my life. That's it. No big deal. Just three stories. The first story is about connecting the dots.*
>
> *… you can't connect the dots looking forward; you can only connect them looking backwards. So you have to trust that the dots will somehow connect in your future. You have to trust in something – your gut, destiny, life, karma, whatever. This approach has never let me down, and it has made all the difference in my life. My second story is about love and loss …*
>
> *My third story is about death. When I was 17, I read a quote that went something like, 'If you live each day as if it was your last, someday you'll most certainly be right.' It made an impression on me, and since then, for the past 33 years, I have looked in the mirror every morning and asked myself: 'If today were the last day of my life, would I want to do what I am about to do today?' And whenever the answer has been 'No' for too many days in a row, I know I need to change something….*
>
> *Remembering that I'll be dead soon is the most important tool I've ever encountered to help me make the big choices in life. Because almost everything – all external expectations, all pride, all fear of embarrassment or failure – these things just fall away in the face of death, leaving only what is truly important.*

From these excerpts, you can see how Steve Jobs used structure powerfully and focused on *three* stories. People remember three points of a speech. When you make sure to have three memorable points, you're on your way to being *memorable as a speaker*.

Larry King, host of CNN's "Larry King Live," described the elements that make someone memorable. He said, "You're a good guest [for my show with] four things:

1. Passion,

2. An ability to explain what [you] do very well,

3. A little bit of a chip on [your] shoulder, and

4. A sense of humor, hopefully self-deprecating."

To explain what you do very well, it helps to form three memorable points. In giving speeches, however, it is often advisable to *leave out* the chip on the shoulder. And we certainly look for people who have energy and enthusiasm.

As I guide my graduate students to make memorable speeches, I tell them, "What's the big idea? Now add two more." Using three memorable points helps you be clear. Being clear puts you on the path to be heard and be trusted.

Now the following interview with Dr. Frank Greene reveals an author using the three memorable points process. In this case, Dr. Greene focuses on three elements with his *VRE model*.

Own Your Strategy for Success

AN INTERVIEW WITH DR. FRANK GREENE

Tom Marcoux: What does it mean to say "Own Your Strategy for Success"?

Frank Greene: This means being personally responsible for your success. Many people have this desire, but often do not have the knowledge tools for making it happen. We have developed a leadership model that is being used by people all over the country to take charge of their lives and "Own Their Success." This leadership model called the VRE model is based on the way successful people operate as leaders in their lives or with others in groups or in large organizations.

All successful leaders meet their challenges by starting with a clear *vision* that creates values for others, they get everyone working together through positive *relationships*, and they *execute* at a very high level by making smart decisions. For the last two years we have been helping people learn how to better succeed by using the *VRE leadership* concepts: *V-vision R-relationships E-execute.*

Tom: Frank, at one point we were talking about how your VRE leadership concepts were used by a team of women entrepreneurs to develop a strategy that helped them gain funding. Would you tell me about how VRE leadership worked in this case?

Frank: Using the VRE leadership concepts they were able to lay out all the elements of a success strategy. They clarified and focused the company vision, they figured who were the right people they needed to have working relationships with who could help them execute their vision. They clarified what to expect from the key people in terms of results to expect and what was needed to get those results. In other words VRE gave them a framework to deconstruct and then reconstruct their strategy into one they are executing.

Tom: What is strategy?

Frank: The strategy is what gets everyone working together to meet a common goal. A strategy has the following elements and describes the leadership challenge and how this creates an opportunity, the factors that need to be addressed in order to be successful, the vision, the relationship rules, and the practices for execution. Many times this is documented in what are called strategic plans. Successful execution of complex strategies means that many people have to take on leadership roles. We use the VRE leadership model to make a *one page strategy* document. So the strategy can be referred to everyday!

Tom: So how did the VRE leadership strategy help the team of women entrepreneurs?

Frank: They needed to submit a proposal for funding, but they were struggling in how to describe their business – as a matter of fact, how to think about their business. I went through this VRE process with them, starting with creating a vision statement for the business. Then, they looked at themselves – what was their passion? What was driving them to proceed with this business? I helped them develop a strong positive description of why they were building the business. They talked about the relationships with their customers and how they were creating value for their customers. Another important part of the VRE leadership strategy is how they were creating value for their customers and the people they work with. They used the VRE structure, and they did a great job of figuring out how to address those points. Then they put together what they had already executed and how they would use the money to help them move their business forward. They became winners of the competition to gain money to help them with their business.

Tom: That's terrific! And now what do you think is critical that new entrepreneurs might miss?

Frank: I have given VRE leadership workshops around the country and what most entrepreneurs tell me is that they do not read the traditional leadership books that are 200 to 300 pages long. What entrepreneurs are looking for is help in developing some practical leadership skills so they can get their work done right now. The VRE leadership model gives a way to immediately understand your leadership strengths. By the way I have found that *everyone* has leadership skills. By understanding the leadership process they have already used in their lives they can now build on that knowledge. Building on existing knowledge is why we get the dramatic leadership learning in our workshops, based on the comments from attendees.

Tom: Yes! I see that under "execution" you emphasize Daily Leadership Practices. Would you give me an example of that?

Frank: Sure. People who are successful at business stay absolutely focused on customer success. A daily focus on customer success was a leadership imperative for me as I developed two software companies that had an average growth rate of about 50% per year for over 10 years while being profitable every quarter.

Tom: Great! Now, if you were to give the one most important piece of advice to a rising entrepreneur, what would that be?

Frank: That's like saying, "I need to bake a cake. What is the one most important ingredient to bake a cake?"

Tom (smiling): Yes.

Frank: Here is something that I personally use. I'll sum up with talking about the *Serenity Prayer*:

> *God grant me the serenity to accept the things*
> *I cannot change; courage to change the things*
> *I can; and wisdom to know the difference.*

REINHOLD NIEBUHR

For anyone who is starting a new challenge in life, and certainly being an entrepreneur is that, you need courage. It takes wisdom to know how to apply your courage so that you are not foolhardy. That's another reason why you need daily leadership practices.

Because it is through practice and learning that you get smarter and your wisdom base grows. It is through your wisdom that you will have the knowledge skills to "Own Your Strategy for Success."

Tom: How can a person get more information about the VRE leadership model?

Frank: We have VRE based leadership books and workbooks and we offer workshops. For more information go to www.Go-Positive. com.

Dr. Frank Greene, is a highly accomplished venture capitalist, operating business executive, and technologist with four decades of experience. He holds a Ph.D. in Electrical Engineering and has been in private venture capital since 1986. In 1993, he started New Vista Capital to assist start-up companies in business planning and raising capital. Subsequently, he served as founding General Partner of the New Vista Capital Funds I & II. From 1971 to 1989, Dr. Greene was the founding CEO of two information technology companies, Technology Development Corp. (went public in 1985) & ZeroOne Systems (sold to Sterling Software). He took two companies through Initial Public Offerings (IPOs) and was instrumental in the merger or acquisition of several more. Prior to 1971, Dr. Greene developed high-speed semiconductor computer memory systems as a member of the technical staff at Fairchild Semiconductor R&D Labs, and participated in the development of high-performance computers as an electronics officer in the U.S. Air Force. Moreover, he has taught electrical engineering & computer science courses at Stanford University, Santa Clara University, Howard University, American University, and Washington University in St. Louis, MO. Dr. Greene is currently a Member of the Board of Reach Communications & Compliance Coach, and a Board Observer for ZNYX Corporation. He is a past Chairman of the American Musical Theatre of San Jose, Board Member of the National Conference of Community & Justice, and Emeritus Member of the Board of Trustees of Santa Clara University.

www.NVcap.com

Dr. Frank Greene's VRE leadership strategy is an example of the power of focusing on *three* elements.

You will greatly enhance the clarity of your message if you keep your main points to three.

Principle:

People remember three points of any speech.

Power Question:

What are the three most important, life-changing points of your speech? What would make you feel great for the audience to remember?

CONCLUSION TO PART X

In Part X, we explored the S.P.E.E.C.H. process:

S – Summarize

P – Prepare your first sentence and last sentence

E – Express an anecdote

E – Enter with a benefit

C – Conclude with "Thank you"

H – Honor three memorable points

Everyone thought I was bold and fearless and even arrogant, but inside I was always quaking.

KATHERINE HEPBURN

The good news is that when you use the S.P.E.E.C.H. process, you will appear confident. You will have a proven structure for your speech.

If you always do what interests you,
at least one person is pleased.

KATHERINE HEPBURN

Make your three memorable points with details that excite *you*. You will be pleased, and your audience will enjoy your presentation.

An interviewer asked me, "What if you have to make a presentation for work and you don't like the subject?" I replied, "You need to dig deeper. Look for a relevant anecdote that can express your point in a way you enjoy."

In Part XI, *Great Communicators Persuade with Ease*, you will discover how to influence people and get them to enjoy saying yes to you.

Let's move forward …

Part XI

Great Communicators Persuade with Ease

HOW WOULD YOUR LIFE be better if you could persuade people with ease?

To organize a persuasive speech quickly, it helps to use the P.E.R.S.U.A.D.E. process:

P – Point to the benefit

E – Emphasize personality styles

R – Request a response

S – Say a story

U – Use personal brand (credibility)

A – Ask questions

D – Demonstrate and involve them

E – Energize the emotional brain

The information I share with you is hard won, gained through my own efforts. During one of my first speeches, at seven p.m. on a Friday, a man in the audience actually *snored*. Scared and concerned, I immediately set forth to become a dynamic speaker who could enthrall audiences. I quickly learned to infuse my speeches with humor and good pacing. Wouldn't you have done the same?

> *A good scare is worth more to a man than good advice.*
>
> EDGAR WATSON HOWE

> *Never, ever underestimate the power of "I'd like that."*
>
> JOHN MAYER

Like other professional speakers, I was moved by speeches I'd heard. Listening to an audio program on communication gave me an edge in my business interactions. Later, when I saw a certain speaker, I felt, "Hey! I could do that!"

Now you will learn the skills that will enable *you* to persuade with ease.

POINT TO THE BENEFIT

"If I could show you how to become a billionaire in just eight years, would that be of value to you?" I asked my audience. Imagine their rapt attention!*

• •

*The process of how Ross Perot became a billionaire in only eight years is revealed in my book, *Wake Up Your Spirit to Prosperity – for Couples*, available at www.TomSuperCoach.com/SpecialOffer.htm.

> *Imagination is everything. It is the*
> *preview of life's coming attractions.*

ALBERT EINSTEIN

Engage people's imagination. Have them imagine and see the good outcomes that can occur if they receive your message.

As mentioned earlier, the *Three Ws* are the audience's subconscious questions:

- Who are you?

- Why should I listen to you?

- What's in it for me?

Answer these Three Ws in your introduction. You can say, "Today I will show you how to do … Then you will save time and gain money by …"

> *Life will give you what you attract with your*
> *thoughts. Think, act, and talk negatively and your*
> *world will be negative. Think and act and talk with*
> *enthusiasm and you will attract positive results.*

MICHAEL LEBOEUF

Mention the benefits at the beginning of your speech and you will capture your audience's attention.

Principle:

Begin with compelling benefits.

Power Questions:

Where is your audience hurting? How can you take away their pain? What benefits that your audience is clamoring for can you offer with your speech?

EMPHASIZE PERSONALITY STYLES

How do you connect with audience members when something you say can appeal to some and *turn off* others?

The only thing that will redeem mankind is cooperation.

BERTRAND RUSSELL

The greatest communicators know that diverse individuals listen to their speeches. The idea is to provide various details that appeal to the different personality styles. In essence, you *cooperate* with each individual's personality style.

A powerful way to make a connection *is to use insights related to personality styles.* Authors Dr. Tony Alessandra, Michael O'Connor, Nicholas Boothman, and Roger Dawson have discussed personality styles. In what follows, I put my own spin on their research.

Over the years that I have conveyed this material, I have found that using images related to animals makes these insights more memorable. Here is the brief sketch of the four personality styles that I revealed earlier:

Lion: A hard-charging leader, who may be considered abrupt or bossy.

Dog: A supporter, who likes routine and cares about the feelings of others. This person may be slow to accept change.

Peacock: An extrovert, who loves to stand out in a crowd and gain approval. This person may be ineffective when it comes to follow-up.

Beaver: An analytical person, who likes tables, graphs and lots of details. This person wants to appear intelligent, and may make decisions slowly due to a great fear of making a mistake.

Ways you can reach each personality style when speaking

Lion: *Write a list of points and check off the completed points as you go through the speech. (You can use a flipchart or computer-based solution.)*

Beaver: *Write a list of points and check off the completed points as you go through the speech.*

Peacock: *Talk with the Peacock before your speech. Then, during the speech, say, "Sam had a good idea about pre-screening the applicants. Sam, how about telling the group your idea?" (This gives Sam a chance to "look good.")*

Dog: *At the beginning of the speech, ask, "What were you hoping and expecting I'd talk about? What topic would help you if I addressed it, so that you'd go home saying, 'I got exactly what I needed from the presentation'?" Listen carefully. Thank each person. Write five or six of the comments on the board and check them off during your speech.*

Principle:

The greatest communicators provide benefits that appeal to a variety of personality styles.

Power Questions:

What personality styles are likely to be represented in your audience? How can you provide benefits customized to each of these personality styles?

REQUEST A RESPONSE

How do you keep your audience awake and receptive to your message? Request a response. Many effective speeches are really a form of dialogue. And, just like a good trial attorney, when you are going to request a response, plan in advance *the questions whose answers can help* you.

> *The things that get rewarded get done …*
> *People do what gets measured.*
>
> MICHAEL LEBOEUF

You need to rehearse so you can smoothly and effectively request a response. In order to make sure that you rehearse, set up a schedule. Even nine minutes a day will help. You can ask five friends if you could rehearse a two-minute section with each. To identify what a good response would be, you need to pre-plan the overall affect of your speech.

> *My [television] show [Roseanne] showed a family with unconditional love. … I went through daily battles to reach that goal, and refused to say lines that would humiliate Dan [the husband, portrayed by John Goodman]. Standup [comedy] taught me to author my own work. Standup taught me discipline … Standups want to make the world right … by pointing out what's wrong and having you laugh at it. You have to have a core that you're true to … The belief to lift*

people. I have a strong belief in God. Nothing that has happened to me [as an incest survivor] has taken that from me … I want to leave something good behind, and what a blessing [it is] to know you can.

ROSEANNE BARR

The point here is, focus on your goal. When you are going to ask for a response, be sure to pre-plan your request so you get the response you're looking for. You, too, can leave your audience with something great.

Principle:

Pre-plan the requests for responses that you will use.

Power Questions:

What would be the best ways for your audience to respond to your request? What would be okay responses? What would be terrible responses, and how would you recover from them?

SAY A STORY

How do you avoid stimulating any natural resistance in your listener? Tell a story.

Hearing stories acts as a kind of mental flight simulator, preparing us to respond more quickly and effectively.

CHIP HEATH & DAN HEATH

My life is my message.

MAHATMA GANDHI

The best stories are often ones from your own life. For one thing, the story will be original. When you tell your own story, you have complete credibility and authority. To guide your listeners to realize the benefit, sum up the story with, "What I learned was … "

One of my mentors, international speaker and author Dottie Walters, emphasized the *value of stories*. Dottie Walters was a master storyteller, who lives on in my heart and in my books. She was my first mentor in the speaking industry. I learned from Dottie the spirit of service that the great speakers embody.

I had the privilege to be coached by Dottie in person a number of times and to interview her for my books, too. When I was with Dottie, she infused me with the confidence that I could do just about anything, that I could rise from where I was, serve people and live abundantly.

For this book, I asked Dottie, "Knowing what you know now, what would you have done differently?"

"I would have believed in myself and not been so frightened," she replied. She told me about her childhood in a family troubled by domestic violence. Her father's last comment before his final departure from home was, "She's not worth going to college." Dottie told me that his comment was like "knocking a kid down the stairs." Her self-esteem was crushed.

But her mother encouraged Dottie's reading and took her to the public library. There Dottie discovered private coaches, as she read the biographies of Albert Einstein, Joan of Arc, Amelia Earhart, Benjamin Franklin and others. These individuals showed her the way. Dottie would say that Einstein seemed to be telling her, "Dottie, stop focusing on the problem and start concentrating on solutions."

One time, as Dottie was relaying this story to an audience, a woman said, "Who do you think you are? He didn't write that for you!"

Dottie responded, "Didn't he write it for all of us who needed him?"

The truth is that Dottie did rise to believe in herself, and she raised thousands of people up with her. She opened a whole new world for me. Her inspiration led me to expand my journey from motion picture director to communicator and to add to my life, authoring ten books, speaking in cities across the United States and being a faculty instructor to graduate students and a guest instructor at Stanford University.

Dottie is with me every time I step in front of my audiences and students.

Dottie Walters passed away February 14, 2007.

Her company, Walters International Speakers Bureau (www. Walters-Intl.com), continues to thrive under the leadership of her grandson, Michael MacFarlane.

For more information about the books *Speak and Grow Rich* (coauthored by Dottie) and *Share and Grow Rich, The Dottie Walters Effect* (Dottie's biography, featuring her advice to Jack Canfield, Mark Victor Hansen, David Bach, Tom Marcoux and others, which helped them launch their speaking and publishing careers) go to speakandgrowrich.com.

Dottie Walters's rejoinder, "Didn't Albert Einstein write it for all of us who needed him?" reminds me of Mark Twain's comment, "The man who *does not* read good books has no advantage over the man who *cannot* read them." Both Dottie and Mark Twain invite to us to continue reading. When we read, we get access to empowering quotes and stories that can *enhance our lives.*

Principle:

An effective story engages the mind, moves the heart and melts resistance.

Power Questions:

What are three stories that have moved you the most? What characteristics do these stories have? How can you make sure your story has similar elements?

USE A PERSONAL BRAND (CREDIBILITY)

> *My philosophy is that not only are you responsible for your life, but doing the best at this moment puts you in the best place for the next moment.*
>
> OPRAH WINFREY

As I mentioned earlier, the audience has subconscious questions, the *Three Ws*:

- Who are you?

- Why should I listen to you?

- What's in it for me?

Answer the Three Ws and you have credibility. Use your personal brand to answer all three questions. Your personal brand is about credibility.

In my books *Wake Up Your Spirit to Prosperity* and *Nothing Can Stop You This Year!* I go into depth about the personal brand. Here I am emphasizing the essence of your personal brand. It's what makes you unique and trustworthy to your listener. Your personal brand is the answer to the question, "What are you best known for?"

*A professional is someone who can do his best work
when he doesn't feel like it.*

ALISTAIR COOKE

All top professionals have devoted significant time and practice to coming up with the few powerful words that convey their competence and trustworthiness.

Sometimes you can borrow credibility. How? You can talk about having interviewed someone who provided special information. For example, when I interviewed Susan RoAnne, bestselling author of *How to Work a Room*, I asked, "Knowing what you know now, what would you have done differently?"

She replied, "When my book was profiled in *USA Today* and *The Wall Street Journal* … I would have tripled my fees."

Be sure to write out your answer to the question, "What are you best known for?" Practice saying the answer, and you're ready to wow a job interviewer or potential customer.

Principle:

People listen when the speaker has credibility. The clearly expressed personal brand provides this credibility.

Power Questions:

What are you best known for? How can you express your personal brand in ways that inspire audience members to feel they will gain big benefits?

ASK QUESTIONS

In my public speaking class, I emphasize, *I can't persuade you if I don't know you.*

How can you get to know your audience? Ask questions.

> *Instead of 600 books on the secrets of selling, try this:*
> *Ask. Just ask people to buy. Ask, ask, ask, ask, and ask.*
> *Become a master asker.*
>
> LARRY WINGET

When you ask your audience questions, you create a rapport. Once rapport is created, you can influence them to accept the value of your ideas.

> *I'm intensely curious. And I have no agenda … I go in trying to learn. I ask short questions. I leave me out of it. I don't use the word 'I'.*
>
> LARRY KING

Demonstrate that you are interested in your audience's well-being. Ask gentle questions and listen intently. Ask follow-up questions.

If possible, *don't take a stance that is directly opposite to an answer given by an audience member.* You can respond, "That's part of it, and the detail we can emphasize now is … " or, "Let's keep that one on the table here … "

It helps to pre-plan some of your questions. For example, I often ask, "How many of us have ever procrastinated on something at some time in our lives?" I raise my hand, and many audience members respond by raising their hands. Some audience members don't.

"Those of you not raising your hands are procrastinating on raising your hands." The audience laughs in response.

First, I have lightened it up. Then I ask a follow-up question: "When you absolutely need to get something done, what breaks your procrastination?"

Often, an audience member will reply, "Fear. For example, I'm afraid of tax penalties." At that point, my audience is fully engaged. Do you see the power of questions?

Asking questions of your audience keeps them engaged. A question-and-answer session can make a powerful impact.

Here are helpful strategies:

1. **Avoid ending your speech with a question-and-answer session.** The greatest communicators regain control of their speeches after the Q&A session and end with a rousing summary. To stay in control, you can say, "In a moment, I will take a few questions. Then I will summarize."

2. **Handle the silence that may happen when you ask, "Any questions?"** You can comment, "That's okay. People are thinking. We'll take a moment here."

3. **If the silence continues, you can say, "Oh, in the meantime, I have a question."** Then state a rhetorical question that relates to one of the points in your speech, and answer your own question. By doing this, you have given your audience time to formulate their questions.

4. **To end your question-and-answer session, say, "I can take two more questions."** Then continue with, "I can take one question … Now I will summarize."

We have the power to turn a question into a gift
– even if it was thrown like a spear.

TOM MARCOUX

How to handle tough questions

Sara is giving a presentation aimed at gaining funding for her new company. From the audience of potential investors, a man asks, "How can you expect us to go with you when your previous company went bankrupt?"

Sara takes a few steps toward the questioner and replies with composure, "John, I hear your concern. In the five years since my previous company, I have dived into this segment of the industry. My experience as a Vice President at Acme Company showed me how … "

With this response, Sara demonstrates what I call the *Power-Three for Handling Tough Questions*. I share the Power-Three for Handling Tough Questions with CEOs and my graduate students. To make this technique clear, I will break down Sara's response and show how to win the audience over.

1. Catch the question (an aikido blending move).

Sara replies, "John, I hear your concern." In the martial art aikido, one "blends" with the opponent's energy. Sara does not contradict John's question. (I demonstrate how one catches a question for my CEO clients and graduate students by having someone toss me a book and catching it gently in a pillow.)

2. Answer the question.

Sara makes sure to answer John's question: "In the five years since my previous company, I have dived into this segment of the industry. My experience as a Vice president at Acme Company showed me how … " She can continue, "I have learned how to deal with Problem A in this segment of the industry."

3. Shine light on a diamond.

Only after Sara has answered the question does she shine light on what she *wants* to talk about. In effect, she has earned the right by answering the question. ("Earn the right" is a phrase emphasized by speech coach Jerry Weissman.)

Novice politicians sometimes make the mistake of ignoring a question and jumping right back to their talking points. The audience is too sophisticated for this move. It is better to answer the question. If you do not have the data you need to answer the question *at the moment*, you can mention this fact.

When you are preparing a speech, remember that you have not finished until you have written the ten worst questions you can receive and two possible answers to each question. Remember, *courage is easier when you're prepared.*

Network effectively with a high ranking individual

Effective questions can help you when meeting top-level professionals, who can ultimately assist your career, like CEOs, bestselling authors, or producers. You need to pre-plan your questions, so that at any moment when you happen to meet a top-level person or celebrity, you are prepared to ask effective questions.

Remember, top professionals are repeatedly accosted by people who want something from them. Many of them are jaded. Here are tips for when you meet them:

1. *Say something specific.* When I was talking with a motion picture director at the screening of his new feature film, I said, "You really held the tension in the bank scene. I wanted to yell at the character, 'Don't ruin your life!'"

2. *Use the powerful way to give a compliment.* Be specific: "I really appreciate how you did … (Specify.) How did you do that?" or "How did you learn to do that?"

3. *Ask, "What's next for you?"* or "What are you looking forward to?"

4. *Be brief and be gone.*

Principle:

Ask questions and you connect with people's hearts and minds.

Power Questions:

Write a list of ten questions. Which of these questions feels most appropriate to you? Which questions touch on what truly bothers your audience members? Then write down at least two answers to 10 tough questions you might receive. (Before giving a speech, you can connect with an insider and learn about the questions that most concern that particular audience. Or you might use a brief questionnaire that you can send through e-mail.)

Demonstrate and Involve Them

I hear and I forget.
I see and I remember.
I do and I understand.

CONFUCIUS (KONG QIU)

As I faced my graduate students' *Professional Presentation* class, I wondered, "How can I get these students to feel the difference between a destructive reaction and a gentle, blending response?"

I demonstrated the difference between karate and aikido. I invited one student to stand up and had the student mime a punch. I showed how force meets force and creates pain during a karate block. Then I showed the gentleness of an aikido move. One shifts position, grabs the arm, and guides the person to the floor. I stopped in time so the student didn't go all the way to the floor. That would have been awkward.

I did this to illustrate the power of providing feedback that avoids creating resistance. It's important to realize that *getting the audience involved* makes your point memorably. One way to get the audience involved is to have people pair off as two-person "teams."

The power of having audience members partner up is that *we often feel better when we can express ourselves* and be heard. Secondly, we feel good about ourselves when we help someone by listening and supporting that person.

Helping others makes *us* feel better. When I met Gerald "Jerry" Jampolsky, MD, bestselling author of *Love is Letting Go of Fear*, I was filled with a great energy. Jerry is so inspired that he practically glows. He teaches that when you help someone, *you* naturally feel better.

One of Jerry's favorite examples is about two boys, Paul and Tony. At 13 years old, Paul had a brain tumor. At 10, Tony had bone cancer severe enough to necessitate the amputation of his leg. When Tony was in the hospital during the scary and painful treatment, Jerry asked Paul to talk with Tony on the phone.

Paul was suffering, too; he looked almost dead. But Jerry noticed that Paul suddenly *came alive* when he was telling Tony jokes. As they talked, a close friendship emerged. While Paul was helping Tony, *Paul* felt better!

Not only did Paul help Tony, but he also inspired 50 million people who saw this story on "60 Minutes." I saw this video segment when Jerry invited me to visit The Center for Attitudinal Healing, which he founded. I went to the Center, in Sausalito, California, to discover how I might help Jerry's work. One of the things I am doing is bringing stories like this to the attention of audiences and readers like you. Here is the Web site: www. AttitudinalHealing.org.

At this Web site we learn, "At the heart of Attitudinal Healing is the belief in the extraordinary ability of ordinary people to be of help to one another, and the idea that we have the power to choose our attitude in any given moment, regardless of circumstances." Please go to the Web site to learn of the 130 locations worldwide.

It often happens that being hit with some form of loss makes people feel somehow less effective and less complete.

By helping another person, we see and feel that we are *still* effective and strong enough to make a difference in that person's life. This is powerfully nurturing. This is an affirmation:

*I help someone and feel the helping
process heal us both.*

Here is how this applies to giving a powerful speech: you help someone when you make the person *part of your demonstration*. For example, you can place the brochure or product in her hand.

Principle:

Demonstrate and involve audience members.

Power Questions:

How can you have audience members participate? Can you get them (a) moving, (b) talking with a partner or (c) talking with you directly?

ENERGIZE THE EMOTIONAL BRAIN

What if you had information that you knew was crucial for the well-being of your audience? What could you do to seize their attention? You could show the audience how to avoid a loss.

Researchers have shown that the emotional brain consists of the amygdala and the brain stem. To energize the emotional brain is to give the listener an experience of the pain that occurs if the listener does not implement your suggestion.

A man who is afraid will do anything.

JAWAHARLAL NEHRU

When love and skill work together, expect a masterpiece.

JOHN RUSKIN

A.L. Williams, author of *All You Can Do Is All You Can Do, But All You Can Do Is Enough!* endured the pain of financial disaster when his father died unexpectedly. Since his father did not have life insurance, William's family was left without financial support. After this extreme experience, Williams became an evangelist for adequate insurance coverage. He *combined love and skill*. A.L. loved to help people protect themselves and their loved ones from financial disaster.

Your emotion moves the *audience's* emotions. Your passion for your topic can provide the wind beneath the audience's wings. For example, Danny Glover (star of *Lethal Weapon IV*, with Mel Gibson), said, "First you have to determine whether or not you have a passion for acting. I believe that persistence and passion can overcome anything … Remember that what you do is an act of giving, an act of love. It has to be an act of love …"

Danny also said, "I never really considered art as anything other than a vehicle to move people." Danny reminds us that our passion for something is the source of our strength. He wanted to produce and star in a feature film entitled *The Prince of Fort Washington*, so he made a deal with the studio. The plan was for Danny to star in another *Lethal Weapon* movie, and in exchange the studio would advance funds for the motion picture he really wanted to do. Danny *combined love and skill*. I had the opportunity to meet Danny when he presided over a San Francisco screening of his completed film.

People have four basic preoccupations:
self-preservation, romance, money, and recognition.

ROY GARN

To effectively stimulate the buyer's emotional brain, we need to become *comfortable about money*. For many of us, this is a tall order. Here is a story related to the process of getting comfortable about the issue of money:

> The bat felt good in my hands. The ball flew toward me. Thwaaack! My bat connected with the ball, and it soared toward the faraway fence, center field. I was stunned. I had never hit a ball that far. It was going, going, almost out of the park, when …
>
> Whump! Judy, my fellow camp counselor, caught the ball. Judy and I enjoyed pats on the back from our teammates and gave each other a hug. Minutes later, we received simple awards: Best Slugger and Best Catch.
>
> The game and the bat in my hands were tools to bring the camp counselors closer together in our shared vision of enriching the lives of the children in our care. On that day, I used the bat as a tool for goodness and closeness. However, you sometimes hear of someone using a bat for an inappropriate, violent purpose.
>
> *The bat and, yes, money are neutral tools.* It is time that we become comfortable with how we relate to money.

Comfort about money ties in with the emotional brain.

Lots of us have been conditioned to feel bad about money, as if having money makes one less – less spiritual, for example. If you feel bad about money, you won't be strong enough to use all the tools you need, such as stimulating a potential buyer's emotional brain. Remember, the emotional brain is focused on feelings of loss.

An interviewer asked, "Why would someone be unlikely to stimulate the buyer's emotional brain?"

I replied, "Let me give you a specific example. Joe is a novice salesperson. If he feels bad about money, he will be reluctant to be in that pain. That will make him hesitate to make the potential buyer feel bad, too. It is as if Joe tells himself subconsciously, 'I'm a bad person to focus on gaining money. And I'm a worse person to make the potential buyer feel bad temporarily.'"

The interviewer then asked, "Why is Joe making the buyer feel bad temporarily?"

"Because sometimes, someone won't buy a thing that is good for him until he feels how he could be hurt by not having the product," I replied.

Again, A. L. Williams helped people imagine the pain of the financial disaster that would ensue if one died without adequate life insurance coverage. Only when his customer could imagine a painful consequence did the person buy insurance.

Make gaining financial abundance *a positive path*. Many top achievers and millionaires have discovered ways to help people on a significant scale. Financial abundance then arrives as a by-product.

Peter McWilliams, author of *Wealth 101*, notes that wealth refers to "health, happiness, abundance, prosperity, riches, loving, caring, sharing, learning, knowing what you want, opportunity, enjoying and balance." A spiritual view of wealth includes being grateful for the blessings we currently enjoy, and being comfortable with the idea of going for more. You can see that we can have *both*.

Film provides an opportunity to marry the power of ideas with the power of images.

STEVEN BOCHCO

As in film, when giving a persuasive speech we can combine the power of ideas and images. Express a *word picture* and you inspire an image in the listeners' minds.

Here is an example of a word picture that I mentioned earlier: "When I'm waiting for you, I'm like a puppy on a raft in the middle of the Atlantic Ocean, not knowing if a rescue boat will ever arrive." In this word picture, we vividly see the power of energizing the emotional brain. The listener can empathize with the sense of loss – loss of feelings of security, or even the loss of hope.

Remember, to truly energize the emotional brain, give the listener a temporary feeling of loss. Then show how your solution provides relief from such painful feelings.

Principle:

To ensure that audience members are moved to take action, connect with their emotional brain.

Power Questions:

What parts of your speech get your audience to imagine potential loss? How can you make this experience vivid and then provide the salve – your solutions?

CONCLUSION TO PART XI

What is essential to living a fulfilling life? Persuasion skills. Communication is about expressing what you want in a way that invites cooperation from the listener. Without effective persuasion skills, people may irritate their listeners, causing them to put up barriers. But with good persuasion skills, you can build bridges and make dreams come true.

Persuasion is often more effective than force.

AESOP

The real persuaders are our appetites, our fears, and above all our vanity. The skillful propagandist stirs and coaches these internal persuaders.

ERIC HOFFER

As we have seen in Part XI, it is valuable to help people access their own emotions.

The man who can make others laugh secures more votes for a measure than the man who forces them to think.

MALCOLM DE CHAZAL

If I can get you to laugh with me, you like me better, which makes you more open to my ideas. And if I can persuade you to laugh at the particular point I make, by laughing at it you acknowledge its truth.

JOHN CLEESE

True persuasion involves making a connection. Gentle humor can often foster such a connection.*

The truly skilled ethical persuader helps people discover how a product will serve the listener's personal needs and desires.

> *People are usually more convinced by reasons they discovered themselves than by those found by others.*
>
> BLAISE PASCAL

In Part XII, *Secrets about Networking and the Media – Building Relationships & Winning via the Internet*, we will explore effective communication skills that help people learn the true value of what we're offering. First you need to seize their attention.

Let's learn how to express compelling messages …

---

* Humor is so important to warming up business and personal relationships that I share "30 Secrets for Creating Humor" in my book *Wake Up Your Spirit to Prosperity*. Visit TomSuperCoach.com/SpecialOffer.htm.

Part XII

Secrets about Networking and the Media
Building Relationships & Winning via the Internet

NETWORKING AND BUILDING relationships, utilizing the Internet, and working with the media are vital skills.

Powerful shortcuts to devising a strategy for interacting with the media and creating a compelling Web site are found in Personaltainment Branding™, which I revealed in my book *Wake Up Your Spirit to Prosperity*. Personaltainment Branding focuses on the P.E.C. Triangle. P.E.C. refers to personalized, entertaining and connecting.

- Personalized means you are *important to me.*

- Entertaining is giving the customer an enjoyable experience.

- Connecting helps fill the customer's empty feeling of loneliness.

An interviewer asked me, "Loneliness?"

I replied, "Yes. On some level, people feel alone with their problems. They want support and a feeling of connection."

To use Personaltainment Branding, take out your personal journal and note these questions to ask your listener.

Five Personaltainment Branding questions

1. What about this is working for you? (*personalized*)

2. When did this become fun for you? (*entertaining*)

3. What's most important about this for you? (*personalized*)

4. What has to happen in order for you to know that you have what you want? (*connecting*)

5. How can we make this work better for you? (*connecting*)

   (Another version of the second question above is, "When *could* this become fun for you?")

When you design your Web site or media release around the Personaltainment Branding questions, your message becomes compelling. It gets people to take action that is favorable to you.

An interviewer asked me, "How do these questions make this happen?"

"It's about accessing people's emotions," I replied. "When you help people feel important and give them an enjoyable experience, they want to return again and again. For example, my buying experience through Amazon.com is quick, easy – and yes, for me it's fun. I love books, and hearing about what readers think about the book I'm considering. It is obvious that the creative team of Amazon.com has pre-planned ways to get readers enthralled. This is what I guide clients to do when they use the Personaltainment Branding questions as a springboard for designing Web pages and media releases."

How can you use the Internet for networking?

Bestselling author Guy Kawasaki uses his blog to solidify relationships with his current customer base and with new people who come into his Web site via Google.com and other search engines. When I contacted Guy about this book, I knew what a fast-moving person he is. I suggested that he might repurpose something from his e-newsletter or his blog, which is entitled *How to Change the World*.

So here is an excerpt from Guy's Blog (blog.guykawasaki.com):

October 25, 2007

A Night in the Life of Guy Kawasaki
Plus Cool Stuff Friday

GUY KAWASAKI

It's 10:30 pm, and I'm sitting on a baggage cart on the tarmac of the Monterey, California airport. My U. S. Airways flight was set to depart and then an engine warning light went on – this was two hours ago. The reason we're all on the tarmac is that a fire alarm went off, so we had to evacuate the terminal.

Still, this is better than the last time I flew on U.S. Airways. That time one of the plane's engines died, and we made an "unscheduled stop" in Kansas City and then had to wait four hours for another plane to fly in. What's all of the got to do with this entry?

Nothing except that I've had two hours to compile a short list of cool stuff.

It's been one of those days. This afternoon I spoke for my buddies at Cisco [Systems]. Just before the speech, I discovered that the recently dry-cleaned pants that I packed were my son's, not mine, so I had to give the speech wearing jeans. One high point: Reggie Jackson was on the flight too, but he left after two hours of waiting. He was giving out autographs – though he didn't ask me for mine. :-) If I get to Las Vegas anytime soon, I'm speaking for the Entrepreneurs' Organization.

[On Guy's Blog, each of the below titles was an active link.]

"25 Tools to Compile an In-Depth Dossier on a Competitors' Site." This article contains description and links for you to scope out your competition's Web site. It covers topics such as ownership, traffic, links, trademarks, and browser compatibility.

"The Web Entrepreneur's Customer Service Toolbox: 100 Hacks and Resources." This is a compilation of useful tools and services to maintain a high-level of customer service. These tools help you keep in touch, run meetings, do accounting, provide support, and solicit feedback.

MeVu. This site enables you to create a page of links to all your Web presences. This means that people can go to one location for your profiles on Facebook, MySpace, and LinkedIn; pictures in Flickr and PhotoBucket; videos in YouTube; and musings in multiple blogs. Here is a sample. [Guy had a link here].

Catalog Choice. This is a not-for-profit that helps you reduce the amount of tree-killing, dump-filling, money-wasting catalogs that you receive (19 billion catalogs are printed each year in the U. S.). You denote which catalogs are coming to you, and Catalog Choice tells the companies to back off. It's a free service.

Best Book Combo. The site searches the catalogs of AbeBooks.com, Amazon.com, BetterWorld.com, and Alibris.com and determines the best total price (that is, including shipping and handling) of a book. For example, the AbeBooks price for [Guy's book] *The Art of the Start* was $17.54 compared to Amazon.com's $18.20.

[Guy's blog is filled with links so that his readers can gain lots of valuable information fast!]

Guy Kawasaki of Garage Technology Ventures, Author of *The Art of the Start: The Time-Tested, Battle-Hardened Guide for Anyone Starting Anything*

www.GuyKawasaki.com

More methods for working with the Internet and the media

If you want to build a ship, don't herd people together
to collect wood and don't assign them tasks and work,
but rather teach them to long for
the endless immensity of the sea.

ANTOINE DE SAINT EXUPÉRY

Antoine's comment inspires us to touch people's hearts and create a feeling of longing in them. The old journalistic comment is, "If it bleeds, it leads." We notice that news broadcasts often begin with intense stories about hurricanes and other calamities. If you can *show people how to protect themselves* from some kind of loss, you can seize their attention.

Perfection is achieved, not when there is nothing more
to add, but when there is nothing left to take away.

ANTOINE DE SAINT EXUPÉRY

Simplicity counts. We live in a sound bite culture. You need to get your message down to a simple, clear, hard-hitting point. "Your brand is the shortest distance to trust," I advised the audience of my sixth annual presentation to the National Association of Broadcasters Conference, in Las Vegas.

Here's how you can use the Internet and the media to create more profit. We will use the acrostic B.R.A.N.D.:

B – Begin with questions

R – Reveal stories

A – Alert to benefits and loss

N – Nurture relationships

D – Dig for information

BEGIN WITH QUESTIONS

How do you make your brand stand out and compel people to take action? Design your Web site to answer the questions a first-time Web visitor has in mind. In my book *Online Secrets to Build Your Brand*, I reveal those questions:

- Who are you?

- How can you help me?

- How can you show me that you're trustworthy?

- Why must I take action now? (*e.g.*, click on a hyperlink)

Ensure that your Web site includes your name, a moniker (such as "Success Coach"), and powerful testimonials to your trustworthiness. Use hyperlinks that identify how you help (for example, "increase your profit"). Remember, people don't buy services. They buy solutions.

As I mentioned when talking about Personaltainment Branding™, make sure that your interaction with the Web visitor is personalized, entertaining, and connecting (what I call the P.E.C. Triangle). Design your Web site based on answers to these questions:

1. What about this is working for you (the Web visitor)? (personalized)

2. When did this become fun for you? (entertaining)

3. What's most important about this for you? (personalized)

4. What has to happen in order for you to know that you have what you want? (connecting)

5. How can we make this work better for you? (connecting)

Related to the first, third and fifth questions ("fun," "most important for you," and "make this work better for you"), a good example of Web design is found in Nightingale-Conant's Web site, which includes a computer-designed Personal Mission Statement that you create by typing in your own answers. For the third question ("most important to you"), effective Web marketers have designed hyperlinks to lure Web visitors. Oprah. com's hyperlink, "Get Better Sleep," is enticing.

REVEAL STORIES

Many years ago, when she first coached me, author Dottie Walters impressed me with her stories. I always remember how vividly she conveyed her beginnings. She talked about placing cardboard in her shoes to cover the holes and using pillows to convert a one-seat stroller into a two-seat stroller, which allowed her to take her children with her to an important meeting.

Dottie energized me to feel that I could start from where I was and climb the staircase of success.

Now I use attention-grabbing stories: "When I was hanging by my fingertips to the hood of a speeding truck, I wasn't thinking about the movie cameraman capturing the stunt. I was only concerned about … " About what? This is the element of a good story. The reader needs to respond, "What happened then?"

This leads us to the use of a personal brand in building your Web site. Mark Victor Hansen's personal brand is "The Master of Mindset." My personal brand is "America's Communication Coach."

Use your personal brand with well-chosen phrases on your Web site, in your e-mail and e-newsletters. For example, "I'm known as America's Communication Coach because I help clients and audiences create a Wow! experience so their clients buy and they get breakthrough results … In fact, Jaclyn Freitas, a meeting planner who booked me said, 'Using just one of Tom's methods, I got more done in 2 weeks than in 6 months.'"

ALERT TO BENEFITS AND LOSS

What reliably gets a Web visitor to click on a hyperlink? Alert the person to a potential loss. Fear of loss will get people to take action. To build your brand and sell items through the Internet, always include a *deadline*.

On a Web page that offers a product, begin with the product's benefit. Then point out how the person will lose without the benefit this product offers. The reason for this sequence is that if the first detail emphasized loss, a positive person might be turned off. However, when the first point is the benefits that are offered, a person who is loss-oriented will just read past those benefits, then key into the loss and buy your product.

NURTURE RELATIONSHIPS

Build your brand online by creating a harmonious dance between your e-newsletter and a special-target Web page. For example, I wrote an e-mail message to be sent by persuasion expert David Barron to his list of thousands of subscribers. My e-newsletter message began, "I never expected to write *Darkest Secrets of Persuasion Masters: How to Protect Yourself and Turn the Power to Good*. But I was angry and I had to stand up for you."

I begin a relationship with the reader: "I had to stand up for you." I tell the truth about getting angry, and the reader sees me as a real human being. But this is not my usual positive way of communicating, so a few lines later I add, "This *Darkest Secrets* material is so intense that I am only releasing it with my most uplifting books: *Wake Up Your Spirit to Prosperity* and *Wake Up Your Spirit to Prosperity – for Couples*." The reader can then click to a specific Web page that includes the same information.

Please note: I reveal that I stand up for the reader; I'm a real person; and I provide vital information that protects the reader from misfortune.

DIG FOR INFORMATION

Effective Web marketers learn about their Web visitors. One method is to offer two free e-books and see which title pulls.

My team tests my e-book *Make Your Impossible Dreams Come True* against my e-book *What I Learned from Really Successful People – that Made All the Difference.**

Stay open to feedback. I named my Web site TomSuperCoach.com because a television host asked, "How do you spell Marcoux?"

When I interviewed Carly Fiorina (former CEO of Hewlett-Packard), she said, "You need to find the people who believe as you do. They're out there." The secret is to reinforce your brand by making your Web site, e-newsletter and business card tell the same compelling story.

Author Danek Kaus shows us how to interact effectively with the media.

How to Be a Media Darling

DANEK S. KAUS

You've probably heard these quotes:

> *Ask not what your country can do for you,*
> *ask what you can do for your country.*

PRESIDENT JOHN F. KENNEDY

> *Speak softly and carry a big stick.*

PRESIDENT THEODORE ROOSEVELT

* To see how this works, go to www.TomSuperCoach.com/GetYourEbook.htm.

Float like a butterfly and sting like a bee.

MOHAMMED ALI

What do these lines have in common?

They are memorable. They create powerful images and/or stir emotions.

That's what the media want from you – great quotes.

Let's face it; we live in a sound-bite world. So one great way to get the media to love interviewing you, and to want to come back for more interviews, is to give them great quotes to use in their stories.

How do you create great sound-bites?

There are several techniques you can use. One is the metaphor.

Let's say you're a martial arts instructor who is being interviewed about the value of your training for children and teens.

You might say something like, "Martial arts offer children an island of sanity and security in a world drowning in drugs and self-destruction."

Another way to be quotable is to say something controversial: "Martial arts prepare children for life in ways our failed public schools can't."

Now if you have a good relationship with the local schools, you're not going to say something like that, but you get the idea.

So if you have a media interview coming up, think about ways to be quotable by incorporating images, metaphors and controversy.

Danek S. Kaus, is the author of *You Can Be Famous: Insider Secrets to Getting Free Publicity* and the coauthor (with David R. Barron) of *Power Persuasion: Using Hypnotic Influence to Win in Life, Love, and Business.* He has published hundreds of articles on business and personal development in dozens of publications and Web sites. Mr. Kaus is available for publicity consultations. Write to him at:

dkaus@sbcglobal.net
winnersedge.blogspot.com

smallbusinessgoldmine.com

Conclusion to Part XII

It is helpful to remember these three powerful principles when interacting with the media:

1. Hone your message so that you say (or write) it briefly.

2. Be sure to seize the attention of the media person and her audience with something that appeals to the emotions.

3. Remember that pain is an important element of a message. If you can help someone prevent a personal loss, you have her attention.

A Final Word and Springboard to Your Dreams

Thank you for your attention and efforts. We have focused on skills so that you can truly *be heard and be trusted*. When your communication accomplishes these two objectives, your life improves. You attract more opportunities. People cooperate easily with you and make decisions that are favorable to your dreams and goals.

Remember to return to these pages again and again to reenergize yourself. You will get more value each time you review the steps covered in this book – and take action!

Please visit me at TomSuperCoach.com to get free reports and my free e-newsletter, *Success Secrets*. I also work with clients one-on-one in person and over the telephone, and I present workshops and speeches to associations and companies.

On the following pages, you will find special discounts, presentations, and empowering audio programs and books that will help you continue your education and expand your prosperity. The best to you,

Tom Marcoux
America's Communication Coach
Motion Picture Director & CEO, TomMarcoux.com, Inc.

Special Offer for My Readers

Bring Tom to your company, conference, or church and get a 10% discount on his fee. TomSuperCoach@gmail.com.

Tom's popular topics:

- Be Heard and Be Trusted
- Truth No One Will Tell You
- Nothing Can Stop You This Year!
- Power Time Management
- Double Your Sales in Half the Time™
- 10 Best Kept Secrets of Persuasion Masters
- Wake Up Your Spirit To Prosperity
- Empower Your Personal Brand

To view a downloadable page of these topics, go to:

bureau.espeakers.com/simp/viewspeaker5261&multimedia

Don't miss a special offer for readers of *Be Heard & Be Trusted* at:

www.TomSuperCoach.com/ReaderOffer.htm

Get FREE reports and a FREE e-newsletter subscription ($195 value!), *Success Secrets*. You can also orde books and CDs, see the list of titles at front of this book.

Glossary

A.C.T.I.O.N. **Process** – This method helps you strategically put energy into preparation and assists you to learn what others truly value.

> A – Approach them in ways they prefer
>
> C – Communicate vividly
>
> T – Touch them five times
>
> I – Invite action
>
> O – Open to personal value
>
> N – Note value and gratitude

Brand, Personal – It is what makes you unique and trustworthy to your listener. Your personal brand is the answer to the question, "What are you best known for?"

People listen when the speaker has credibility. The clearly expressed personal brand provides this credibility. Here are six elements of your personal brand:

> 1. What are you best known for?
>
> 2. Ideally, what do you want to be best known for?

3. What high visibility details of your job are important to your boss, the supervisor above her or him, to the company, CEO or shareholders?

4. Identify two anecdotes.

5. Use a sound bite.

6. Develop a moniker.

B.R.A.N.D. Process – Here's how you can use the Internet and the media to create more profit:

B – Begin with questions

R – Reveal stories

A – Alert to benefits and loss

N – Nurture relationships

D – Dig for information

Branding, Personaltainment – *See*, "Personaltainment Branding"

Bring Calm Steps – Take the following steps to guide someone to be more cooperative, by bringing them to calm.

1. Release your own disquiet.

2. Breathe deeply before seeing or calling the person.

3. Match tone, volume and pacing.

4. In graduated steps, lower your tone and volume … and in graduated steps, slow down your pacing.

Buying Anxieties, Five – These were first identified by author Gene Bedell.

1. Reluctance to give up options

2. Fear of making a mistake

3. Social pressures

4. Fear of losing

5. Perceived cost

Charisma – A charismatic person expresses compelling messages – messages which have a powerful and irresistible influence. These messages overpower inertia, low moods, and procrastination.

Choice-Market Testing™ – To market test a title, use my process of *Choice-Market Testing*. For example, for a film I was producing and directing, I had two poster concepts created. Then I asked people, "Which movie would you pay to see?" It's crucial to give people a choice, because many prefer to be polite and thus avoid providing critical feedback. If you show them only one cover or title, they say, "That's nice." For real feedback, I always give two choices. I ask, "I have two titles for my new book. If you were in a bookstore looking for a book for yourself or a friend, which title would you buy?" I watch their faces. They pause and give a useful answer. Then I gently ask, "I see that you prefer title number two. What do you think that title is about? What about it grabs your interest?"

C.O.M.P.E.L. Process – We want people to cooperate with us, to take action in the direction we're proposing. Here is a process to achieve that objective.

C – Connect with the listener's pain

O – Open with genuineness

M– Maximize leverage

P – Pull with a story

E – Ease

L – Lift

Courage – Ambrose Redmoon stated, "Courage is not the absence of fear, but rather the judgment that something else is more important than fear." I emphasize to my audiences: courage is easier when you're compared.

Dog – *See,* "Personality Styles, Four"

Effort Goals – *See,* "Goals, Effort"

Excel on Another Horse – Here is a critical process for taking control to create your own opportunities, as an alternative to seeking out existing opportunities rife with competition.

1. Observe what is *not* working.

2. Reconnect with your real goal (what brings you fulfillment).

3. Seek another method ("another horse").

4. Take a new action.

Expert – An expert is someone who has devised a system that people like and use.

Finishers – *See,* "Implementers"

Goals, Effort – This is a goal defined in terms of the effort required, rather than the result desired. It is a goal harmonized with the perspective that a journey is its own reward. Effort Goals contrast with Result Goals. Effort Goals are much less likely to be met with frustration.

Goals, Result – This is a goal defined in terms of the result desired, rather than the effort required. This is most peoples' paradigm of a goal. Result Goals contrast with Effort Goals. Result Goals can be frustrating, since outcomes are often not within our control.

Good Story, A – Stories reach us on our subconscious and emotional levels, going around our natural resistance.

> 1. Begins with a *grabber*
>
> 2. Has *suspense*
>
> 3. Has *vivid details*
>
> 4. Includes *word pictures*
>
> 5. Ends with *"What I learned was …"*
>
> 6. Has a *call to action*

High-Visibility Tasks – High-visibility tasks help you do a great job, and they help others *see* that you're doing well for the company. They often involve vital tasks which would cause trouble if any errors occurred.

Horse, Excel on Another – *See*, "Excel on Another Horse"

Idea-People – Some people are idea-people or "starters." They can come up with good ideas, but they're *not* interested in becoming experts at the tasks that are involved in implementing those ideas. It helps when idea-people team up with implementers.

Implementers – Implementers are "finishers." They get a lot of joy out of finishing a task well.

I.M.P. R.E.S.S. Process – To be effective in job interviews, we use the I.M.P.R.E.S.S. process:

I – Inquire

M– Mention how you fulfill criteria

P – Prepare for questions

R – Review just before

E – Engage connection

S – Send scarcity messages

S – Save money for last

Influence, Principles of – In his book *Influence*, researcher/author Robert Cialdini noted the principles of influence, including:

1. Reciprocity, create

2. Commitment and consistency, principle of

3. Social proof, demonstrate

4. Perception of scarcity, enhance

5. Liking, set the stage to be liked

6. Authority

To influence someone, focus on helping her in some way.

Input Style, Preferred – We receive input all day long. There's some input we like, some we don't, and some we are indifferent to. Matching your message to the preferred input style of the listener assures it will be heard more effectively.

Visual: "I need to see some sample work."

Auditory: "I'd like to hear comments from your references."

Kinesthetic (touch): "We need to find out if you'd work smoothly with the other team members. The next step is for you to have interviews with team members."

Journal, Personal – A vital record of your journey through this book. To get the most from this book, be sure to write down the answer to each exercise in your personal journal as you proceed.

L.E.A.D.S. Process – To thrive during a crisis, you need to lead yourself and others to calm.

L – Listen

E – Engage

A – Act

D – Decrease downers

S – Shift to inner sources of happiness

Least Acceptable Result (LAR) – Your *Least Acceptable Result* (LAR) is the minimal deal that you will accept. As long as you do better than your LAR, you know you're successful. For example, a speaker whose regular fee is $9,000 may agree to accept $6,000 when she wants to enter a new market. If her LAR was $4,000, then she's still done well. Author Herb Cohen writes about MSP and LAR.

Leverage – Leverage is when you strategically apply a small amount of effort for a big result. "Leverage," Donald Trump says, "is having something the other guy wants ... needs ... or best of all, simply can't do without."

Leverage is a product of effective action, which occurs when you:

1. Know what you want.

2. Know how to tell when you have what you want.

L.I.K.E.–M.E.–N.O.W. **Process** – Being likeable is a big component in getting a job, a movie role and other opportunities. (You can call this the *liking factor*.) How can you encourage someone new to like you?

> L – Listen
>
> I – Interview
>
> K – Kindle similarity
>
> E – Express gratitude
>
> M– Monitor time
>
> E – Engage the person's concerns
>
> N – Note ideal clients
>
> O – Open to humor
>
> W – Watch and help

Lion – *See*, "Personality Styles, Four"

Listeners, Effective – People trust and like individuals who listen well. The truth is that you need to be an effective listener, so that other people can feel that you truly heard them, opening the door to their truly hearing you in turn.

> 1. Turn their body so that their heart faces the other person's heart.
>
> 2. Lean forward.
>
> 3. Make listening sounds like "mm-hmm."
>
> 4. Mirror feelings by saying things like, "That sounds frustrating."
>
> 5. Confirm that they understand by saying, "So you want _______. Do I have that about right?"

Love Languages, Five – Dr. Gary Chapman's book, *The Five Love Languages*. In this book, Gary Chapman points out that each person has a personal "love language." If you speak the person's language, he or she will truly *experience* your gratitude.

1. Words of affirmation

2. Gifts

3. Quality time

4. Acts of service

5. Physical touch

Low Mood First-Aid Kit – This is a toolkit for coping when a crisis snatches away our external sources of happiness. The tools selected are those which connect us with our internal resources for self comfort.

M.A.K.E.–L.U.C.K. **Process** – By creating an atmosphere of good will, the great communicator leaves many doors open. The more valuable you become to other people, the more opportunities will open for you.

M– Make yourself prepared

A – Align your persuasion skills

K – Keep searching

E – Excel on another horse

L – Look to help

U – Use everything for networking

C – Course-correct constantly

K – Keep going for what you really want

Maximum Supportable Position (MSP) – The Maximum Supportable Position (MSP) is the best deal you believe you can make. Your MSP is not a crazy offer. It is something you can support with good reasons. Author Herb Cohen writes about MSP and LAR.

Moniker – Have you heard a label like "America's favorite financial adviser"? That's a moniker. Monikers sound like:

- The go-to person for software

- The Tech Wizard of Department M2

- The results coach

- The big jobs manager

Peacock – *See*, "Personality Styles, Four"

P.E.C. **Triangle** – Powerful shortcuts to devising a strategy for interacting with the media and creating a compelling Web site are found in Personaltainment Branding™, which I revealed in my book *Wake Up Your Spirit to Prosperity*. Personaltainment Branding focuses on the P.E.C. Triangle. P.E.C. refers to personalized, entertaining and connecting.

- Personalized means you are *important to me*.

- Entertaining is giving the customer an enjoyable experience.

- Connecting helps fill the customer's empty feeling of loneliness.

Personality Styles, Four – Lion: *A hard-charging leader, who may be considered abrupt or bossy.*

> **Beaver:** An analytical person, who likes tables, graphs and lots of details. This person wants to appear intel-

ligent and makes decisions slowly due to a great fear of making a mistake.

Dog: A supporter, who likes routine and cares about the feelings of others. This person may be slow to accept change.

Peacock: An extrovert, who loves to stand out in a crowd and gain approval. This person may be ineffective when it comes to follow-up.

Observe their personality styles, then you can get your own preoccupations out of the way and speak in a way that will immediately make the other person feel comfortable.

Personaltainment™ Branding – This is a powerful technique for structuring your services, interacting with the media, and creating a compelling Web presence.

Personaltainment Branding Questions, Five – Design your Web site based on answers to these questions:

1. What about this is working for you (the Web visitor)? (personalized)

2. When did this become fun for you? (entertaining)

3. What's most important about this for you? (personalized)

4. What has to happen in order for you to know that you have what you want? (connecting)

5. How can we make this work better for you? (connecting)

P.E.R.S.U.A.D.E. **Process** – To organize a persuasive speech quickly, it helps to use the P.E.R.S.U.A.D.E. process:

      P – Point to the benefit

      E – Emphasize personality styles

      R – Request a response

      S – Say a story

      U – Use personal brand (credibility)

      A – Ask questions

      D – Demonstrate and involve them

      E – Energize the emotional brain

P.H.O.N.E. Process – Learn how to skillfully connect via the telephone.

      P – Practice smiling

      H – Honor personality styles

      O – Own your energy level

      N – Note timing

      E – Earn her trust

Platinum Rule – "Do unto others as they would like done unto them." Formulated by Dr. Tony Alessandra and Michael J. O'Connor.

P.O.W.E.R.–B.R.A.N.D. Process – To create credibility, learn the secrets of creating and expressing a brand. Here is the P.O.W.E.R.–B.R.A.N.D. process:

      P – Point out the warranty

      O – Open with USP

      W – Wring out feelings

      E – Energize a category

R – Ramp up "the first"

B – Bring one message

R – Repeat the "one word"

A – Arrange to lead

N – Nominate one person

D – Duck the "spreading brand" tendency

Power-Three for Handling Tough Questions – I share the Power-Three for Handling Tough Questions with CEOs and my graduate students.

1. Catch the question (an aikido blending move).

2. Answer the question.

3. Shine light on a diamond.

Power-Three of Influence – The process in which you ...

1. Show how much you care.

2. Show that you and your interviewer have common concerns, traits and feelings.

3. Demonstrate that you're a trusted advisor.

Rapport – A (1) relation characterized by harmony, conformity, accord, or affinity; (2) confidence of a subject in the operator (as in hypnotism, psychotherapy, or mental testing) with willingness to cooperate. *Merriam-Webster's Medical Dictionary.*

R.E.D.U.C.E. Risk Process – In this section, we have explored the way to lessen the risk of any action through the R.E.D.U.C.E. process. When you reduce risk, you significantly reduce your resistance to action.

R – Revise options

E – Envision solutions to mistakes

D – Disengage from the fear of loss

U – Unleash yourself from social pressures

C – Cover the cost

E – Engage rehearsal

Result Goals – *See*, "Goals, Result"

Reciprocity – Reciprocity occurs when one person gives something and the other person feels compelled to return the favor.

Serenity Prayer – "God grant me the serenity to accept the things I cannot change; courage to change the things I can; and wisdom to know the difference." This prayer is by Reinhold Niebuhr.

Solution-for-Error Plan – A 10-minute method that helps you quickly learn from a mistake and do better. The idea is to harvest wisdom from your experiences.

1. What's the error and what led to it? What are the painful consequences, or the feelings you want to avoid?

2. How can you avoid the error? What can you do better?

3. How can you compensate for your own tendency?

4. What did you do right?

5. What does the solution look like? What does it feel like?

6. What are the benefits of the solution to you? To the team?

7. How can you reward yourself for taking action?

Sound Bite – A sound bite is the expression of your message boiled down to a simple, clear, hard-hitting point.

S.P.E.E.C.H. **Process** – If you are confronted with the situation of needing to give a speech within one week, or even within five minutes, you can use the following S.P.E.E.C.H. process:

> S – Summarize
>
> P – Prepare your first sentence and last sentence
>
> E – Express an anecdote
>
> E – Enter with a benefit
>
> C – Conclude with "Thank you"
>
> H – Honor three memorable points

Starters – *See*, "Idea People"

Three-Fs Process – This is a process to become stronger. It includes answering specific questions in a particular order:

> 1. *Find It* – What are you afraid of ?
>
> 2. *Flip It* – What do you really want?
>
> 3. *Forward It* – What can you do? What can you relax into?

We can take our fear and convert it into empowering energy by using the *Three-Fs* process:

> *Find your fear* ⇨ *Flip it* ⇨ *Forward It.*

Touch Them Five Times – Water can touch an object in many places. Similarly, researchers have noted that in order to close a transaction, it's necessary to ask an average of five times. Have at least five ways to *ask for the sale*:

1. So, you're ready to go forward with this?

2. This will work for you, right?

3. Would you okay this? (instead of: Sign here)

4. How about we take care of the paperwork now?

5. You'd like delivery when?

T.R.U.T.H. Process – About the T.R.U.T.H. process: In order to do better financially, you need to stretch and take appropriate risks.

T – Transform to "Yes."

R – Run in better races.

U – Untangle from the money-for-time trade.

T – Take on risk.

H – Hone your persuasion skills.

Truth No One Will Tell You, The – This concept encompasses the four reasons people fail to express the truth:

1. They don't know the truth.

2. They don't want you to know the truth so they can exploit your weakness.

3. They care about you and want you to avoid getting hurt.

4. They can only guess about what is best for you because *your inner truth* is only revealed by *your answers* to effective questions.

Truth-Revealing Questions – This is a method for discovering your inner truth as revealed by your answers to effective questions.

- What do you really want?

- What do you want to feel?

- Where are you grieving?

- How can you take better care of yourself now?

- Where are you "contracting"?

- How can you have some "expansion" in your life?

Unique Selling Proposition (USP) – Have you heard the phrase, "Fresh, hot pizza to your door in 30 minutes or less, guaranteed!"? This is a USP, or Unique Selling Proposition. It focuses on a specific detail – when people call for pizza delivery, they are *hungry*.

W.I.N.–T.H.E.–P.R.I.Z.E. **Process** – This is a process to prepare before your next interaction with someone who may seem to be your opponent. Effective preparation may enable you to defuse the situation so that you do not have an opponent, but rather an associate, with whom you can achieve a mutually beneficial outcome.

W – Walk up the chain of command

I – Impress the person that you're staying

N – Nudge politely

T – Tune in to language

H – Hone your approach

E – Establish your credibility

P – Persist

R – Record notes

I – Itemize "this or that"

Z – Zero in on de-escalating

E – Encounter the reputable

Word Picture – A word picture creates an image with words, making your communication vivid.

Further Reading

The following list of books and audio programs provides the reader with select landmarks in the rich literary landscape which has informed this book. Enjoy!

Adler, Bill *see* Winfrey, Oprah & Bill Adler

Alessandra, Dr. Tony, *CHARISMA: Seven Keys to Developing the Magnetism that Leads to Success,* 2000, 288p, Business Plus, 978-0446675987

__________ & Michael J. O'Connor, *The Platinum Rule: Discover the Four Basic Business Personalities and How They Can Lead You to Success,* 1998, 304p, Grand Central Publishing, 978-0446673433

Allen, Marc, *The Greatest Secret of All: Moving Beyond Abundance to a Life of True Fulfillment,* 2007, 128p, New World Library, 978-1577316190

Barron, David R. & Danek S. Kaus, *Power Persuasion: Using Hypnotic Influence to Win in Life, Love, and Business,* 2005, 108p, Robert D. Reed Publishers, 978-1931741521

Bass, Ellen, *The Human Line,* 2007, 96p Copper Canyon Press, 978-1556592553

__________ & Laura Davis, *The Courage to Heal: A Guide for Women Survivors of Child Sexual Abuse,* 4th edition (20th Anniversary), 2008, 640p, Collins Living, 978-0061284335

Bedell, Gene, *Three Steps to Yes: The Gentle Art of Getting Your Way,* 2002, 256p, Three Rivers Press, 978-0609807194

Ben-Shahar, Tal, *Happier: Learn the Secrets to Daily Joy and Lasting Fulfillment,* 2007, 224p, McGraw-Hill, 978-0071492393

Bloom, Linda & Charlie, *101 Things I Wish I Knew When I Got Married: Simple Lessons to Make Love Last ,* 2004, 256p, New World Library, 978-1577314240

Byrne, Rhonda, *The Secret,* 2006, 198p, Atria Books, 978-1582701707

Campbell, Joseph, *The Hero with a Thousand Faces* (Bollingen Series, No. 17), 1972, 464p, Princeton Unviversity Press, 978-0691017846

Canfield, Jack & Mark Victor Hansen, *Chicken Soup for the Soul,* 2001, 480p, HCI, 978-1558749207

Chapman, Dr. Gary, *The Five Love Languages: How to Express Heartfelt Commitment to Your Mate,* 1995, 204p, Northfield Publishing , 978-1881273158

Churchill, Winston, *Never Give In!: The Best of Winston Churchill's Speeches,* 2004, 558p, Hyperion, 0786888709

Cialdini, Robert, *Influence: The Psychology of Persuasion* (Collins Business Essentials), 2006, 336p, Collins Business, 978-0061241895

Dahlkoetter, Dr. JoAnn, *Your Performing Edge: The Total Mind-body Program for Excellence in Sports, Business and Life,* 4th Ed., 2007, 264p, Pulgas Ridge Press, 978-0970407986

Davis, Laura *see* Bass, Ellen & Laura Davis

Disney, Walt, *Quotable Walt Disney,* 2001, 272p, Disney Editions, 978-0786853328

Dyer, Dr. Wayne, *Inspiration: Your Ultimate Calling,* 2007, 272p, Hay House, 978-1401907228

__________, *Your Erroneous Zones,* 1993, 320p, Avon Books, 978-0061091483

Einstein, Albert, *The World As I See It*, 2006, 128p, Filiquarian Publishing , 978-1599869650

Emerson, Ralph Waldo, *Emerson: Essays and Lectures: Nature: Addresses and Lectures / Essays: First and Second Series / Representative Men / English Traits / The Conduct of Life*, 1983, 1150p, Library of America, 978-0940450158

Fettke, Rich, *Extreme Success: The 7-Part Program That Shows You How to Succeed Without Struggle*, 2002, 288p, Fireside, 978-0743223140

Franklin, Benjamin, *Benjamin Franklin: Autobiography, Poor Richard, and Later Writings* (Library of America), edited by J. A. Leo Lemay, 2005, 816p, Library of America, 978-1883011536

Gandhi, Mahatma, *An Autobiography: The Story of My Experiments With Truth*, 1993, 528p, Beacon Press, 978-0807059098

Gilbert, Bill *see* King, Larry & Bill Gilbert

Hansen, Mark Victor *see* Canfield, Jack & Mark Victor Hansen

Hepburn, Katherine, *Me: Stories of My Life*, 1996, 432p, Ballantine Books, 978-0345410092

Jampolsky, Gerald "Jerry," MD, *Love is Letting Go of Fear*, 25th Anniversary Ed., 2004, 144p, Ten Speed Press, 978-1587611964

Kaus, Danek S., *You Can Be Famous: Insider Secrets to Getting Free Publicity,* 2009, 176p, Robert Reed Publishers, 978-1934759110

Kaus, Danek S. *see* Barron, David R. + Danek S. Kaus

Kawasaki, Guy, *The Art of the Start: The Time-Tested, Battle-Hardened Guide for Anyone Starting Anything,* 2004, 226p, Portfolio Hardcover, 978-1591840565

Keller, Helen, *The Story of My Life: The Restored Classic, Complete and Unabridged*, Centennial Ed., edited by Anne Sullivan et al., 2003, 352p, W. W. Norton & Company, 978-0393057447

King, Larry & Bill Gilbert, *How to Talk to Anyone, Anytime, Anywhere: The Secrets of Good Communication*, 1995, 224p, Three Rivers Press, 978-0517884539

Lao-Tzu, *Te-Tao Ching - A New Translation Based on the Recently Discovered Ma-wang-tui Texts* (Classics of Ancient China), tranlated by Robert G. Henricks, 1992, 430p, Ballantine Books, 978-0345370990

Lee, Michael Soon, MBA & Sensei Grant Tabuchi, *Black Belt Negotiating: Become a Master Negotiator Using Powerful Lessons from the Martial Arts*, 2007, 224p, Amacom Books, 978-0814474617

Levinson, Jay Conrad, *Guerrilla Marketing: Easy and Inexpensive Strategies for Making Big Profits from Your Small Business*, 4th Ed., 2007, 384p, Mariner Books , 978-0618785919

Luskin, Dr. Fred, *Forgive for Good*, 2003, 240p, HarperOne, 978-0062517210

____________, *Forgive for Love: The Missing Ingredient for a Healthy and Lasting Relationship*, 2009, 240p, HarperOne, 978-0061234958

MacFarlane, Michael, *Share and Grow Rich: The Dottie Walters Effect*, 2007, 207p, Elevate, 978-1601940087

McWilliams, Peter, *Wealth 101: Getting What You Want-Enjoying What You've Got*, 1999, 532p, Prelude Press, 978-0931580185

O'Connor, Michael J. *see* Alessandra, Dr. Tony & Michael J. O'Connor

Parnell, Aaron Lloyd U., *Living with Vitality – The Dynamic Power of Extraordinary Health*, 2007, 204p, PZQ Press Divison, 978-0615143323

RoAnne, Susan, *How to Work a Room*, Revised Ed., 2007, 336p, Collins Living, 978-0061238673

Robbins, Anthony, *Awaken the Giant Within: How to Take Immediate Control of Your Mental, Emotional, Physical and Financial Destiny!*, 1992, 544p, Free Press, 978-0671791544

Robbins, Mike, *Focus on the Good Stuff: The Power of Appreciation*, 2007, 240p, Jossey-Bass, 978-0787988791

Savage, PhD, Elayne, *Don't Take It Personally! The Art of Dealing with Rejection*, 2002, 242p, iUniverse, 978-0595255757

__________, *Breathing Room – Creating Space to Be a Couple*, 2001, 210p, New Harbinger Publications, 978-1572242210

Siegel, Dr. Bernie, *Love, Medicine and Miracles: Lessons Learned about Self-Healing from a Surgeon's Experience with Exceptional Patients*, 1990, 256p, Harper, 978-0060919832

Spielberg, Steven: Interviews (Conversations with Filmmakers Series), Lester D. Friedman & Brent Notbohm, 2000, 250p, University Press of Mississippi, 978-1578061136

Tabuchi, Sensei Grant *see* Lee, Michael Soon, MBA & Sensei Grant Tabuchi

Tracy, Brian, *Eat That Frog!: 21 Great Ways to Stop Procrastinating and Get More Done in Less Time*, 2nd Ed., 2007, 128p, Berrett-Koehler Publishers, 978-1576754221

Waitley, Denis, *The Psychology of Winning*, 1987, Nightingale-Conant, 0671520679, audio recording (also available in paperback)

Walters, Dottie & Lillet "Lilly" Walters, *Speak and Grow Rich*, 1997, 288p, Prentice Hall, 978-0735203518

Wieder, Marcia, *Making Your Dreams Come True*, 1999, 235p, Harmony, 978-0609606087

Williams, A.L., *All You Can Do Is All You Can Do, But All You Can Do Is Enough!*, 1997, 219p, Ballantne Books, 978-0449001103

Winfrey, Oprah & Bill Adler, *The Uncommon Wisdom Of Oprah Winfrey: A Portrait in Her Own Words*, 2000, 290p, Citadel, 978-1559724197

Ziglar, Zig, *Goals - Set goals...and reach them!*, 1988, Nightingale-Conant, audio recording

Index of Names

King, Stephen   169
Knight, Phil   229

— L —

Lao-Tzu   8, 31, 98–100, 104, 356
LeBoeuf, Michael   295, 298
Lee, Bruce   199
Lee, Michael Soon   186–188,
     204, 356
LeGuin, Ursula   7
L'Engle, Madeleine   13, 14
Leno, Jay   159
Levinson, Jay Conrad   274–275,
     356
Linda   146, 182
Lipson, Benjamin   168
Livingston, MD, Gordon   7
Luskin, Dr. Fred   47–49, 356

— M —

MacFarlane, Michael   301
Mackay, Harvey   66
Mac Leod, Johanna   vii
Malamud, Bernard   246
Maltin, Leonard   214
Marcoux, Tom   iii, 16, 51, 66,
     84, 88–89, 91, 114, 120,
     131, 133, 137, 140, 151, 168,
     176, 228, 235, 239, 244,
     253, 261, 279, 286–289,
     301, 306, 326, 331,
     369–370
Marcy   151
Marina   63
Martha   133
Martin, Steve   5
Matt   196
Maxine   238
Maxwell, John   122

Mayer, John   294
McWilliams, Peter   314, 356
Merriam-Webster's Medical
     Dictionary   185
Meyer, Paul J.   83
Michael J. O'Connor   346
Michelle   265
Mirnah   250
Mondale, Walter   157
Morita, Lindsay   113
Morrissey, Mary Manin   51

— N —

Nadia   265
Nehru, Jawaharlal   69, 311
Newman, Paul   235
Nichols, Mike   270
Niebuhr, Reinhold   289

— O —

Obst, Lynda   192, 253
O'Connor, Michael J.   179, 296,
     353
O'Malley, Austin   141
Orman, Suze   41
Osteen, Joel   140, 147, 148, 261
Ovid   53

— P —

Pan, Peter   93
Parnell, Aaron Lloyd U.   14–15
Pascal, Blaise   317
Paul   310–311
Pausch, Dr. Randy   86
Pavese, Cesare   115
Peale, Dr. Norman
     Vincent   209
Pearce, Joseph Chilton   56

Index of Subjects

About the Author

Tom Marcoux
America's Communication Coach

Tom Marcoux helps people like *you* accomplish big dreams. He helps clients influence people, especially "*When they need to make them go 'Wow!'*" Further, Tom helps people get more done and feel good doing it.

Tom is also a prolific author. Including *Nothing Can Stop You This Year!*, He has published 10 books and 21 audio programs, with sales in 15 countries. Prominent among his publications are *Online Secrets to Build Your Brand* and *Communicate to Win* (which was a required textbook at Cogswell Polytechnical College, the expanded and retitled edition is the book in your hand.)

When you want to influence others, join Tom's many clients who benefit from his secrets on branding. Tom is described as "the Personal Branding Instructor" by the *San Francisco Examiner*. Helping people become more effective job candidates, he has presented to ProMatch and chapters of Experience Unlimited (affiliated with the California Employment Development Department).

Holding a degree in psychology, Tom is also a personal/professional coach and guest expert on TV and radio, in addition to being featured in technology/communication magazines. He is the recipient of a special award at the Emmys Awards.

Tom is an award-winning speaker and corporate workshop leader (to professionals from IBM, Wells Fargo, Sun Microsystems, Silicon Valley Bank). For six years, he has addressed the National Association of Broadcasters Conference in Las Vegas on topics like, "Online Secrets to Build Your Brand." Tom is a member of the National Speakers Association.

Tom is a faculty lecturer at Academy of Art University; guest lecturer at Stanford University, DeAnza College, and California State University at Los Angeles; in addition to being an online class instructor, the author of three online courses, and a workshops presenter to other faculty at the Academy of Art University's Teacher Conferences.

Tom also wrote, directed, and produced a film that went to the Cannes Film Festival market, where it obtained international distribution. Presently, Tom is leading teams working on book-film projects titled *Crystal Pegasus* (children's fantasy) and *TimePulse* (science fiction).

When you need to enthrall audiences or effectively communicate your message to the media, engage Tom as your media coach. Tom helps clients clarify their message, build confidence in speaking, and craft compelling sound bites and stories for the press. Tom will help you excel!

(415) 572-6609
TomSuperCoach@gmail.com
www.TomSuperCoach.com

COLLOPHON

This   book   was
designed and set by gBambo
of the design atelier:

Kunſt+Aventur

It is named for *Kunſt und Aventur* (Art & Enter-
prise), published in Strasbourg, France in 1440, in
which Johannes Gutenberg (*c.* 1398 – 1468), a Ger-
man goldsmith, unveiled his epochal invention – the
mechanization of printing.

Text was set in Minion Pro and Gill Sans Standard.
Minion was designed by Robert Slimbach and based
on classical old ſtyle types of the late Renaissance.

The design was executed in Adobe's Creative Suite
4, using Photoshop, Illuſtrator, and InDesign.

Photography used a Nikon D70 + Nikkor
ED AF-S 24-120mm 1.3-5.6 G VR lens.

kunſt.aventur@gmail.com
for inquiries

Get what you really want …

use the methods found in Tom Marcoux's books!

For special discounts, order at:
www.TomSuperCoach.com/SpecialOffer.htm

For more QuickBreakthrough resources, see
www.TomSuperCoach.com